Praise for *Because of a Dog*

"Matthew Sigman has created something special in these pages: an inviting space where anyone who has ever grieved the loss of deep love—and isn't that all of us?—can gather to bathe in the healing waters of shared human experience. I found myself rereading entire passages for the sheer elegance of the writing and its ability to transport me to places my heart had not visited in a very long time. Sigman has that rare gift of storytelling that invites the reader along on the adventure, not as observer but participant."

—John Grogan, *New York Times* bestselling author of *Marley & Me*

"*Because of a Dog* had me laughing out loud in one line and unexpectedly reaching for the tissue box and browsing flights to small Italian towns in the next. It's a rare blend of wit and poignancy that will deeply move anyone who has ever loved a dog."

—Christina Hunger, *New York Times* bestselling author of *How Stella Learned to Talk*

"*Because of a Dog* is as delightful as the singular Italian village in its pages. Matthew Sigman's terrific memoir is many tributes all in one: to a very good dog, to an exceptional place, and to the healing powers of food, travel, and friendship. A tender, witty, captivating story of grief, healing, and transformation."

—Justine van der Leun, author of *Marcus of Umbria: What an Italian Dog Taught an American Girl About Love*

BECAUSE OF A DOG

How an Enchanted Italian Village Mended a Broken Heart

MATTHEW SIGMAN

sourcebooks

Cover design by Philip Pascuzzo
Portrait of Augie by Bachrach Photography
Cover images © Tjarko Evenboer/The Netherlands/Getty Images,
Petekarici/Getty Images
Internal design by Tara Jaggers/Sourcebooks

Published by Sourcebooks
1935 Brookdale RD, Naperville, IL 60563-2773
(630) 961-3900
sourcebooks.com

Cataloging-in-Publication Data is on file with the Library of Congress.

Printed and bound in the United States of America.
LSC 10 9 8 7 6 5 4 3 2 1

For Augie

Contents

Prelude

Now shrugging off fate, now reaching for the right word, now shifting gears, now fiddling with the radio, now shouting into the phone, now texting. To his credit, there was an artfulness to Valerio's driving: He steered with his knees.

I had come to Europe for a summer of peace after a winter of sorrow. Now, blown off course like Gulliver, I was facing death on a switchback mountain road at the hands of a madcap Italian innkeeper. My right hand gripped the Jesus handle so fiercely that my fingernails gouged half-moons into my palm. My throat struggled to hold back the lovely lunch I had enjoyed on a sun-washed terrace overlooking Lake Maggiore. After six months on the Grief Diet, having lost forty pounds, I had finally indulged in a proper (and properly expensive) meal, and I was about to hurl it all on a roller-coaster ride to Quarna, a medieval village perched in the Italian Alps.

There was no mention of the twenty-three hairpin turns

in the Airbnb description of Valerio's inn, no warning when he picked me up in the piazza of Stresa, not even a hint as we reached Omegna, the town on Lake Orta where the ascent began. As my face went from ashen to green, sweat soaking my shirt, Valerio assured me I was not alone in my distress. Recently, an Australian couple, driving on their own, arrived at the inn so distraught that they stayed just long enough to curse him, demand a refund, then turn around and leave. He snickered telling the tale. The downhill drive, with a superior view of the plunge, was far more terrifying.

As the turns tightened, I prayed Valerio might finally grab the steering wheel. My prayers were not answered. The phone, however, was.

"Pronto!" he shouted, the phone nestled in the crook of his neck.

A car swerved toward us from a blind curve ahead. In an effortless instant, Valerio zigged, the other driver zagged. They exchanged a friendly wave.

"Sì!" Valerio said into the phone. "Sì-sì-sì!"

A sputtering three-wheeled truck tooted from below as a motorcycle approached from above. Valerio bobbed, the truck weaved, the motorcycle passed through the eye of a needle.

"Sì-sì!" he continued, the tone of each "sì" conveying a different meaning: affirmation, dispute, forgiveness, affection. It seemed that *sì* was the most common word in Valerio's vocabulary.

Valerio waved hello to every passing car and every driver waved back in kind. I was curious as to whether each greeting was to an acquaintance or the wave was just a common courtesy. I unclenched my throat long enough to squeeze out a word.

"Amici?"

My Italian vocabulary was mostly limited to musical terms learned from violin lessons that began at age six. That vocabulary expanded as my passion for classical music grew and I cultivated a taste for opera. I could communicate well with a consumptive nineteenth-century courtesan, not so well with a crazed twenty-first-century driver. But *amici*, "friends," I could utter with confidence. I have lived for more than twenty-five years in New York City's West Village, my tiny apartment around the corner from the building that served as the facade for *Friends*. It is a guidebook destination for tourists from around the world who wish to pay homage to their dear, dubbed television pals: Monica, Rachel, Chandler, Joey, Phoebe, and Ross. On their pilgrimage, they often get tangled in the neighborhood's cockeyed streets. As a middle-aged man walking a dog, the international symbol for a friendly local, I was stopped daily for directions to "the *Friends* house" in every imaginable language.

It got to the point where Augie, my trusty mutt, could smell the weariness in their socks and instinctively lead the pack. Civic-minded by nature, Augie was always eager to extend any hospitality, particularly any hospitality that would extend his walk. *Amici. Amigos. Amis.* Augie was a friend in any language.

Valerio smiled and threw both hands in the air.

"Amici! Sì-sì! In Quarna, tutti sono amici!"

Even Augie could have figured that one out.

That I should stumble into such a precarious situation was not completely shocking. Serendipity has always been a companion on my travels, especially to Italy. In my teens, as a student exploring Tuscany, I was nearly trampled by knights on horseback in Siena. I had unwittingly arrived on the day of the Palio, the medieval pageant held but twice a year. In my twenties, as a music journalist traveling on assignment, my departure from Venice was thwarted without notice. I was attempting to leave on the day of the Regata Storica—all canals were closed, all trains were canceled. In my thirties, pursuing an *inamorato* in Rome, I was enjoying a gelato on the Spanish Steps when an explosion of hysteria erupted from above. The bomb I feared turned out to be a bombshell: Madonna, on tour, was leaving her hotel.

Encouraged by devoted parents eager to see their four children discover the world beyond Toledo, Ohio, I was infected at a young age with what John Steinbeck in *Travels with Charley* calls "the virus of restlessness." There were artfully planned journeys to Europe, detours on American business trips, and adventures for the sake of adventure: rafting down the Grand Canyon, snorkeling on the Great Barrier Reef, discovering the shtetls of my ancestors. And yes, there were pursuits of the heart and the loins. My wild oats were widely sown.

In those bachelor years there was no one to check with, no fish to feed, not even a plant to water. I was free to ramble, free to roam. After Augie came into my life, everything changed. The itch to travel did not fade, only now all guides included the word dog: *Traveling with Your Dog*, *Hiking with Your Dog*, *Camping with Your Dog*, *Best Dog Beaches*. An inveterate city-dweller with no need for a car, for Augie I bought my first: an ancient Ford station wagon with faux wood paneling, maroon velour upholstery, and a wayback big enough for him to stretch and snooze. Road-trip timetables were calibrated for dog-friendly breaks, routes optimized for dog-friendly trails, restaurants selected for dog-friendly outdoor seating. Even when we were home in the West Village, errands once mapped for expedience were remapped for exploration. For eighteen years, wherever I went, however I went, I preferred adventures with Augie to adventures without.

No journeys were more sacred than those involving water. A pond, a lake, a bay, a marsh, a river, a stream, but most of all, the ocean. How he raced along the shore! How he leapt across the dunes! How his joy became my joy!

It was at the beach I cast his ashes.

Lemuel Gulliver's discovery of Lilliput began with a shipwreck. Hugh Conway was lured to Shangri-La after a plane crash. Tommy Albright got lost on a hunting trip and stumbled onto Brigadoon. My discovery of Quarna began on a chilly January afternoon when I came home to find Augie, my beloved companion, silent in his bed by the window. I pressed my head to his chest, praying he was just sleeping soundly, praying his heart was just beating quietly, praying the bellows of his lungs would soon restore the breath of life. But there is no sound louder than a heart stilled. Except perhaps two hearts stilled.

Despite his chronological age, he had only recently become frail—his eyes dulled, his hearing faded—but the evening before he ate well, bopped around the apartment, and went for an uneventful walk. Afterward, he came to my side of the bed, gave me a lingering gaze, and joined me and Collin in bed for a cuddle. The following morning, he awoke at his usual time, bid us good morning, and signaled his need for relief. Not even on his dying day would Augie soil the sanctity of his home.

It was supposed to have been an ordinary day of writing, with Augie at my feet, but Collin received an early morning text that our wise and wonderful friend Rick was fading fast at Sloan Kettering. For five years, Rick had been treated there on and off—mostly on—for an insidious bone cancer. He had taken a turn for the worse in the night, so I gave Augie a quick kiss on the snout, and Collin and I raced uptown. A stylish physician and philanthropist, equally at home in the shops on Madison

Avenue and the favelas of Brazil, Rick was now a vacant shell in a soiled gown trapped in the tentacles of modern medicine: wires, shunts, IV lines, machines whirring and blinking in the harsh fluorescent tableau of a hospital death.

"Please, God, don't let Augie die this way," I thought. I had long prayed that when his time came, I would summon a compassionate veterinarian with a potent syringe and, holding Augie in my lap like a pietà, sing him to everlasting sleep with a lullaby. My greatest fear was that I would panic, scoop him up, and he would die on a table in the tentacles of modern veterinary medicine in the harsh fluorescent tableau of an animal hospital death.

Had there been a potent syringe at Sloan Kettering, I would have put Rick down on the spot. Mercifully, a few hours after Augie's death, Rick joined him on the journey. That Rick died so cruelly at the age of sixty-two was heartbreaking. That his death was expected, even welcome, made it easier to bear. That I was furious at Rick for depriving me of Augie's last moments felt shameful (after all those years of suffering, he couldn't have waited one more day?), but I knew that Rick, the most selfless person I have ever known, would have been the first to validate my emotions. Among his survivors was Donatella, a French bulldog ever at his side.

Augie's death, on the other hand, was neither expected—soon, certainly, but not that day—nor welcome. Had I missed some sign? Was there a message in his bedside gaze the night before? Had I been blinded by denial? That he had died alone was as traumatic as the death itself. Was he frightened? In pain? Looking for me? Waiting like Argos for one last glimpse of Ulysses? I would never know.

When I called the vet, he let out a quiet gasp. He and Augie bonded at first sight, and he had examined him just a few days before.

"I came home and he was gone," I said.

"Lucky," the vet said, in a whisper.

Lucky? At first it seemed a tactless thing to say, but I quickly realized it was the soul of empathy. Lucky me, I had not seen Augie struggle or suffer, nor did I have to make the agonizing decision to put him down. Lucky Augie, he did not die in the fluorescent tableau of an animal hospital. He died in a sunbeam, an old dog in his bed.

Chapter 1

The Beginning

Augie came into my life before the internet did the legwork for pet adoption. I visited several shelters in New York City and sadly found them better at rescue than placement. "Take a look around and let me know if you see one you like," said an attendant at a shelter known for its society galas, as if it were a used car lot. At another distinguished adoption center, pay stubs, tax returns, bank statements, and references were required before I could see a whisker. At The Humane Society of New York, a nondescript building on the East Side, the culture of caring was evident the moment I entered the tiny lobby. Volunteer walkers with their charges were coming and going as if it were rush hour at Grand Central, tails wagging with excitement on the way out, tongues hanging with exhaustion on the way in. I was greeted immediately by an effervescent young volunteer in scrubs whose first words were, "Come, let's meet the dogs!"

We wandered up and down rows of large cages, where well-kept dogs put on their soft-eyes acts or bayed for attention. I was introduced to each dog by name and provided a backstory. Some had physical or behavioral challenges, making them unsuitable for adoption by an inexperienced owner. I was introduced to the new arrivals in an open space where puppies and kittens mingled, but the Humane Society was averse to placing puppies with first-time adopters. Too often, cute puppies became defiant adolescents and were returned to the system. I wasn't keen on a puppy anyway. I was hoping for a mature dog, perhaps even housebroken with a bit of obedience training. The volunteer—and the dogs, I'm sure—politely suppressed howls of laughter. In a city where walk-up apartments and lurching elevators can challenge the most diligent dog racing the clock, housebroken mature dogs with advanced degrees were snapped up like double-ply cashmere sweaters on sale at Saks.

Next on the agenda was meeting William Berloni, the power agent for animals in theatre, television, and film, who volunteered his time to the Humane Society advising adopters on their prospective choices. A dog whisperer with a rabbinical mien, Bill's most famous client was Sandy, a lovable mutt he rescued from death row and cast for the Broadway musical *Annie*. Bill's style was so relaxed and engaging, his analytic skills so effortlessly veiled, that I didn't realize until later that our conversation wasn't an information session. It was an audition. Bill was presumably there to help find a suitable dog for me, but his equal objective was to ensure that I was a suitable human for a dog. He was the matchmaker who would make me a match.

With just a few questions, he unmasked more about my character than a dozen psychotherapists.

"Do you consider yourself athletic?" Bill asked.

"Ummmm..."

"No sporting breeds for you."

"Do you consider yourself calm?"

"Errrrr..."

"No toy breeds for you."

On the process of elimination went, until finally:

"Do you feel capable of caring for an animal with a disability?"

At the time I did not. In time that would change.

What I don't recall Bill asking was *why* I wanted a dog. The simple answer would have been that, exhausted from the treadmill of ambition—I had pivoted via a Wharton MBA from writing and editing to the front lines of the digital media revolution—I decided on a mid-career hiatus. I quit my corporate job and made a bucket list for a gap year. I wanted to travel freely through Europe without an itinerary. I wanted to live at the beach for a few months. Any beach, as long as it was remote and peaceful. Sand and sea seemed an ideal canvas for reimagining my life. And I wanted a dog.

The deeper answer would have been that a shadow of loneliness had come over me. I'd had one long-term relationship, several short-term relationships, and more trysts than I would admit, but an enduring human bond eluded me. My heart was hungry for love, commitment, affection, and companionship. If I could not find a human being, a reasonable facsimile in canine form seemed a step in the right direction.

The assessment completed, Bill determined that a shepherd mix would be ideal. Such dogs combine intelligence with a calm disposition, he said. They adapt well to city life, are easy to train, and have fewer physical and behavioral issues. A mature dog, he felt, would indeed be more appropriate. There were no matches at the Humane Society at the time, but there was a constant flow of new arrivals. I should stop by from time to time, he suggested. I stopped by two weeks later. And another two weeks later. The staff was always cordial, always welcoming, but there was never a match.

And then I got "The Call." A litter of rescued puppies would soon be weaned and Bill and the staff felt my persistent visits had demonstrated that I was up to the challenge. Their confidence was flattering, but I was hesitant. With a mature dog, I could blame bad behavior on poor nurturing by someone else. What parent does not wish for plausible deniability? With a puppy, I would be held fully accountable. Barking, nipping, and lunging would be testaments to my ineptitude. For sweetness and warmth, the dog would get sole credit.

I raced to Barnes & Noble and pulled every dog book off the shelves. They ranged from saccharine to scientific, with little in the way of practical guidance. "Let the dog choose you," I read over and over until my eyes were sore from rolling. Finally, I found a book with rational advice. The author suggested first picking up each pup and draping it across your arms to assess its comfort with your touch and smell. Later I would read that dogs and humans instantly exchange oxytocin, the same love-and-cuddle hormone that forges the human mother–newborn bond and adult erotic attraction. Humans and dogs don't just choose each other randomly or by physical attributes. They bond chemically and instinctively.

The author's next suggestion was that, if given the opportunity to pick from a full litter, to place each pup separately in a large crate alongside the dominant dog. If the candidate responded to the alpha dog with excessive aggression or submission, it might be too difficult for a first-timer to train, especially in an urban setting where immediate sociability is essential.

As I entered the adoption room, a gangly pup who looked like a fawn was chasing a kitten. There was no apparent malice. The pup simply wanted to play. He was either unaware or unconcerned about the distinction between species. The kitten, however, seemed well aware and highly concerned. With his long legs and pointy ears, the Fawn Dog looked like an alien predator.

The Fawn Dog was part of the litter ready for adoption. He and his three siblings had been picked up by city animal control, along with their mother, from Prospect Park in Brooklyn. Brooklyn's transformation from a dowdy working-class suburb to a gentrified haven for young professionals was still a work in process, and Prospect Park was a notorious dumping ground for unwanted dogs.

The Fawn Dog looked like he had been switched at birth or was a savvy stowaway. His littermates were a matched set of white fluff balls. The Fawn Dog was black, white, and tan. Two of the fluff balls were deep in sleep, the third was yapping incessantly. The Fawn Dog was upright and quiet, with a glint in his eyes and ears at full attention. He seemed enraptured by his new world.

Were they *sure* the Fawn Dog was from the same litter? I asked. Yes, they were sure. How was this possible? Two theories were offered. One was that the Fawn Dog was simply a genetic outlier, the proverbial black sheep in a litter from a singular sire-and-dam hookup. The other theory amazed me. Canine estrus, it was explained, can last up to ten days, and a female dog in heat wandering in Prospect Park would likely have attracted multiple suitors. The Fawn Dog could well be a brother from another father. The mother's genes being constant, if the Fawn Dog's senses seemed sharper or his intelligence more refined or his temperament calmer (or had they been the opposite), it was simply the luck of the paternal genetic draw. He could have been a poet or a bum. It was the luck of the draw for me too.

I moved forward with the two evaluations I had read about.

I picked up each pup in the litter, starting with the three fluff balls. The barker nipped, the snoozers wriggled and fussed. The Fawn Dog relaxed into my arms as if settling into a hammock. His warmth radiated into my chest. His scent was intoxicating.

For the second part of the evaluation, I scooped up the barker and placed him in a spare cage, where he immediately seized a squeaky toy. I then introduced each pup into the crate one at a time. The first fluffy snoozer went to a far corner and resumed her nap. The second one rolled over and peed on herself. The Fawn Dog, curious about the squeaky toy, tried to get in the game from one side, then the other side, then one angle, then another, but the barker, clearly the alpha, would not relent. Finally, the Fawn Dog went to the opposite corner of the cage and barked at some imaginary object in the distance. The alpha, responding to the alarm, dropped the squeaky toy and raced to see what the commotion was all about. The Fawn Dog pivoted in an instant and snapped up the toy. It was an indisputable display of cunning, a calculated misdirection as shrewd as that of a fine magician. Even the Humane Society volunteer was astonished.

"That's my dog!" I said.

Chapter 2

The End

There are things people don't warn you about when you adopt a dog. Things they assume you know. I grew up with dogs in a lively household, but I had never heard of the expression "zoomies" or witnessed an outbreak. (Possibly because the frenetic behaviors of four children were indistinguishable from those of a dog.) The first time Augie jumped up from a deep sleep, raced about the apartment like a ferret on speed, then crashed on the sofa as if nothing had happened, I thought he'd had a seizure.

They don't warn you about cheese teleportation, that even a silent thought of cheese can beam a dog to your side from a distant galaxy.

They don't warn you that the delirium of "puppy love" unleashes a capacity for affection you never imagined you had.

And they don't warn you that the clock of anticipatory grief starts at hello. You don't have to be a profound neurotic with an attachment disorder to hear the tick-tock of mortality. You don't have to be an actuary to know that you will likely outlive your dog. And nobody warns you how fast dog years fly by. With those years come hijinks and adventures beyond your expectations. And vet bills beyond comprehension. Augie was a robust dog, but over the years he had a litany of ailments and treatments that kept us on edge: a heart murmur, hypothyroidism, a vestibular disorder, fractured molars, paw fissures, dermatitis, cancer, a fractured leg that required amputation, and a dozen diagnoses and procedures and medications I've surely forgotten.

Augie didn't just overcome his afflictions. He *soared* over them. Nothing slowed him down. *Nothing.* His resilience duped us all into the illusion of invincibility. One of his veterinary specialists, who knew him as a puppy and treated him again eighteen years later, was astonished to see him so vital.

"Augie may actually live forever," he said in a tone so lacking in irony, for a moment I wasn't sure if he was joking. I'm not sure if he was sure either.

Eventually, when Augie turned eighteen, I accepted the inevitable. There is only so much a benevolent God and a phalanx of veterinarians and a chunk of your life savings and a mountain of credit card debt can do. Even though he was still in fine form, I started to make arrangements. When the inevitable arrived, I did not want logistical panic on top of sorrow. I didn't want the vet shipping him off to some processing center and mailing him back to me in a cardboard box. Anything other than a respectful burial seemed impossible. I picked up the phone and called Hartsdale Pet Cemetery just north of New York City. I cried so hard I could not get a word out. The kindly man was silent.

"This is more difficult than making arrangements for my parents," I finally got out.

"We often hear that," he said.

I made an appointment and drove up to Hartsdale. As I passed through the wrought iron gates, I felt transported into a hallowed resting place rivaling the great human cemeteries I have visited: Père-Lachaise in Paris, La Recoleta in Buenos Aires, Bonaventure in Savannah. There were extravagant monuments (as with humans, there is no budget for the broken-hearted), simple footstones, and epitaphs from solemn to witty. There was a palpable sense of community in knowing others had memorialized their pets without shame. The only thing missing was an endless verdant meadow where the ghosts of dogs could gambol and run and drink from streams and pee and poop wherever they pleased.

"This grave is the only grave I visit with any regularity—in fact, it is the only grave I visit at all," wrote E. B. White in "Bedfellows," a 1956 essay honoring Fred, his dachshund. White buried Fred in a corner of his farm in Maine. "I have relatives lying in cemeteries here and there around the country, but I do not feel any urge to return to them," he confessed. But he did expect to check in now and then to see what Fred was up to. I have never felt the urge to return to Toledo to visit the graves of my parents and grandparents. I fully expected to visit Augie's grave, if only on the anniversary of his death, to say hello and see what he was up to.

There was sanctity at Hartsdale and a staff that radiated pure compassion, but even a modest burial package—plot, stone, perpetual care—gave me pause. There seemed more charitable uses for the money. I set aside burial and decided that when the time came, I would enlist the good people of Hartsdale to retrieve Augie and privately "transition" him from dog to dust with ceremony and dignity. I could not bring myself to say the word *cremate*. As for *cremains*, what creep invented that ghastly portmanteau?

There was still the matter of place. Where would I scatter his ashes?

When I brought Augie home from the Humane Society, I had fulfilled two of the three bucket list goals for my gap year: I had traveled for three months in Europe without an itinerary and I had adopted a dog. Now it was time to fulfill the third wish: to live at the beach. The genie who granted that wish was my friend Kim, a globetrotting businesswoman who was off to London for a year. For a modest rent, she offered me her modest summer house in Springs, a quiet hamlet adjacent to the chic Long Island village of East Hampton. I sublet my apartment in the West Village for a tidy profit, packed up the station wagon, and took up residence with Augie in Springs, as close to the pristine Hamptons beaches as a nonbillionaire can get.

Whether blistering hot or bitter cold, Augie and I drove every day to Two Mile Hollow, the most desolate of the East Hampton beaches. He raced along the shore and, at a break in the dunes in front of an old windmill, leapt through a wardrobe into a Narnia of his own, a paradise where he would roam and chase and hunt and ponder undisturbed. He would disappear long enough to test my nerves, leap back over the dunes to check on me—his eyes radiant—and then return to his adventures. I would walk along the shore in my own world of imagination. Eventually, exhausted from his adventures, Augie would join me on the walk back to the car where the dream would end for the day, to resume the next. Off season, when the summer hoards were gone, we saw the occasional fellow traveler with a dog—a silent nod was the unspoken rule for both species—but there were days we saw no one for miles. On windswept days, there were no prints in the sand other than my feet and his paws. We might as well have been the first man and dog on Mars.

Kim's assignment in London was extended a year and I extended my gap year accordingly. The sand-and-sea-and-dog fantasy was no longer a virtual canvas for reimagining my life. The so-called "gap," I realized, was life itself.

I was not naive. I knew the gap could not last forever. I didn't have the assets to sustain the lifestyle, and I knew the longer I was off the corporate treadmill, the harder it would be to get back on. But while the gap lasted, I was grateful that I had the self-awareness—so rare to myself and others—that this long moment in the present with Augie would likely be the happiest time of my life. Which is not to say there were not happy times in the past or there would not be happy times in the future, but I knew that every minute of every day during our two years at the beach we were both living our best lives.

So the answer to the question "Where would I spread his ashes?" was easy: the break in the dunes in front of the old windmill at Two Mile Hollow Beach in East Hampton. It was his portal to joy in life. It would be his passage to paradise in the afterlife.

On that awful January day when I came home to find him gone, the arrangements I had made went as planned. We brought Augie to the vet, the good people of Hartsdale retrieved him, and a private transition was scheduled two days later. Adhering to Jewish tradition, I wanted to commit him to earth as soon as possible. Collin and I wished to be present for this next step of the journey—every element became ritual—so we put on our good suits and drove up to Hartsdale. Augie had been placed in a closed coffin in their little chapel. Yet again, adhering to Jewish tradition, there was no viewing. Members of the Hartsdale staff served as pallbearers, conveying Augie's casket along a stone path from the chapel to the transitioning center. It was a procession worthy of a dog of his stature.

"It's sad when they die so young," said the pallbearer who had prepared Augie for his coffin.

So young? Collin and I were amused.

"He was eighteen," I said.

The pallbearer looked stunned. It was understandable. Yes, there was salt and pepper on Augie's snout and his eyes were a little rheumy, but his coat was thick and lustrous. There were no bald spots or fatty lumps or skin tags. Yes, he was absent a hind leg, but he was not withered. He died a handsome dog.

I feared I might have a last-minute change of mind and opt for traditional burial. Or cryopreservation. Or taxidermy. Or cloning. Or sati. But I did not. I touched my hand to the coffin and said yet another goodbye, one of many goodbyes along the way from death to dust. Skewing slightly Egyptian, I handed the pallbearers a few items Collin and I wished to have placed with Augie for the journey: snacks, in case he got hungry; a favorite toy, in case he got bored; and, from each of us, an unwashed undershirt so he would be comforted by the scent of our love.

By the time the transitioning was over, it was too late to drive out to East Hampton, so we brought Augie home and set the temporary urn on the windowsill so he could watch the world go by one last time. The following morning, we drove out to the beach. The scene was just as Augie would have wished: a freezing day, not a soul in sight, a heavenly sun turning the ocean from gray to azure and the sand from brown to gold. We followed Augie's exuberant ghost down the beach until we reached the break in the dunes. We each said a few words of gratitude, we said the Lord's Prayer, and we said the Mourner's Kaddish, the traditional Jewish praise of God recited graveside. I opened the urn and began to pour. A gust came out of nowhere and the ashes swirled into the dunes, undeniably the breath of God carrying Augie to the heavens. He was now at one with wind and water and earth and sky.

Chapter 3

Grief Begins

I had checked all the boxes. I had fulfilled the rites and rituals and prayers of my tradition. Augie was now committed to earth with dignity. I had done my duty to my loyal friend. My sorrow was great, but I was calm and composed as we drove home from the beach. Until I was not. An hour in, somewhere on a barren stretch of the Long Island Expressway, it hit. I started to shake. I got light-headed. I couldn't breathe. My chest was killing me.

"Pull over," I said to Collin.

The nearest exit was some obscure road to nowhere. We were hoping for a fast-food joint or gas station where I could have a nice nervous breakdown, but I could not wait. I had to get out of the car. I was suffocating.

"*Pull over!*" I said to Collin.

I bolted out the door, across the gravel shoulder and onto a patch of grass. There the damn burst. I had cried plenty in the days since Augie's death, but this was beyond crying. An order of magnitude beyond crying. This was now a sound from within my soul, the likes of which I had never heard. I was *wailing*. I was on my hands and knees begging God to bring him back.

"*I want him back*," I said over and over. "*I want him back.*"

It wasn't a wish. It wasn't a prayer. It wasn't a negotiation. I was actually begging God to bring my dog back.

"*Just a little more time, please! A little more time to hold him and comfort him!*"

I escalated from pious to pissed. For a supposedly compassionate deity, it was heartless to take him without letting me say goodbye.

From an old friend with a penchant for medical curiosities, I once learned about Takotsubo cardiomyopathy, also known as "broken heart syndrome." Takotsubo feels like a heart attack and looks like a heart attack, but it is not a heart attack. There is no coronary artery blockage or electrical malfunction. Instead, there is a sudden ballooning of the left ventricle, most often in response to an emotional shock such as the loss of a spouse or child—even a surprise birthday party. *Takotsubo* is the Japanese word for an octopus trap, which is what the heart looks like on a scan after such an event. Most people recover. Some do not. The medical literature cites multiple cases of sudden death by Takotsubo in response to the loss of a pet. This is how I assumed it would end for me. Augie would go, then *boom*, my heart would turn to calamari.

It did not happen in the moment when I found Augie dead in his bed on the floor (I was actually a bit disappointed), so I assumed the opportunity had passed. But here it finally was. *This was it.* Death by Takotsubo on the shoulder of an exit off the Long Island Expressway. But I did not die. The cyclone passed. Collin helped me back into the car. There were grass stains on my knees and mud on my hands and snot everywhere. We drove around and around and finally found a McDonald's so I could wash up and have a cup of coffee and a bite to eat.

Were this a traditional Jewish funeral, we would have returned home from the cemetery, washed our hands with a ceremonial pitcher, and then sat down for the *seudat havra'ah*, the mourners' first meal. Friends would have organized a buffet of tuna salad, blintzes, a sweet noodle kugel, and bagels with cream cheese and lox. My *seudat havra'ah* was a Filet-O-Fish meal, super-sized. It may not have been tradition, but packed with carbs and fat and sodium, it was the equivalent of a Valium. My brain went into twilight mode and we drove safely and silently home.

I observed *shiva*, the seven days of Jewish mourning, during which one is commanded to abstain from work. I went to a

Jewish bookstore to buy a seven-day memorial candle. I had a brief crying jag. The elderly woman behind the counter offered a compassionate look.

"Your mother?" she asked.

I had to mask laughter beneath the tears. I considered saying "a friend" in order not to seem disrespectful, but my heart took over.

"My dog," I said.

She touched my hand.

"They are family too," she said.

Equally commanded in the rites of Jewish mourning is a return to the world when shiva ends. I went back to the magazine article I was to be writing on the day Augie died. I slowly began the process of getting rid of Augie's things so the apartment would not look like a shrine. Certain mementos I boxed up and put on a high shelf in a closet. Others I put into storage. Some will always be within reach.

In *The Year of Magical Thinking*, Joan Didion, as rational a writer who has ever lived, says she could not let go of her late husband's shoes, in case he came home and needed them. Augie's leash still hangs on a hook by the door, in case he needs to go out.

Why, as an assimilated Jew, did I turn to such traditional rituals? Because they are too deep in my bones to ignore. They were part of most deaths I had experienced—grandparents, parents, aunts, uncles, and friends. I knew the rituals and I needed them. It was instinctive, but it wasn't rote. It was devout. I was on an emotional roller coaster out of control. Jewish ritual was my safety bar.

In the months after Augie's death, I did a deep dive into the literature of pet loss, from the sentimental to the academic to the religious. I found numerous examples of mourning rites among Christian, Buddhist, and Hindu sects (Oh, how the Japanese mourn their cats!), many of which are rooted in an intersection of human and animal spirituality. I found little in the Jewish tradition. In the Torah, there are detailed commandments for the care and slaughter of livestock, but there are no references to mourning companion animals. The absence, says Elijah Judah Schochet in *Animal Life in Jewish Tradition*, is deliberate. Affirming an invisible monotheistic God required a "radical demythologization of the animal kingdom." No more idolatrous animal totems, no more animal-human hybrid gods. In *The Loss of a Pet*, Wallace Sife cites the late Rabbi Balfour Brickner, a leader of modern Reform Judaism, who allowed that a pet, "having brought joy to the life of its owner, is as deserving of loving care in death as it was in its lifetime." Reconstructionist Rabbi Susan Schein, and other rabbis in the more liberal branches of Judaism, have constructed a burial service for pets, with poetry and biblical quotes. But across all formal Jewish denominations, there was one consistent admonition: It is forbidden to say the Mourner's Kaddish for an animal. To do so would conflate the soul of man with the soul of an animal. Furthermore, the Mourner's Kaddish is a communal act that requires a *minyan*, a quorum of ten. One cannot risk insulting traditional mourners—parents, children, siblings, spouses—by equating the loss of an animal with the loss of a human.

Disputation being at the heart of Jewish law and tradition, I agree and I disagree. I agree there are boundaries between private and public mourning. I agree it would be callous to say Kaddish for a cat in the company of a mother who has lost a child. But I disagree that one cannot honor the soul of an animal without conflating it with the soul of a human. I have met many soulful animals and even more soulless humans.

"Prayer evolves with empathy," I have heard Rabbi Amichai Lau-Lavie preach at Lab/Shul, New York's "Experimental Community for Sacred Jewish Gatherings." In his view, an individual can construct their own spiritual path to healing and seek out a community that will embrace their needs. I did not belong to such a community when Augie died, nor was I aligned with any specific Jewish denomination, but I needed faith, I needed prayer, and I needed ritual. So, out of empathy for myself and for Collin—who, while not Jewish, was also in need of solace—I constructed my own spiritual path and stretched the letter of the law. We said the Mourner's Kaddish at Augie's graveside when we cast his ashes, and we would say it again each year when we visited his graveside on his *yahrzeit*, the anniversary of his death. The heart grieves what it grieves.

Saying Kaddish for Augie was not the only Jewish law I would violate. Cremation is strictly prohibited. Among the reasons is that in the World to Come, only those buried whole will be resurrected. If indeed there is an afterlife, the thought that I might not share it with Augie in one form or another was disconcerting. So, again flouting rabbinical law, I asked Collin and my siblings to break from tradition, have me cremated, and scatter my ashes at the break in the dunes in front of the windmill at Two Mile Hollow Beach in East Hampton. If, at that future time, East Hampton is too much of a schlep, any dune at any ocean beach will do. Anywhere there is wind and water and earth and sky, I will be with Augie.

Chapter 4

The Augie Years

As I get older, I have started measuring time as my parents and grandparents did, not by specific years, but by world events and personal milestones. "Before my time." "During the Depression." "After the war." Before marriage, after divorce. Before, during, and after children, illness, college, jobs, love affairs. My life will always be divided like a play in three acts: Before Augie (feckless youth and professional ambition), the Augie Years (responsibility and devotion), and After Augie (healing and gratitude).

Before Augie, I flew without fear. Work, family, vacations. I loved to fly. Jumbo jet, turboprop, turbulence, snowstorm, I didn't flinch. I was a devotee of airplane disaster films. During the Augie Years, I panicked at the slightest shudder. *Who would care for Augie? Who would know his favorite walks? His favorite treats? His friends? His quirks?* After Augie, my fear of flying evaporated. I worry less about crashing and more about my sciatica.

Before Augie, I could leave for work early in the morning, have drinks and dinner with friends in the evening, or suffer through an obligatory work-related event—the latest wunderkind director's godawful, five-hour intermissionless immersive opera. The only bladder I had to worry about was my own. During the Augie Years, there was a mandatory detour home before any evening event. Or a dog walker to schedule. Or, better yet, an undefined "prior engagement." After Augie, staying home and bingeing old movies became my prior engagement.

Before Augie, I was smoker. A pack-a-day smoker. A wake-up cigarette, a before-and-after-meal cigarette, a cigarette with every coffee or drink, a cigarette after sex. In olden times, I smoked with abandon in bars and on airplanes. Before Augie, I quit frequently—a day, a week, a month. Before Augie, quitting was about health, self-esteem, and social acceptance. Quitting was about *me*. During the Augie Years, quitting was for a puppy who wanted nothing more than to snuggle, whose little lungs needed protection from carcinogens. Quitting was for a dog who loved to hike and climb, which meant my lungs needed more capacity. Quitting was about *him*. During the Augie Years, quitting was easy. No behavior modification, hypnotism, acupuncture, pills, patches, gum, or odes to willpower. I just thought of Augie. Not a single cigarette until the day he died. After Augie, walking home with Collin after bringing his body to the vet, I picked up a pack of cigarettes and a lighter at the first bodega we passed. I lit up and inhaled deeply, as if the smoke could extinguish the fire within.

Before Augie, I went through the occasional stoner phase. Marijuana was still illegal and clandestine, all the more fun when it was part of a classic "downtown" New York City social occasion. When paying a call on my source (to call Iris, a woman of a certain age, an uncertain accent, and a scathing wit, a "dealer" would be rude), one didn't swing by for a nickel bag of cheap weed. One showed up at her Tribeca loft with a chilled bottle of white wine. Good jazz was on the stereo. A salon of oddball sophisticates might be gathered. She procured only the finest domestic and imported blends and presented each varietal like a sommelier. One could zone out and chat for hours as if in an opium den of a bygone era.

During the Augie Years, I dialed down my indulgence so I could be sufficiently present to attend to his needs. He reciprocated by being equally present to attend to my needs. He was the perfect sober buddy. Whether I was at home staring at the ceiling or walking the streets staring up at the streetlights or sprawled on the grass at the house in Springs gazing at the stars, he was a willing companion. He understood the concept of a waking dream. And he understood the concept of munchies. Doritos being unhealthy for dogs, he got his favorite dog biscuits. After Augie died, without him as my sober buddy, I started having bad trips. I quit marijuana in all its forms. I haven't touched it since.

Before Augie, love was an ideal, an uncertain mix of adolescent infatuation and Hollywood romance. During the Augie Years, my heart grew and my brain developed. My understanding of relationships matured. I bonded with Collin in no small part because of the capacities Augie forged.

When I adopted Augie, I thought I was just a bachelor adopting a companion. A dude and his dog. I thought the math was additive: One plus one equaled two. I was wrong. It was transformative. One plus one equaled family. The moment he came home, I went from an *I* to a *we*.

Our little family became part of my larger family. My siblings never failed to inquire about him when we spoke, and my seven nieces and nephews never really knew Uncle Matt without Augie. "Where's Augie?" was their first question when I walked in the door. Far from feeling insulted at the look of disappointment on their faces, I was happy to be second banana. He was playful and patient with them. He never griped about a pulled tail or a tugged ear or a too-tight hug. Never in his life did he growl or snap or nip at a child.

Augie redefined my relationship with my parents. Before

Augie, I had no great hostility toward them beyond the minimum required by psychoanalysis. They loved me and I loved them, even if the rapport was often awkward. My mother, tightly wound, chattered endlessly of her ailments and expounded dramatically on all matters political and cultural. She was not much of a listener. My father was a steady presence, a hard worker devoted to his family, but stoic in demeanor. He was not much of a talker. During the Augie Years, communication with my parents flourished. Suddenly they were more alive and engaged, not just in his life but in mine too. When we visited them in Toledo, my mother read poetry to him and he was her willing audience. She spared no nuance of rhythm or expression. My father was delighted to have a silent companion for the Weather Channel or an excuse for a contemplative walk. In his final days, when dementia erased his children's names from his memory, my father would light up and shout "Augie!" when we entered his room. Like President Kennedy, who bemoaned that his presence in Paris was outshone by the attention focused on his elegant wife, I was merely the man who accompanied Augie to the nursing home.

In the Augie Years, both my parents died. Their deaths were sad but not unexpected and, compared to Augie's death, mourning and grief went through natural cycles. After Augie died, there were times I felt ashamed that I grieved more for him than for them, but I had gone off to college at seventeen and lived an independent life ever since. I shared a home and life with Augie longer than I shared a home and life with my parents.

Before Augie, my urban social life had begun to thin out. Single straight friends married, had children, and moved to the suburbs. Single gay friends became coupled and forged new social circles (and, as the law evolved, got married, had children, and moved to the suburbs). Among my high-achieving peers, affluence—which always eluded me—increasingly became a social divider. I wasn't poor, but I couldn't afford impromptu getaways to Caribbean islands or dinners at celebrity-chef restaurants. I got B-listed.

In the Augie Years, my social life flourished. He helped me cultivate new friends in the West Village and in Springs. Much like parents who become friendly with the parents of their children's friends, my human friendships became a function of his canine pals—Shiloh, Milo, Mabel, Foley, Fabrizio, Dylan, ChouChou—and their owners. There were invitations to dinners, a wedding, a Yankees game. Unquestionably, his best friend was Dash, the longtime companion of Geoff, a landscape designer with whom I became great friends in Springs. Geoff and I were both Midwesterners, exactly the same age, gay and single, and shared the same bawdy sense of humor. We were "cool" year-round Springs people with modest houses who held our noses high looking down on the obnoxious summer Hamptons mansion crowd. But as much as we bonded in laughter and bitchery, we owed our friendship to Augie and Dash, who met at the beach. Dash was a nearly identical shepherd mix—same coloring, same ridiculously long legs and big ears—except three times Augie's size. He looked like Augie's big brother and acted like it. Dash welcomed Augie into his world, even if he was occasionally annoyed by Augie's little-brother clinginess. They raced in tandem on the beach, chasing birds far out of their reach. They went rabbit hunting in the woods. They ate from each other's bowls. They crashed on Geoff's cool tile floor side by side to nap. When Augie and I visited for play dates, I never had to worry about him wandering too far. If he was out of sight, I knew he was safe with Dash.

In the Augie Years, West Village neighbors who had never made eye contact with me stopped to say a cheerful hello to Augie, and eventually to me. He charmed shopkeepers, inspiring many of them to begin the practice of keeping dog treats behind the counter; he should have received a percentage of the sales from the customer acquisition strategy he inspired. We lived around the corner from Henrietta Hudson Bar & Girl (sic), the city's biggest lesbian bar. On weekends, no matter how long the queue of women, Augie accepted every scratch, kiss, and nuzzle with grace as if he were royalty in a receiving line.

After Augie, people still stopped to say hello, but it was with wistful memories. Then the hellos dwindled to nods as they walked by. The proprietor of a pet shop where I had been a regular kibble customer for a decade drew a blank when I passed him on the street. In fairness, he wasn't alone. People I'd known for years did not recognize me without Augie.

Before Augie, I was terrible at picking up men. I was not a

bar-talker or a club-goer or part of The Scene. During the Augie Years, I had a wingman: dalliances and romances were sparked by his charms. Johnny, a fellow Augie seduced in Central Park, was a young artist with whom I remained close after the affair faded. A few years later, Johnny died unexpectedly. When his sister called with the sad news, she said her mother specifically asked that I bring Augie to the memorial service. They had met several times and she associated Augie with happy memories of Johnny. It was a long drive to Knoxville, Tennessee, for the service, and there were disapproving glances from other guests, but Augie behaved like a gentleman the entire time and was a tremendous comfort to a grieving family. It was one of his finest moments.

In the Augie Years, I always felt safe on the city streets, even when we occasionally wandered into sketchy unlit blocks. He was my bodyguard night and day. One morning, in broad daylight, walking him in my bucolic neighborhood, I was mugged by a crackhead who appeared out of nowhere. Augie barked and the mugger fled. I called 911 and filed a report. After the police apprehended her, I was called in to view a lineup. I was out running errands with Augie, and I explained to the officer that I had to take my dog home first.

"Bring him along," the officer said. I thought, comically, that Augie might be part of the identification process. No, he said, the guys at the station house just liked dogs.

A few weeks later, I was summoned to appear before the grand jury at the woman's indictment (she had multiple prior violent offenses and was facing jail time). The district attorney said it was not necessary to bring Augie to court, but during my testimony he asked for a description of Augie, including his age and breed, whether he had any prior violent offenses, or if he exhibited behaviors that might have provoked the attack. I was asked to state his name for the record. Somewhere in the annals of New York City crime, you will find "Augie."

He was my metronome: His heartbeat defined the largo of a nap, the andante of a stroll, the presto of play. He was my clock: His basic needs tolled morning, noon, and night. He was my calendar: His nose sniffed out early blossoms, impending snowfalls, the dew of summer grass, the muck of autumn leaves. He was my compass: He guided me to places familiar and places unknown. That I know my neighborhood so well is because of him. There are streets in the West Village I would never have walked without his tug; my instinct was for the shortest distance between two points, his for the road less traveled. I walked with him every day for eighteen years, rain or shine, city or country, tethered by a leather umbilical cord to unremarkable deeds of the day and remarkable moments in history, tethered through seventy-two seasons and six thousand five hundred and fifty-three days.

Before Augie, I was singular. During the Augie Years, I was connected. After Augie, I was adrift.

Chapter 5

Escape

Absent Augie's daily hoovering, the kitchen floor was dirtier. Or so Collin told me. I was not in the kitchen much—I wasn't cooking or eating—so I hadn't noticed. The only appetite I had was for coffee and cigarettes. Normally averse to exercise (walking Augie was my aerobic sport) I developed an obsession for the gym. In the morning, in the afternoon, and sometimes in the evening, I stretched, biked, lifted, and crunched. Within a month, I could see my cheekbones. In two months, I downsized my jeans twice. For the first time in decades, I could wear a tight T-shirt without holding my breath. I got a buzz cut. In the gay world, I was transformed from a Bear to a Daddy. I turned heads.

Coffee, cigarettes, gym.

Neighbors stopped me on the street and said, "You look great!"

Coffee, cigarettes, gym.

I bought concealer for the dark circles under my eyes.

Coffee, cigarettes, gym.

Neighbors stopped me on the street and said, "Are you okay?"

Collin was sure I had some sort of grief-induced cancer.

"I'm fine," I said.

"You may be *fine*," he said, "but you're not *you*."

He was right. Without Augie, I was no longer me. I was not even who I was Before Augie. I was irrevocably changed by loving him, and now I was irrevocably changed by losing him.

Joan Didion combed the literature on grief and found repeated observations that the progression of bereavement from "normal" to "complicated" most often occurs when the survivor and the deceased are unusually dependent on one another. "Were we unusually dependent on one another?" she asks of her forty-year marriage to fellow writer and frequent collaborator John Gregory Dunne. "Or were we unusually lucky?" I read this passage and wondered: Are dependency and luck mutually exclusive? Augie and I were unusually dependent on one another *and* we were unusually lucky. Unquestionably, I had skipped "normal" grief and gone directly to "complicated."

Despite the guidance of a longtime therapist, as the weeks and months went by, I was getting worse. I never experienced suicidal ideation, but the depression was specific, deep, unrelenting, and unresponsive to medication. I tried a pet loss support group at the Animal Medical Center, but my capacity for reciprocal empathic engagement was limited. The others in the group had lost a pet. I had lost Augie.

One young woman's story jolted me. Her rabbit had died the year before, and she was still distraught. *All this because of a rabbit?* I thought. *An animal with such limited sentience?* Later, while reading legendary psychiatrist Elisabeth Kübler-Ross's classic, *On Grief and Grieving* (cowritten with David Kessler), I was stunned to learn that her foundational encounter with grief was the death of her pet rabbit, Blackie. Growing up in Zurich between the World Wars, rabbits were a source of food for her impoverished family. She was regularly sent to take one from the warren for slaughter, but she always made sure that Blackie, her "special bunny," was not chosen.

> He was mine, the one love object I had that belonged only to me. Blackie got pretty fat because I kept giving him extra food, and of course the dreaded day came when my father told me it was time for me to bring Blackie to the butcher. I could not allow it. I begged Blackie to run away, but the more I shooed him away, the more he thought I was playing and would run back to me. No matter what I did, he kept coming back, and my pain only escalated when I realized that he loved me too.

From the grave, Kübler-Ross was a better therapist than many of the living ones I have seen. In a single paragraph, she instilled a greater empathy toward others—and toward myself.

Yes, all this because of a rabbit. Yes, all this because of a dog. Yes, all this because of any creature who gives and receives love.

I have had a lifetime of therapy, a vaudeville of diagnoses and treatments. This time was different. I was snobbishly accustomed to pedigreed psychiatrists, psychoanalysts, and psychologists with degrees from the finest schools. I had turned to two of them as my grief intensified, but despite their good-faith efforts, neither could penetrate the darkness. Sensing the depth of my depression, a support group leader at the Animal Medical Center suggested a therapist who specialized in pet loss. I scoffed at the idea. I suspected a charlatan with New Age woo-woo rituals.

I was wrong. Jeremy, the pet loss counselor to whom I was referred, understood the specificity of my sorrow immediately. There was no cant or medicalizing or analytic orthodoxy. He did not want to talk about my mother or my dreams or attachment disorders. He wanted to talk about Augie. He wanted to see pictures of Augie. He wanted to hear about Augie's life. He wanted to hear about Augie's death. With Jeremy's guidance, color began returning pixel by pixel into my sepia life.

Just as I was starting to get my shit together, a shitstorm came pouring down. The magazine story I had been working on in Augie's final days was killed, the first time in my career as a writer that a commissioned article was rejected. That I had been paid was consolation, but it was a story of which I was proud, to which I had devoted countless hours of research and interviews, and now it was trash. Other editors seemed to smell the rot. Magazine assignments dried up, corporate writing gigs dwindled, and a bread-and-butter client of fifteen years did not renew my contract. I had done nothing wrong, the client said. They loved my writing, they said. They were simply switching to "a crowd-sourced digital content delivery platform," which was a polite way of telling a horse he has been replaced by a self-driving taxi.

Con Edison launched a massive six-month street dig under our window. The radiators died. The kitchen ceiling collapsed. My burger-and-movie buddy moved to the suburbs.

Then came the ultimate dump: Collin, the devoted, warm, caring, patient man with whom I shared my life for ten years, wanted out. His discontent had been brewing for more than a year, he said, but he had suppressed it during Augie's decline. He had tolerated my mercurial temperament, but now I had turned hostile, morose, and self-destructive. He was done. No, there was not another man. Yes, he had been looking at apartments.

Perhaps his anger was misdirected grief? I suggested. Collin came into my life when Augie was a mere eight years old. Augie wagged his approval on our first date. Collin and I met when we were both living in Savannah, spending time with our respective families. Our courtship blossomed on evening walks through the elegant squares of the city's historic district under oak trees dripping Spanish moss. Augie always walked between us, not as a divider, but as a connector.

When we settled back in New York City, walking Augie brought us even closer together. Walking him was what we did on a beautiful day, on a snowy evening, or for no reason at all. Augie was the inspiration for weekend trips to the Catskills or the beach. If our voices were raised, Augie made peace. He curled at our feet under the dining table. At night he slept in the tangle of our legs.

Perhaps we needed time or counseling to regain our post-Augie equilibrium? I suggested. No, Collin said. He didn't want time. He didn't want counseling. He wanted out.

A temporary détente was negotiated. Long-planned family celebrations were imminent. He agreed to a charade so as not to spoil them. There was furniture and there were friends to be divided. There were legal, financial, and health insurance issues. He agreed to a grace period. One last favor: I wanted to travel. Would he mind the store? He would.

With Augie gone, Collin going, my career and apartment crumbling, I felt like Gulliver, adrift and uncertain where the currents would take him. Miraculously, a lifeboat arrived. Mari, a cherished friend of decades, reached out from Switzerland, where she and her family lived. I poured out my heart and she mopped it right up. The rest cure, she insisted, was to sit in her garden in Lausanne, overlooking Lake Geneva. I was welcome to come right away and stay as long as I liked, but I was warned there would be a parade of summer guests and there might not be much in the way of solitude.

I'd had plenty of solitude, I thought. Perhaps forced socialization might be a tonic.

Guests there were at Mari's. Lots and lots of guests. In the house, on the lawn, in the bathroom, in the kitchen. Guests for a meal, guests for a day, guests for a week. An Australian noodle chef, a Chicago parole officer, a Belgian soprano, a Russian painter, a Taiwanese orchestra conductor, an expat California attorney, a cat food marketing executive, a race car driver, a makeup artist, the neighborhood pharmacist, a cattle breeder, and a research scientist actually on the verge of a cure for cancer. The motley cast was cheerful, but within a fortnight, I needed to escape my escape. I ventured west to France, where I sampled mustards in Dijon and men in Lyon. Back in Lausanne, I began planning a venture east to Italy. I didn't have the energy for the tourist destinations of the south and knew little of the north. Like most Americans, I thought the northern border of Italy ended in Milan. All I knew of Piemonte and the Lake District was that George Clooney had a hideout on Lake Como.

I presented my dilemma to Mari's eclectic jury of guests at the dinner table.

"What about Stresa?" Teresa, the expat California attorney suggested. "Not even two hours by train. The town is charming and Lake Maggiore is beautiful. But it's the Borromean Islands you go for. You zip across the lake by water taxi to palaces, gardens, and a tiny fisherman's island with marvelous little restaurants. Spend a night or two, take a passeggiata along the lake, and eat lots of gelato."

An easy train ride. Palaces, gardens, lunch, a *passeggiata*, lots of gelato, and a quiet hotel. A perfect little idyll in Italy.

Perfect until I searched online for a hotel. The grand Belle Époque hotels in Stresa were seven hundred euros a night. Even the modest hotels along the lake were three hundred euros. Airbnb listings were all family-sized vacation houses, but when I expanded the parameters, up popped a modest inn just ten kilometers from Stresa. In the thumbnail picture, the smiling innkeeper and his wife looked sane, and the description was enchanting: "Located in a quiet town, our charming inn offers everything you need to spend a few days in peace with nature."

Those who have survived budget hotels in Europe know that *charming* means worn carpeting, *quiet* means the clanking tram beneath your window stops at midnight, and *nature* means a sketchy urban park is a block away. Adding to my suspicion, the inn was in a village called Quarna, a speck on a map, even when magnified on my phone to 200 percent. But I was tired of searching and for one night I could deal with a Podunk pensione. And ten kilometers was an easy train or bus ride or a good solid walk on a nice day.

The email exchange with the innkeeper, Valerio, had the tone of sitcom dialogue:

ME

Greetings. I am an American on holiday and wish to visit Stresa. Might you have a room available at your inn for one night?

VALERIO

Sì-sì! Where you drive from? I give you directions.

ME

I have no car. I will take the train or bus from Stresa to Quarna.

VALERIO

(laughter crackling through the ether)

Is no train to Quarna from Stresa! Is bus, but two changes, two hours. Maybe. Taxi is forty minutes. Seventy-five euros each way.

No train, no direct bus, seventy-five euros each way for a ten-kilometer trip to an inn in the middle of nowhere? It was either the truth, a misunderstanding, a con, an absurdity, or some combination of any or all.

ME

Thank you, but it would be crazy for me to spend a hundred and fifty euros on taxis for one night. I regret I must cancel.

VALERIO

Sì-sì! You crazy. But I have idea. I bring you and give you to Stresa for fifty euros. Is good? But one time only. No here-there-here-there.

ME

(suspicious, confused, intrigued, and exhausted)

Thank you. In return for your kindness, may I stay two nights?

VALERIO

Sì-sì!

Chapter 6

Discovery

Stresa was indeed the escape Mari's friend Teresa said it would be. I wandered through the grand hotels, one more opulent than the next, with gilded old-world dining rooms and manicured gardens and plump Belgians and Germans lounging by the pools and barking into their phones. The town of Stresa was unnavigable, its alleyways packed with tourists and tchotchke shops. But the Borromean Islands fulfilled their promise. The palaces and gardens were glorious. Speeding across the lake in a water taxi on a hot summer's day, doused in sun and spray, was life-restoring. My long lunch on the fisherman's island was superb: gingered carrot soup, pungent porcini risotto, glistening pike, a perfectly composed caprese salad, and gelato served with a trio of macarons—coconut, pistachio, chocolate—that collapsed on the tongue. All washed down with an Aperol spritz, two glasses of wine, and a heart-attack espresso. Topped off with a cigarette, of course.

When I arrived stuffed and tipsy at the designated rendezvous point in Stresa and saw Valerio's megawatt smile, broad chest, and jiggling pasta belly—a white trilby perched on his head—it was bromance at first sight. He was a manly Italian man absent an iota of oppressive Italian man pheromones. And not a *ping* on the gaydar. *Thank God.* The last thing I needed was Cupid shooting a poisoned arrow in my ass. What I needed was laughter, adventure, and friendship. Aside from his driving, Valerio seemed the perfect guide out of melancholy.

We made the final hairpin turn into Quarna, and a jumble of terracotta roofs rose up on the horizon. Baked by the brilliant August sun, waves of heat rising from the tiles shimmered like a celestial aura between heaven and earth. As we drew deeper into the village, we entered a twisting, narrow canyon of stucco houses awash in coral, ocher, pink, and white. Now and then, squeezed between the immaculate houses were crumbling stables on the verge of collapse, their wooden beams sagging perilously under ancient stones, their thatched roofs long since washed away and replaced by corrugated tin. To the left and right, cockeyed alleys meandered into courtyards where rainbows of laundry stretched across balconies. The canyon opened up to a sunny irregular piazza where, on the terrace of a small café, young adults drank beer, old men nursed wine, women chatted over coffee, and dogs snoozed under tables. Across the piazza, teenage girls flirted with teenage boys perched on motorbikes, their neon helmets like mating plumage. A Baroque church with a soaring clock tower stood guard over time itself.

What was absent was equally stunning: There were no tourists. No guides, no selfie sticks, no sensible shoes, no gift shops, no "authentic" local crafts made in China. Terraced hills of pine and birch rose in the distance. Petunias and begonias cascaded from window boxes. Down an embankment to the left was another piazza where children frolicked around a cobblestone mosaic of a giant horn. Musical symbols—clefs, notes, instruments—were carved into walls and forged into iron railings. I did not yet know that music was embedded in the stones of Quarna and the bones of the Quarnesi, that for centuries Quarna had been home to workshops where woodwinds and brass instruments were crafted by hand. I did not yet know that the creepy, crumbling mansion high on a hill to the left was still very much alive with skilled artisans cutting, hammering, bending, punching, polishing, and engraving saxophones. Or that the dilapidated cinderblock building high on a hill to the right was a long-shuttered clarinet factory, now the town's dream of a performing arts center they hoped would be the cornerstone of their cultural survival. I did not yet know that the town band was as central to its spiritual life as the church.

We reached a fork in the road where a plaster saint in a

flowing blue robe stared down from a roadside altar adorned with silk flowers.

"Who is she?" I asked.

"Santa Rita," Valerio said.

Later I would look her up and smile. Lovely Rita is the Patron Saint of the Impossible. What could be more impossible than a depressed, gay American Jew seeking respite in an Italian mountain village with a vigorous Italian mountain man as my guide?

Valerio, beaming with pride, pointed to a yellow stucco house with an emerald-green lawn and lattices of climbing roses. It was his home and the inn. Unlike the tangle of conjoined houses in the village center, Valerio's detached house and the houses perched farther up the mountain were separated by lawns, gardens, fences, stone walls, and vegetable patches. Many were grand multistory homes that looked like the McMansions of American suburbia. He laughed when I asked if this was the rich neighborhood. Yes, farther up there were summer villas for wealthy families from Milan and Turin, but most of these houses were family homes divided into multigenerational flats: elderly grandparents on one floor, their children and their children's children on another, with a peculiar aunt or uncle tucked away in a garret. The huge stones of the original foundations, some hewn centuries ago and dragged from local quarries, could support as many additional floors as there were generations.

Valerio's house had originally been built by a beloved aunt

with savings from her job polishing dental instruments at a small local factory. Like many Quarnesi of her generation, she did additional piecework on a foot-powered lathe in her home workshop. When she died, she willed the house to Valerio, who converted the upper two floors into a home for his wife and daughter and the ground floor into the inn. They both had full-time jobs down the mountain: He managed service for an auto dealership; she worked at a flower shop.

The inn was a welcome sight. In a woman's travelogue, it was the perfect moment for a nice cup of tea. In a man's, it was the moment for a stiff drink. In my story, it was the moment for an Alka-Seltzer.

Before the clutch could cool, there was an invitation.

"You want first to go to Belvedere?" Valerio asked.

The question was phrased as if I knew that Quarna's Belvedere was a not-to-be-missed destination. As if a guidebook had brought me to this crossroads! I did my best to suppress a moan. To my seasoned tourist ear, the word *Belvedere* usually meant a crumbling castle with a tortuous climb to a sweeping view of a predictable panorama.

Before I could decline, Valerio kindly accepted the invitation on my behalf.

"Sì-sì! You want to see Belvedere!" he said.

If Jews are notorious for answering a question with a question, I quickly learned that the Quarnesi will inevitably answer a question with an answer.

You want a beer? You want pasta? You want to hike the mountain? You want to see the church? You want to meet my daughter? "No" is never an option, so you drink the beer, eat the pasta, hike the mountain, see the church, and meet the daughter.

And you go to the Belvedere.

Getting to the Belvedere required six more turns and crossing a boundary of time and culture. There were, Valerio explained, two Quarnas, separated by less than a kilometer: Quarna Sotto, the lower village through which we had arrived, and Quarna Sopra, the upper village through which we were passing en route to the Belvedere. According to various mash-ups of fact and lore, the villages were settled separately in the thirteenth century by nomadic tribes from Switzerland, France, and Germany seeking mountain pastures in warmer climes. Quarna Sotto was settled by Walser people, Quarna Sopra by Frankish Celts. Or both. Or neither. There had been various schisms between the two Quarnas over the centuries, the result of which was that they were still distinct municipalities, each with its own mayor, city council, post office, church, cemetery, booster club, and ancient dialect. Old Quarnesi who spoke modern Italian just fine often conversed in their respective *dialetti*. Young Quarnesi peppered their modern Italian with the occasional *dialetto* word or expression. Much like the Yiddish of my grandparents, *dialetto* was mostly reserved for color, curses, and coded messages in front of children.

The descendants of each community were differentiated by common surnames. In Quarna Sotto, some two-thirds of the population were named Coppi, Maggi, Lanza, Rampone, and DeBernardi. In Quarna Sopra, the prominent names were Quaretta, Piana, Bertoli, Corbetta, and Ciacco-Vasino. And in a twist worthy of the political factions of Lilliput, where Tramecksans wore high heels and Slamecksans wore low heels, the people of Quarna Sopra were tall and lean, and the people of Quarna Sotto were short and stout.

There had been perpetual conflicts between the villages over the centuries, with an array of feuds and hostilities and insults. Valerio told me that not long ago his mother, a native of Quarna Sotto, happened to be in Quarna Sopra and stopped by the post office to mail a letter.

"Why don't you use your own post office?" a Quarna Sopra woman snapped.

The squabbles of yore were over land and water and illicit romance between young lovers and football. During the Fascist regime, the authorities forced the two villages to combine their administration. Within hours of the demise of Il Duce, the villagers voted to separate. Two days of (separate) celebrations followed. In recent times, as the populations and municipal revenues dwindled, skirmishes focused on the consolidation of clergy, schools, football teams, and bands. Nomenclature was strict. Traditionalists adamantly referred to the villages separately: There was Quarna Sotto and there was Quarna Sopra. *Basta*, that was that. Forward-looking young people, schooled together and raised with a broader sense of community, referred to the two villages collectively: There was Quarna, singular.

Valerio snaked through the alleys of Quarna Sopra until we arrived at a nondescript gravel parking lot. Up a modest hill, a stone tower loomed. In my imagination, it was an ancient Roman signal tower. I could see smoke and fire alerting the emperor's centurions to barbarians invading from the north! As with most archaeological fantasies I would have in Quarna over the years, this one turned out to be false. A signal tower indeed it was, but for different media. Originally built for radio antennae, it was adapted for satellite dishes and now cellular phone relays.

Across from the tower was a grassy patch where families gathered at folding tables laden with food and drink. Children dashed about, while dogs napped in any spot of shade they could find. These were not the allegorical or aristocratic dogs of Italian Renaissance paintings. These were scruffy family dogs savoring the scent of summer and waiting for what scraps might fall or be tossed their way.

It was not hard to envision Augie insinuating himself into the company of Italian dogs and Italian village life. Augie fit in anywhere, country or city, human or canine. And at nearly forty pounds with long legs and big ears (he never grew into them), he was no pocket pooch. Long before it was common practice in New York City, I took him everywhere: the bank, the post office, the library, shops, hotels, casual cafés, bars, the subway, buses, taxis, trains, boats. We often took the ferry to and from Staten Island just so he could stand on the prow, snout raised high like a carved figurehead on a grand merchant ship. I never asserted false privilege by claiming him as an "assistance" or "emotional support" animal. I never had to. His black, tan, and white coat was a natural camouflage. Ever polite, he heeled close and never barked and God knows never lifted a leg in polite company. I respected the obvious limits—I would never take him to a fine restaurant or a museum, or to a party without a specific invitation—but every place else was game. We were never thrown out or asked to leave. Not once. Every New York City dog owner should be grateful for the contribution Augie made to advancing the acceptance of dogs in public life.

Mercifully, at the Belvedere there was no castle or staircase, just a flat stone platform that, as we approached, appeared to float on air, hovering over a dazzling panorama. Down below was Lake Orta, its waters reflecting the light of an early summer evening. It looked as if an artful glacier had scooped out a bowl for golden soup, Renaissance masters had painted the rim with a border of pine-covered mountains, and God himself had covered it with a cloche of sky. To the south were the plains of Lombardy, to the north the high Alps of Switzerland, to the east a faint glimpse of the Apennines. In every direction, church spires sprouted from the villages on the hillsides. The air was so clear, Valerio told me, that when the breeze was just right you could hear people chatting from the valley.

"You want picture?" Valerio asked. "You want picture!"

Normally I would decline. In the analog days of travel, I never carried a camera or posed in front of a monument. Nor in the digital age had I joined the selfie generation. But this image was not for posting or sharing or boasting or liking or tagging. This image was for me. This image was to document the first moment since Augie died that I felt happiness.

Chapter 7

Exploring

After the revelation of the Belvedere, we finally arrived at the inn. Valerio's wife, Tati, a curvaceous blond whose radiant eyes matched her husband's radiant smile, and their daughter, a seven-year-old who glowed as if she had swallowed a pink lightbulb, delivered "Ciao-Ciao!" greetings from an aboveground pool in the side yard. It seemed a bizarre anachronism—a neon-blue, vinyl monstrosity planted among pear trees, blueberry shrubs, bean stalks, and a tin-roofed firewood lean-to—but what should I expect? Nymphs carousing in a wine vat with Bacchus? It was a scene no different from a hot August day from my childhood, my siblings and I splashing around a neighbor's identical neon-blue, vinyl monstrosity.

Ryk, a wriggly English setter, raced over to inspect me.

"Vai! Vai!" Valerio shouted. "Go! Go!"

Ryk didn't budge.

"Dumb dog," Valerio said, with a shrug of apology and exasperation.

"Dog before so smart, so special," he said.

His eyes welled with tears. He looked away. It took every bit of fortitude for me to hold myself together watching him hold himself together. He was a member of the quiet society I had come to know: those who have lost a spirit animal for whom enduring grief remains easily provoked.

Far from the cat-lady worn-carpet dive I feared, the inn was a shelter magazine dream: cool marble floors, warm walnut doors, polished fixtures, a modern kitchenette, and an antique armoire just to shake things up. There were only two guest rooms, each with its own blindingly clean bathroom. Every tile and line of grout seemed freshly scrubbed with a toothbrush. Beyond the sliding glass doors of each bedroom was a patio with cushioned wicker furniture and a view of the mountains. My inner New Yorker ran the numbers. At the rate Valerio charged, I could stay for a month at half the price of my West Village apartment. Breakfast included.

Let Collin keep the apartment, I thought. I could be happy here. Happier living in a mountain village inn. The only thing missing was Augie. How he would have romped and snoozed with the dogs at the Belvedere. How he would have greeted the townsfolk on our walks—human, canine, feline—and how they would have greeted him in return. He would have found the inn enchanting. He loved hotel rooms. After a long car drive, he would bolt inside and dash to the toilet for a drink before I could fill an ice bucket with fresh water. Then, his mouth dripping, he investigated every corner and tested the bed. Having seen my share of television exposés and crime shows where ultraviolet light reveals the stains of humanity on a hotel bedspread, it was my habit to remove it immediately and toss it in a corner. Augie would leap on top, do his circle dance to smush it down, take a deep breath and let out a sigh, and crash in his bedspread nest. For a human, it was a petri dish of horrors. For a dog, it was a sachet.

He might have been disappointed with the immaculate condition of Valerio's inn.

"Too clean," I could hear him say. "Nothing to lick."

And he would be right. Valerio obsessively vacuumed and mopped wall to wall every day. There was not a crumb to be found anywhere. The linens, I was sure, would pass any ultraviolet examination. But Augie would make do. If not on the bed or the cool marble floors, he could find a place in the sun on the patio where, instead of dregs of humanity, he would inhale the perfume of mountain air and pine trees and gardens and hear the sound of critters washing over him, their language universal and inviting.

As I curled up for the nap I so desperately needed, I clutched my pillow thinking of Augie. I had long since shrugged off any "object-dependence" psychobabble with regard to pillow clutching. I wasn't traveling with a stuffed animal or a blanket like Charlie Brown's friend Linus. Now and then I just needed something to hold on to, something to fill the void. Happy memories of Augie existed in the conscious realm, but still overshadowed by grief, I had to remind myself to think them. Happy memories had not yet entered the unconscious realm where dreams of Augie might appear. Fortunately, there were no nightmares. The mind—conscious or unconscious—has an impressive capacity to block pain. Repression is often underrated.

I had been napping for an hour when Valerio knocked at my door. He apologized for waking me, but dining choices in Quarna were limited and reservations required. Ironic, I thought. Here I was, in a hamlet four thousand miles from New York City, and it was still hard to get a table on a Saturday night. The summer crowd—tourists who came for hiking and descendants of old families who opened their ancient houses for August—filled every seat in town.

"You go for dinner at eight? You go for dinner at eight!"

Valerio conveyed my choices with an explanation that was part culinary, part cultural. Just as the French are particular about their dining categories (never confuse a café, a bistro, a brasserie, and a restaurant), so too are the Italians specific in their hierarchy (never confuse a bar, a taverna, an osteria, a trattoria, and a ristorante). In Quarna, the choices did not conform to these traditional categories. Down the hill was Locanda Posta, affectionately known as "Posta," which in old times was the post office, newsstand, and concession for cigarettes, coffee, sugar, and salt. It had evolved into a pub that served a traditional Italian breakfast (espresso and a sweet brioche), a simple lunch and dinner, and on weekends, umpteen varieties of pizza. The mood was cheerful, the service relaxed, the tables set with fork and knife roll-ups and paper placemats.

Up the hill was Circolo, which defied traditional dining categories altogether. Founded in the early twentieth century as a social club for working men, it had evolved into something approaching a ristorante, while maintaining its sense of community. The entrance was dominated by a long bar where men, standing in the Italian tradition, drank and argued. At a corner table, teenagers played card games. Children, like cats in front of a fish tank, stared at ice cream treats through the glass doors of a freezer case. Beyond the bar was a large dining room. Unlike the modest table settings of Posta, every table at Circolo was dressed in crisp white linens with proper glassware and flatware and oil and vinegar cruets. On weekdays, workmen had their ten-euro, two-course *pranzo* lunch as equals among affluent citizens. On weekends, families gathered at long tables for festive meals.

Circolo was run by a young couple: Valentina, a waitress-dominatrix who strictly enforced reservations and the menu, and her husband, Alessio, who was the chef. Unlike his strict wife, he was an affable fellow, with a man bun, tattoos, and a peculiar Italian-Rasta accent from time spent in Jamaica.

Naturally, Valerio chose the restaurant for me.

"You go to Circolo tonight! You go to Posta tomorrow night!"

At Circolo I was given the worst seat in the house: a small table, short on legroom, directly behind the dining room door against which everyone bumped coming and going. But the view compensated for the discomfort. In the foreground was the dining room, filled with vivacious families as if from a classic Italian film. In the background were enormous windows looking west to the mountains and the setting sun. Valentina, the hostess/waitress, was Goth-perfect: kohl-lined eyes, high Doc Marten lace-ups, and an affect as flat as Morticia Addams. Her English was adequate if a little too literal. My *primi* choices were "pasta with cream," "pasta with ham and cream," and "pasta with tomatoes." My *secondi* choices, as I understood them, were "cow with sauce," "pig with sauce," "veal with sauce," or a plate of "meats and cheeses."

"Solo pasta con pomodoro," I answered, my Italian sufficient to process "just pasta with tomatoes." My lunch had finally settled, but a modest bowl of pasta was all I wanted.

"Solo pasta con pomodoro?" Valentina replied. Her mockery of my flat Ohio vowels was spot-on, but her tone was ambiguous.

It was not clear whether she was sneering at my pretense or pronunciation or at my ignorance in Italian dining culture. Only one course? It was as if Oliver Twist had said, "No more, sir. I'm full."

"Sì," I said. "Solo pasta con pomodoro."

"No bread, no wine, no water, no salad, no meats? Solo pasta con pomodoro?"

Clearly I had tripped a cultural wire. The wiser course of action seemed to concede.

"Okay, okay," I said, this time sticking to respectful English. "Salad, bread, wine, and water."

She shrugged and walked off.

My gaze went back and forth between the glow of the sun setting behind the mountains and the boisterous families around me. The men argued, the women chatted, the children ran about.

Valentina plopped a Flintstones-sized platter of pasta on my table and dashed off. I assumed there was an error. I flagged her down.

"This must be a mistake. I'm just one person," I said.

"Is for one!" she snapped.

It was, I would learn, a grievance that even the Quarnesi held against Circolo. It was an inverse of the old joke about the customer who complains, "The food is terrible and the portions are too small!" At Circolo, the food was wonderful and the portions too big. My pasta was fresh and tender, the tomatoes kissed with a pinch of sugar and salt, but it was an impossible feat.

As I was wiping my platter with the last piece of bread, a bout of singing began, first at one large table, then at another. Folk song? Pop song? Drinking song? I was curious.

"What are they singing?" I asked Valentina when she came to clear my plate.

She scowled and stomped off.

Soon a man arrived at my table, fortysomething, thin as a birch, with calm eyes and a salt-and-pepper beard. He spoke in halting English. He looked concerned.

"Is a problem?" he asked.

"No, no," I said. "No problem. I just wanted to know what song they are singing."

"Ah," he said. "Is football song. Their team wins."

He stroked his beard as if to coax out the words.

"Where you are from?"

"New York City," I said.

"New York City! Is not like Quarna! You like Quarna?"

"Yes, it is beautiful."

"Where you stay?"

"The inn," I said, pointing up the hill. I did not yet know that Valerio's two rooms, along with two rooms above Locanda Posta, made up the entire lodging capacity of Quarna.

"You are hiker?" he asked.

"No," I said. I did not yet know that the mountains above were destinations for Italian, Dutch, French, and Swiss trail enthusiasts.

"You are here for Mandali?"

"No," I said. I did not yet know of the Mandali Retreat Center, a meditation destination perched on a bluff in Quarna Sopra.

"You are musician?"

"No," I said. I did not yet know of the village's history of instrument craftsmanship and the saxophone factory up on the hill.

He seemed to have exhausted the options, as if hiker, meditator, or musician were the only three reasons anyone would come to Quarna.

While we were speaking, Valentina placed a platter of prosciutto, bresaola, and mortadella on the table. Apparently, a *secondi* was nonnegotiable. "Meats and cheeses" it was. It was plated like a perfect rose blossom. It was too beautiful not to eat.

"You want another glass of wine?" he asked. He waved to Valentina, pointed at my glass, and the refill promptly arrived.

A rapport now established, I felt I could turn the tables.

"You are from Quarna?" I asked.

"Yes," he said.

"And what do you do?"

He pulled up a chair.

"I am Renato. I am policeman," he said.

Had I acted in a manner so suspicious as to alert the authorities?

"Am I under arrest?" I asked.

His laughter put us both at ease.

No, I was not under arrest. He was just the nearest English speaker the exasperated Valentina could find.

There were no arrests in Quarna because there was no crime in Quarna, he explained.

"In Quarna most people do not lock doors," he said. "There is nothing to steal."

Disputes between neighbors? The backlog was two hundred years. Drunk drivers? By the time they were reported, they were asleep at home. Speeding tickets? He laughed. He would have to ticket every driver twice every day: downhill in the morning and uphill in the evening. Fights? Only on the football field, where they were handled by the referees.

He was silent for a moment, as if contemplating whether to tell the truth or the whole truth. Yes, he said, there were dissonant notes in village harmony: drug dealers to oust, altercations to negotiate, domestic abuse to resolve. Renato shook his head in dismay, but the gloom quickly passed.

"You want limoncello?" he asked when the level of my wine glass was getting low. He signaled Valentina. The limoncello appeared. I didn't protest.

Absent crime, what did Renato do all day? He drove the school bus, directed traffic during processions, opened and closed the cemetery, posted municipal notices, cleared fallen branches, mended fences, and soothed petty disputes.

"I go to work in the morning with nine problems," he said. "By noon I fix seven and then have twelve."

Renato spoke of his family and of village traditions. He spoke of the community's fear that Quarna might become a ghost town like so many other mountain villages. I doubt there were a hundred words in his English vocabulary, but like Valerio, he configured them with fluency. He saw the comedy of his people but did not speak of the tragedy he had known, which I would later learn from others. His father was a hiker, climber, and naturalist beloved by the town. He introduced children to flora and fauna, blending folklore and science into magical stories. At the age of forty-six, while scaling Mont Blanc, Renato's father fell to his death. His greatest legacy to his son, I was told, was preternatural kindness.

After well over an hour, Renato took his leave. It was time for him to finish his duties for the day and for me to wander the cobbled streets. The sun was now below the horizon and the streetlamps came on, casting noir shadows. I was disoriented at every turn, but if I went too far down an alley or got lost when the street turned into a dirt path, all I had to do was wait until the church clock tolled. Like Augie guiding me through the cobbled streets of the West Village, the bells of Quarna were my wayfinder home.

There was another sound in my head that evening. It was a bell tone, like the *ding* of the glockenspiel that signals to a musical theater audience that a song is about to begin. In the months of grief since Augie died, I had not written a thing. My journal was perfunctory. I pitched no magazine stories and I received no assignments. There was no great American novel (or even a bad one) in a drawer or sheaf of short stories. I had silenced my voice. My imagination was a void.

But as I wandered Quarna that evening, the elements coalesced: a journey of healing, the accidental discovery of an ancient village, a mountain backdrop, a cast of vibrant characters, and the threat of cultural extinction.

Ding! I heard a song coming on.

Chapter 8

Brigadoon

In the morning, after lazing on the terrace with Valerio's hearty breakfast, I began a methodical walk from the bottom of Quarna Sotto to the top of Quarna Sopra. In the morning light, absent the dazzle of discovery or the blur of wine and limoncello, a certain shabbiness was revealed. Yes, on the main road, there were pastel houses with window boxes spilling waterfalls of red petals, but down the alleys and into courtyards were vacant houses, weeds poking through broken cobbles, rusted tools, broken roof tiles, cigarette butts, a condom wrapper. The old stables that seemed rustic on arrival now looked like dead teeth. This was not a Potemkin postcard village. The mom-and-pop stores were not imitations of a bygone life. The butcher shop had a glass case displaying rough cuts of beef and pork, two lonely whole chickens, an array of bulging salamis hanging from the ceiling, and the occasional fly. The two little grocery stores, one in Quarna Sotto and one in Quarna Sopra, were each the size of a New York City corner bodega. Their inventory was alike: bread and eggs, a few wheels of cheese, cheap wine, packaged cookies, jarred sauces, boxed pasta, and cleaning products. Cleaning appeared to be the primary hobby of older Quarnese women who, in their flowered housedresses and head kerchiefs, dutifully swept the streets in front of their homes.

Yet another revelation of village life presented itself on that first morning. Not a man, woman, or child passed by without a smile and "Giorno!" or "Ciao!" Old people ambling to the grocery, adults bustling to jobs, kids running to playdates. Shopkeepers, construction workers, and even, it seemed, dogs behind fences, cats nestled on the hillsides, donkeys and horses and cows nibbling grass. "Giorno!" I heard at every twist and turn. "Giorno!" I replied. More people said hello to me in an hour than in twenty years in New York.

The counterpoint to the simplicity of the Quarnesi was the grandeur of their churches, one each in Quarna Sotto and Quarna Sopra. Behind modest exteriors, through humble wooden doors, were explosions of color: the gold of glory, the blue of purity, the purple of faith. There were portraits of the life of Mary, carvings of the martyrdom of Christ, painted terracotta saints adorned with crowns of silver and gold, wide marble altars lit with pendants, and eighteenth-century organs. This was not Florence or Venice. There were no Renaissance masterpieces. But what these paintings lacked in richness and perspective was balanced by the exuberance of the artists who painted them. It was astonishing that the offerings of shepherds and craftsmen paid for two elaborate churches, plus several smaller chapels reserved for special occasions.

"How was this possible?" I later asked Roberto, the village sage.

"Dia prima del cibo," he said. God before food.

Two cemeteries flanked the village: one at the base of Quarna Sotto, one at the summit of Quarna Sopra. Old headstones were carved from dark granite and adorned with photographs of stoic men in high collars and stern women in lace. Contemporary footstones were sleek slabs of polished marble. There were Lego cars on the grave of a child. There were grand mausoleums for prominent families. Had I not already made my intentions clear to Collin that I wished to have my ashes cast beside Augie's at the beach, I would be content to spend eternity in Quarna.

On my way back down to Quarna Sotto, I came across an imposing gate adorned with the letters *R* and *C* in gilded script. Through the gates, I could see a crumbling pink mansion connected by a footbridge to a long, low, decrepit building.

R and *C*. Roman Catholic perhaps? A former monastery

where monks once copied manuscripts with quill and ink? Or a convent where nuns once embroidered vestments? I asked Valerio what Catholic institution it once was. He howled. No, the letters stood for Rampone & Cazzani, a saxophone factory owned by his uncle Roberto and managed by Roberto's sons, Claudio and Simone. The pink mansion, abandoned for decades, was the grand home of the Rampone family in better times. The long, low, decrepit building was still very much alive with craftsmen.

Classical music is the genre to which my ears have been finely tuned since childhood, and perhaps predictably for a man of my ilk, I am well-versed in the canon of musical theater and the Great American Songbook. Not that I am a complete nerd. I followed the pop and rock music of my generation, from the Beatles to the Eagles. My first rock concert, at age fourteen, was Styx opening for Queen at the Toledo Sports Arena. "Bohemian Rhapsody" was new, and Freddie Mercury was ecstatically alive. As for jazz, I had little affection. Meandering, absent structure and logic, it went in one ear and out the other. If I went to a jazz club, it was as a guest under duress. But here was another element of the story brewing in my head. How improbable that a music journalist escaping grief would stumble upon a musical instrument workshop in a hamlet in the Alps.

The first hurdle was getting inside the factory.

"Would your cousins show me the factory?" I asked Valerio.

For the first time there was no "Sì-sì!"

"Impossible! They very busy men. Is better you go to the museum."

Museum? Yes, he explained, a small museum, just across the road from Circolo, was dedicated to the history of musical instrument manufacturing in Quarna. The hours were irregular, but he would call to see if an appointment could be made to open it for me.

He could read my determination and conceded. I was welcome to ring the bell at the factory gate and ask his cousin Claudio for a look inside, he said. Claudio was the only one at the factory who spoke English, and Valerio warned me that he was stubborn. Unless I was a virtuoso saxophone player the answer would be no.

I rang the bell and the negotiation began.

ME

(*largo amabile*, slow and amiable)

Hello. I am a music journalist from New York on holiday staying at your cousin's inn. I wonder if I might have a tour of your workshop.

CLAUDIO

(*furioso fortissimo*, loud and furious)

Impossible! We do not give tours. We have important musicians and dealers coming. We are planning for a major trade show. I have no time.

ME

(*ostinato amabile*, persistent and amiable)

I understand. I apologize for the intrusion. Perhaps tomorrow?

CLAUDIO

(*feroce*, fierce)

Impossible!

ME

(*ostinato patetico*, pathetically persistent)

Fifteen minutes?

CLAUDIO

(*marcato*, emphatic)

Impossible!

ME

(*piangevole*, plaintive)

Five minutes?

CLAUDIO

(*sospirando*, sighing)

Five minutes! But not a second more!

Three hours later, Claudio had tutored me on the history of Quarna, the history of Rampone & Cazzani, the history of the saxophone, and the history of his family. His guided tour began in the back of the factory, where sheets of brass, silver, and gold awaited molding and hammering, components awaited machining and assembly, and work in process awaited testing, polishing, and engraving. The scene was nearly identical to the mad inventor's setup in *Edward Scissorhands*; it was as if film director Tim Burton had, like me, stumbled on Quarna, discovered the saxophone factory, and noodged his way in. The instruments' bells looked like heads, their necks looked like necks, their keys looked like eyeballs. Lathes and punches whirred. Men in blue aprons hammered and polished and assembled with precision, some wearing goggles, others wearing surgical magnifying eyeglasses. The floors were covered with shavings and dust. The air reeked of solvents. The only ventilation came from a few old windows propped open to capture what little mountain breeze the midday sun would allow.

Claudio introduced me to the workers and explained their various skills and tasks. None spoke a lick of English, and their hands were too toxic for shaking, but they smiled and nodded. Later I discovered introductions were not necessary, at least not for them. Rampone & Cazzani was Quarna's largest employer, but the glory days in which they employed dozens were long gone. Now there were but fifteen or so craftsmen, all related by blood or marriage or friendship. No family in Quarna was separated by more than two degrees from Rampone & Cazzani. In the three minutes it had taken me to walk from Valerio's inn to the factory gate, Valerio had texted his cousins Claudio and Simone, and a buddy who worked there. They, in turn, alerted cousins and neighbors that a strange American writer was coming to visit the factory. Before I had even pushed the buzzer, the entire factory knew who I was.

Claudio's English was well-honed from international travel, his timbre warm, his cadences elegant. If there was ever a lesson in saxophone appreciation it was in Claudio's voice. Each sentence was a long, melodic line rising and falling, a riff here, a quip there. Each paragraph wandered, changed tempos, and followed variations on a theme.

"Water, wood, and isolation," Claudio explained, were the blessings that sustained Quarna from century to century. Abundant mountain springs enabled nomadic tribes from the north to graze their flocks in more temperate weather. As time passed, nomads established villages and began diversifying from their pastoral and agrarian economies. They harnessed streams to power mills that would crush chestnuts into flour. They harvested lumber and built lathes and repeaters to fashion woodcrafts. They brought their goods to market in villages near and far, carrying their loads up and down rugged trails in heavy baskets balanced on their heads. The isolation, Claudio said, inspired a culture of perfectionism. If you were going to carry milk, cheese, fruit, flour, or kitchen utensils for three hours in any weather, likely with children in tow, better you should come home with money in your pocket than unsold goods on your head.

In the early 1800s, seeking further opportunities, two industrious Quarnesi went to Milan in search of new trades that might match the resources of the village. They learned to make flutes and clarinets and other woodwinds and established a factory in Quarna. Hardwoods and softwoods ideal for the acoustical properties of musical instruments were plentiful on the mountains: Boxwood, laburnum, pear, birch, olive, rosewood, and walnut were harvested and cultivated. Later, cocobolo was imported from Central America and ebony from Africa. Precious metals—brass, silver, and gold—were sourced from distant suppliers for keys and valves. The market for Quarna's instruments expanded beyond Italy to Germany, Austria, and France. Frequent wars were bad for people but good for business. Military bands led regiments into battle. Veterans returned home and formed civic bands.

The ownership of Rampone & Cazzani passed through various branches of the family over the years, with various degrees of acumen and ineptitude. For a time, control fell to outside investors who skimped on quality and damaged the brand. Roberto, Claudio's father, was a workshop craftsman who used every lira of family money to buy the company, restoring its reputation for quality even as finances flickered. "He blew on the flame just enough to keep it lit but not so much as to blow it out," one village elder told me. Roberto was revered for saving Rampone

& Cazzani and, in so doing, saving the fundamental identity of the village as a *paese per la musica*, a place for music.

Claudio, fortysomething, was the outside man, a natural salesman, ebullient and visionary. His brother, Simone, thirty-something, was the inside man, a skilled artisan whose keen eye and swift hands kept the work flowing. Their father was officially retired but still in the office or on the shop floor every day, an enduring source of inspiration and aggravation to his sons. Their mother, Maria Rita, had been the heart of the business. She kept the books, answered the phones, charmed the distributors, soothed the artists, and fed her husband and sons. Her death from cancer the previous year cast a shadow over the family, the business, and the entire village. It was a shadow from which all were still slowly emerging.

By the late 1990s, woodwind and brass manufacturing had shifted to low-cost factories in Asia, where an entire marching band's worth of instruments could be stamped out in a day by industrial cookie cutters. Rampone & Cazzani began to focus exclusively on what it did best: creating connoisseur saxophones for professionals and serious amateurs. Among their customers were virtuosos from around the world who performed in all genres, including jazz, classical, rock, and pop. When saxophonists came to town for repairs, tune-ups, or to test-drive new instruments, their spending trickled down to Circolo, Posta, and Valerio's inn, which he built, in part, for housing visitors to the factory.

Through a combination of frugality, quality, and innovation, Rampone & Cazzani remained on solid financial footing. Claudio bolstered the brand with a strong internet presence and forged partnerships with distributors and resellers around the world. Most importantly, he built enduring one-on-one relationships with musicians. It was not just a matter of selling an artist the right instrument. A sax player could easily find a French Selmer in the tradition of Charlie Parker and John Coltrane. But Rampone & Cazzani could customize an instrument to an artist's soul like a Savile Row tailor. Can you make this note brighter? Shift this valve to accommodate my index finger? Tool this rod for greater speed? Claudio could take the instrument back into the workshop, say a few words to a craftsman, and a tinker or two later, the customer could try it out.

Rampone & Cazzani's brand reached every continent, but Claudio was equally committed to his community. Working with other leaders in the village—the mayors, the band conductor, the president of the music association, and the president of the museum—he organized tentpole events for the summer music series by recruiting distinguished artists to perform, present masterclasses, or simply jam in the piazza.

At the end of my private tour, after the workers had finished their day and the factory went quiet, Claudio picked up a saxophone to play. His voice and the instrument were as one; he played as he spoke and spoke as he played. His passion and his work were as one. He insisted his talent was limited to test-driving each instrument, but his performance was refined and heartfelt. Did I fall in love with the saxophone after a three-hour tour of Rampone & Cazzani and a private recital by Claudio? No. I respected the instrument more and began to grasp its capacity for beauty and virtuosity.

But it was not the saxophone that was catalyzing my romance with Quarna. It was the power of music in the lives of the Quarnesi—the skill of the workshop craftsmen, the pride of the town band musicians, and the passion of the villagers for whom a clef was a symbol almost as holy as a cross. Their passion was beguiling, a force pulling me into an uncertain journey. I wasn't sure if I was Swift's Gulliver, captured and enlightened by distant kingdoms to see the folly of conventional life, or Hilton's Conway, captured and enlightened by the High Lama of Shangri-La to ensure the hidden city's immortality.

On a subsequent visit to Quarna, I met Chris Collins, the noted American saxophonist and devoted Rampone & Cazzani customer. He compared Quarna to Brigadoon, the enchanted Scottish village that appears for just one day every century in the Broadway musical by Lerner and Loewe.

"Each time I return, I'm afraid it is a dream and will disappear for a hundred years," Collins said.

To hedge against fate, he bought a house in Quarna.

After journaling frantically—my brain was flooded—and a long siesta to clear my mental cache, I followed Valerio's instructions for pizza at Locanda Posta. The mood was far more relaxed than at Circolo. Young people lingered over beer at outdoor tables. Old men stood at the bar nursing their wine. The chef was a fiftysomething man with a salt-and-pepper goatee. The barkeep was a flirty thirtysomething babe in a cropped T-shirt. The waiter was a twentysomething stud in shorts and work boots, the rugged antithesis of the groomed-to-perfection Roman "show poodles" over whom Elizabeth Gilbert gawks in *Eat, Pray, Love*.

From the way the three interacted, I sensed the chef was the father, the barkeep his daughter, and the waiter her young lover. Later, Valerio set me straight. I had the Italian family as wrong as a French farce. The chef was the barkeep's brother. The waiter was the barkeep's son.

Returning to the inn bloated from pizza and beer, I saw Renato, his duties for the day complete, sitting on the terrace at Circolo drinking with friends. He waved me over and in his earnest English introduced me to his drinking crew: a paper salesman, a factory foreman, a freight train conductor.

"The American!" said the train conductor, a gregarious fellow with a broad, toothy smile. Sporting a well-loved, well-worn Metallica T-shirt and black jeans, with a ponytail down to his waist, Gabry revealed an idiosyncratic command of the English language: His vocabulary was derived from an obsession with 1960s and 1970s American pop and rock, his sentences an artful fusion of bubblegum and acid lyrics. He talked and sang and smoked and drank while accompanying himself on the air guitar and air drums. The best of the Byrds segued into a medley of the Carpenters, Blue Öyster Cult, Chicago, and Kiss. In between songs were snippets of his life. He lived in Milan, but the old family house in Quarna was his true home, where he spent summers as a child and where he came for weekends and holidays to hang out with his pals.

Valentina, the waitress, was more relaxed now that the dinner rush had ended. Impressed that I had been welcomed by a few locals, she placed a beer in front of me unbidden; it was assumed that a man chatting with men on a summer evening would want a beer. Later, when I went to pay, she waved me off. Someone at the table had picked up my tab. I was beginning to learn that generosity was a sport in Quarna, and that I would have to learn the art of diversion to reciprocate.

Would that I could have stayed in Quarna another night, another week, a lifetime, but I had already committed to celebrating Swiss National Day with Mari and her family and had to catch a morning train back to Lausanne. Valerio delivered breakfast early, curious to hear about my conversations with Renato and the Circolo gang. It was obvious he had heard reports.

"They curious about you," he said.

I was amused. Surely there were plenty of hikers and musicians and Mandali faithful who stopped into Posta and Circolo and chatted with the townsfolk.

"No," he said. "Is not normal. You strange. You talk to Quarnesi. And Quarnesi talk to you!"

The Quarnesi were suspicious of strangers, I would learn. In old times, encounters with outsiders were mostly transactional: buy, sell, barter. Even now, the interactions were not that much different. To outsiders, the Quarnesi were quaint curiosities. To the Quarnesi, outsiders were like customers to be indulged. And here I was, after two days, drinking beer with Quarnese locals, asking about their lives and listening to their stories, and barging my way into the factory for a private tour.

Before I left, there was the obligatory inscription in the guest book. It is my least favorite part of the cozy inn/bed-and-breakfast experience. The hyperbole, the exclamation points, the subtle critiques, the cheesy accolades. My words came quickly:

"I arrived a New Yorker. I leave a Quarnesi."

Who knew that such sentiment might get me killed?

As we drove down the mountain, on top of the twisting and turning and gesturing and texting and knee-steering, Valerio was now crying.

"You arrive a New Yorker! You leave a Quarnesi!" he said over and over, each time bursting into tears anew. It was as if we were driving in a rainstorm without windshield wipers.

Finally, his eyes wiped and dried, we arrived at the train station in Stresa. In seventy-two hours, we had bonded, as random and unlikely a friendship as I could imagine: an ebullient Italian rooted to the land and a depressed American off the urban grid.

And I had bonded with the village itself: to its history, its passions, and its fears. I had seen its glorious vistas and its scruffy underside. I had yet to reconstruct my sense of home in New York, but here, at least for a few days, I had found a sense of place.

"You come back to Quarna?" Valerio asked with a sniffle.

I did not allow him time to answer.

"Sì-sì," I said. "I come back to Quarna!"

Chapter 9

The Blessing of the Elders

I returned to New York and, while absence had made Collin's heart grow slightly fonder, he still wanted out. His peace offering while he searched for an apartment was a Nespresso machine. My peace offering was use of the sofa.

Assignments resumed, therapy resumed, friendships resumed. I cut down on smoking, eased off on the gym, and put on a few more pounds. But the grief was still acute. I felt Augie's presence in my bed like a phantom limb. I saw an apparition beside the bed, that last gaze of his big brown eyes. Was that the signal I had missed? On every walk through the West Village streets, he was beside me. Now and then, I carried his leash in my pocket for comfort.

Friends invited me out, and I did my best not to be a boor, but Augie anecdotes kept erupting: as if my brain was desperate to save memories, images, and sounds, as if forgetting were another act of betrayal. There was the time on a long ago freezing winter day when his tongue got stuck to the pungent sidewalk in the meatpacking district. There was the time Nicole Kidman stopped to say hello (to him, not me), the time Daniel Radcliffe crossed the street to pet him (sweetly asking permission first), the time Yoko Ono, stepping out of a limousine, lowered her enormous Jackie O sunglasses and waved (at him, not me). There was his first major spring shed: he stood up from a nap and left an outline on the carpet like that of a chalked corpse on pavement. There was the time I roasted a duck and he got so hysterical I had to sedate him with a Valium.

And there was the trauma of his first night home. Every dog training guide and many dog owners I admired insisted I use crate training. They said a crate gave a dog a comforting sense of place—his own home within a home—as well as a means for me to secure the apartment against separation anxiety, the ultimate weapon of mass destruction. I bought a sturdy crate, rearranged my tiny bedroom to position it beside me, and nested it as instructed: a comfortable mattress, a water bowl, a ticking clock to mimic his mother's heartbeat, and even a sturdy old-school hot-water bottle wrapped in a plush towel.

The foolproof strategy lasted less than a minute. The moment I fastened the crate door and turned off the lights, his cry pierced my heart. It was the anguished mewling of a hungry newborn abandoned on the steps of a church in the rain. I brought him into my bed and never locked him up again.

Later that night, there was another piercing cry. My own. I had always been a sleep-in-boxers-only guy. That tradition ended on that first night in bed with Augie when, with his sweet, soft head against my chest, he mistook me for his mother and latched on to a nipple. I never slept without a T-shirt again. Not even now that he is gone.

I committed myself to building a relationship with the saxophone. I listened to Charlie Parker and John Coltrane and Stan Getz and Dexter Gordon, and while I did not feel the nuances I cherished in legendary violinists and pianists, I could hear their personalities. The story that I felt coming on that first night in Quarna seemed a solid pitch for a music magazine or travel magazine about a village struggling to survive. That it might be an open-ended journey of discovery (and perhaps self-discovery) did not yet occur to me.

And then it did. I thought of John Berendt, the journalist whose *Midnight in the Garden of Good and Evil* helped rescue Savannah, Georgia, from decline. He had been riding a wave of airline promotions for weekend getaways from New York and was enchanted by a visit to Savannah. An idea for a story began percolating, its narrative uncertain. To find the story, he decided to immerse himself in the city.

"I would spend perhaps a month at a time in Savannah, long enough to become more than a tourist if not quite a full-fledged resident," Berendt writes. "I would inquire, observe, and poke around wherever my curiosity led me or whenever I was invited. I would presume nothing. I would take notes." Over eight years in Savannah, he found himself "involved in an adventure peopled by an unusual assortment of characters and enlivened by a series of strange events, up to and including murder." A murder in Quarna seemed unlikely, but the possibilities for adventure, colorful characters, and strange events felt sufficient for a story, even if the narrative was unclear. A Berendt-style immersion seemed a logical strategy.

I had coffee with my old friend Susan, who has guided the careers of many composers, writers, and artists I admire. I spoke of Quarna: the beauty, the people, the music, the folly of stumbling onto a Brigadoon. She could sense the enchantment.

"Follow that passion," she said.

I mapped out how I might go back to Quarna, interview people, and collect stories.

She stopped me cold.

"You can't just walk into a tiny village and stop people on the street," she said. "They will run you out of town. You have to get yourself invited. You have to get the blessing of the village elders."

My email exchange with Claudio went like this:

"Thank you again for taking the time to show me your factory. I remain enchanted by Quarna—by the warmth of its people, its beauty, and its history, but mostly by the power of music to keep the village alive. This is a story I would like to pursue in greater depth. I wish to return to learn more, to meet civic and music community leaders, and to interview ordinary Quarnesi. Whether it results in a magazine article or a book I do not know, but I believe the story of Quarna is a story to be told."

I hit send at midnight. I awoke to two replies.

"*Impossible!*" the first email said. "It is our busy season and coordinating all that would be too complicated. I do not have the time to make that happen."

His second message, sent five minutes later, was briefer:

"Call me."

After an hour on the phone, we worked out a plan. A magazine story or book could be good for the village and, he implied not so subtly, good for his business. He agreed that I should not proceed until I had the blessing of the village elders. Getting them to agree individually might be possible, he said, but getting them to meet in the same room at the same time and agree collectively? "*Impossible!*" He would test the waters, but I had to be patient. It could take several months. Or even a year.

Two weeks later I received an email:

"Can you be here for lunch next Sunday? They have all agreed to meet with you. Together!"

"Sì-sì!" I said.

As a long-standing arts journalist, I have interviewed hundreds of performers, writers, composers, poets, civic leaders, philanthropists, and volunteers. I have been nervous on occasion, depending on the stature of the interviewee or the delicacy of the subject matter, but when I arrived that fall in pursuit of the Quarnesi and their stories, I had a full-blown anxiety attack. I did not wish to offend the Quarnesi or, worse, reduce them to caricatures. If I were to take their time and stoke their expectations, I would do so at ethical peril. I had raised the capital of good faith, and I knew I must spend it wisely. There was also the value of my time and money. As a journeyman writer, I had never written on spec. I was investing in myself at financial peril.

There was an obvious hitch in the plan: language. My Italian had grown over the years from my multiple visits to Italy and my flourishing passion for Italian film, art, food, and men. But I was a novice beyond light conversation. A full-blown intensive immersion course might have helped me form simple questions but would not prepare me to understand complex answers. Claudio offered to facilitate the meeting with the village elders, but if they approved and I were to stay on in the village interviewing townsfolk, I would have to enlist local English speakers to translate. Fortunately, there were young people who had learned English in school, working people who used English for their jobs, and several men and women who had lived abroad—a salesman, an engineer, an au pair. With their collective help, Claudio was confident I could gather the essential elements for a story.

There was also the matter of identity. How much should I reveal about myself? No matter how diligently I tried to remain an objective professional, if I was asking them to share stories of their lives and families and history and culture, it was logical that they would expect me to reciprocate. It was already a stretch for them to welcome an American in their midst—few had ever met one—but an American *and* a Jew *and* a homosexual? I could already hear the clickety-clack of the nonnas counting their rosary beads.

As for the Jewish component, I was less concerned about blatant anti-Semitism than I was about simply having to explain it. An Italian friend, Nicola, had advised that I would likely be the first Jew most of them had ever met. The advice proved correct. Their knowledge of *Ebrei*, Hebrews, was the stuff of biblical lore, not modern religious or ethnic identity. The gay thing had Nicola more concerned. Italy was progressive on same-sex rights, he said, but tolerance among city sophisticates did not necessarily trickle down to country folk. Younger Quarnesi weaned on anything-goes American culture would likely be indifferent, but older Quarnesi would be uncomfortable, perhaps even hostile. I had already learned from my visit to the saxophone factory that the analog Quarna grapevine was high speed. The digital grapevine, I would learn, was equally swift. These were mountain people, but they were not hillbillies. They were well-engaged with social media, and it would not take much sleuthing to find pictures of me posing with Collin and Augie on Facebook. And a dozen pictures of two men with a dog in various locales is the international symbol for gay.

I would not be the first cultural explorer to shield his sexuality or the first to weave it into subtext. In Richard Halliburton's heyday as a blockbuster adventure writer in the 1920s and 1930s, his readers would have been scandalized by his homosexuality, even though he traveled openly in gay circles and had a longtime companion he did not hide. Only in my thirties, when I reread his *New Worlds to Conquer*, did I see the obvious homoeroticism in his sensual descriptions of men and camp portrayals of women. In the 1990s, Berendt, as the narrator of *Midnight in the Garden of Good and Evil*, was opaque about his sexuality, even when the story he chose to tell is populated with flamboyant gay, bisexual, and transgender characters and he became immersed in Savannah's "bachelor" social scene.

Ultimately, I decided, I would hide neither my religion nor my sexuality, nor would I introduce it into conversation. If asked a direct question, I would answer truthfully and confidently. I am a man in full. I feel no need for fanfare and I am too old to hide. And I already had too much respect for the Quarnesi to lie. If they ran me out of town with pitchforks, so be it. Running downhill couldn't be any more frightening than driving uphill.

When I arrived in Quarna for the blessing of the elders there was a delightful surprise at the inn: The guest in the other room was a chiseled young Russian athlete with rosy cheeks and ice-blue eyes. Valerio explained that my inn-mate had come for an ultramarathon that had just occurred. At various points in the one-hundred-kilometer route up and down the mountains, the Quarnesi set up refreshment stands with water, tea, cake, and pasta. The marathon brought some fifteen hundred people racing through the village, and while it was not a source of revenue—the runners did not stop long enough to spend any money at Posta or Circolo or to see the museum—the villagers hoped their hospitality might trumpet Quarna as a destination for hikers or music lovers. It was also a bid for Quarna to be seen, so as not to be forgotten in the race against extinction.

My bags were barely on the floor—and my eyes barely off the Russian—when Valerio invited me up for dinner. I was flattered that I was crossing the line from public to private in his family life. And equally eager to see the rest of the house. It did not disappoint. High ceilings, polished hardwood floors, a combination of contemporary and antique furniture, incredible lighting, and the pristine small kitchen of my dreams. Adding to the perfection was a splash of disarray. This was a true family home, much like that of my childhood. There was laundry stacked on the dining table, toys on the floor, and papers—bills and such—in a motley pile on the kitchen counter.

Valerio apologized for the simplicity of the meal, but his idea of "simple" was an aperitivo of salamis, cheeses, and elaborate breadsticks, followed by a lasagna his mother-in-law had sent over. Dessert was his homemade panna cotta with crushed walnuts and honey. This was no sumptuous Tuscan cornucopia out of Frances Mayes's *Under the Tuscan Sun*. This was a weeknight, schoolnight, microwaved family meal, Italian style.

It should be noted that, except at Circolo, where Chef Alessio demonstrated his pasta machine with pride, I was never once served fresh pasta prepared in someone's home in Quarna. Not once. Every kitchen in Quarna was stocked with Barilla dry pasta in every size and shape. Northern Italians, it was explained to me, were too busy to make pasta. They worked, sometimes two jobs. Southern Italians, I was told, were unemployed and lazy. They had nothing better to do with their time than make pasta and then ruin it with too much tomato sauce and garlic.

I sliced off a chunk of a mystery salami and popped it into my mouth. It was gamey and greasy and spicy.

"You like?" Valerio asked.

"Sì-sì! I like. What is it?"

"Is cinghiale," he said.

He tapped into his phone.

"Wild boar," he said.

"Where do you get it?" I asked. I imagined it must be a delicacy from a specialty shop.

He pointed to the backyard. The boar had been rooting around his garden, so he shot it. He and a friend loaded the beast into a wheelbarrow and took it to Luigi the Butcher, whose shop was down the hill. In return for a share of the meat, Luigi prepared salami and stew meat that would last Valerio and his family all winter.

"Out here in the country, there was no avoiding the direct link between death and dinner," Peter Mayle writes in *A Year in Provence*. That hunters eat their kill was not strange to me; after all, I grew up in Ohio, where venison fresh from the kill was a staple. And I lived in New York City, where farm-to-table culture was all the rage. But backyard-to-butcher-to-table was a new concept to me.

While Valerio prepared dinner and Tati folded laundry, their daughter, whom I dubbed the "Pink Principessa," was getting restless. With seven nieces and nephews by blood and a dozen more by proxy, I was an expert in such situations. I reached into my kit bag and pulled out "Head, Shoulders, Knees, and Toes" and the "Hokey Pokey." The Principessa's jaw dropped. It was as if I had invented fire and the wheel. First, I taught her the words in English, and then I had her teach me the words in Italian. Valerio and Tati stopped their work to watch. An encore was demanded. Now with Mama. Now with Papa. Now with Mama and Papa together. The following night, when Valerio's parents joined us for dinner, there was an encore with Nonna and Nonno. And Nonna and Nonno and Mama and Papa.

I am a man well-traveled, enchanted by the planned and the unexpected, but I have seen few wonders as magnificent as watching three generations of an Italian village family tapping, touching, bending, jumping, and laughing. Rarely have I been so impressed with myself.

I arrived at Circolo fifteen minutes early for the luncheon with the elders. A cluster of men were chatting at the bar.

"The American!" said a man I did not recognize, before ordering a prosecco for me. A sporty fellow looked me over, clucked disapproval, and began adjusting my shirt collar and smoothing out the wrinkles on my sweater. He seemed a little too handsy, but I would learn that even rugged, straight mountain men in Italy had a strict code of style. They considered it indecent to wear an unironed T-shirt. The men at the bar all knew who I was, why I was there, and with whom I was meeting. They were rooting for me. They did not want me to look like a bum.

From the bar, I could see into the dining room where, against the picture windows overlooking the mountains, the tables were dressed up a notch since my first visit. There were no summer families with children running about or workmen gathered for the daily prix fixe pranzo. The room now reflected the style of a true ristorante. One long table, set banquet-style, was dressed two notches higher in elegance. I was about to ask one of the men what the occasion was when I realized the occasion was me.

The mayor of Quarna Sotto was the first to arrive. In his seventies, with a smooth pate, he was fashionably dressed in a vibrant blue cashmere sweater that matched his eyes. A retired businessman whose family had ties to Quarna for generations, he had spent his professional career in Milan. His English was clear and witty. Then came the mayor of Quarna Sopra, who could not have been more different in style and demeanor. Tall, slender, with a thick tousle of salt-and-pepper hair, he seemed a vigorous outdoorsman in jeans, a Patagonia fleece jacket, and Nike running shoes. A native Quarnese from an old family, he was a manager at a factory down the mountain. His English was rough, but he was far from provincial. He and his family traveled widely and were headed to New York the following day.

"Your first time in New York?" I asked. No, he said, his third. His wife and his daughter liked to shop, and he and his son were die-hard basketball fans. His primary concern for their upcoming trip was the best way to get to the Barclays Center by subway.

Next arrived the president of the music association, so revered as a musician and community leader that he was known to all as "Il Presidente." A conservatory-trained clarinetist, he was long retired from his day job as a teacher of mechanics at a vocational school in Omegna. Finally, the Rampone & Cazzani crew arrived: Claudio, Simone, and their father, Roberto.

Valentina, in such august company, brought out a radiant smile. There was chitchat among the elders, *primi* and *secondi* orders were placed, and wine was poured.

The interrogation began.

What is your objective? What are your qualifications? What is in it for you? Will this just be about music? Will you write about our crafts? Will you write about nature and tourism? Will you write about the history of our people? Of our resilience? Of the bravery of the partisans under the fascists? Will it be translated into Italian? Have you been to the museum? Have you seen the restored mill? Have you heard the band? Have you met Roberto, the village historian?

Claudio, caught in the crossfire, bravely translated in both directions, before, during, and after each course. They asked, Claudio translated. They ate, I answered. They argued among themselves. I asked, Claudio translated. I ate, they answered. Again and again. Back and forth. They scowled, they laughed, they bickered. Hands, arms, shoulders, and elbows flew. It was a miracle no one was injured.

The few questions I was able to squeeze in fell flat. Their answers were polite but blunt.

"How do you provide health care to the elderly?" I asked.

"Our elderly do not get sick," an elder replied.

The journalistic skills of which I was so proud now seemed embarrassingly naive. I had honed those skills writing about artists and institutions whose biggest problem was inevitably money. I had not written about a village of 634 souls whose biggest problem was existence. Still, they answered my questions politely. Perhaps I was a fool, but I was also a guest.

Dessert was served. Coffee was served. Grappa was served.

There was one last round of discussion and a quiet deliberation. Finally, Claudio delivered the verdict.

Chapter 10

The Community of Augie

That New York City is a vast, cold metropolis is a fiction created by sensationalist movies and television shows. The reality is that New York City is a quilt of neighborhoods. Some patches of the quilt are made of steel and glass, paved in asphalt, and filled with snobs and schemers. Other patches, like the West Village, where I live, are made of brick and mortar, paved in cobblestone, and populated by engaging oddballs. Most patches of New York City are stitched into the rectilinear grid established in 1811. The West Village, more than a century older, remains a warren of twisting narrow streets, hidden mews, old townhouses, churches, small apartment buildings, and secret gardens.

The West Village during the Augie Years was as classic as a period film. Within two blocks were a candy shop, a newsstand, a bodega, a pizzeria, a cobbler, a laundry, a butcher, a baker. (And, yes, many years later, a candle-making shop.) For a cheap breakfast, you rolled out of bed into the Greek diner around one corner or around the other corner to Shopsin's, where a caustic hippie and his wife served mysterious concoctions garnished with the occasional insult. For a cheap beer, you ambled to Chumley's, a legendary speakeasy from the 1920s, where literary bohemians like Eugene O'Neill, John Steinbeck, and William Faulkner once bemoaned the human condition. My neighbors in the Augie Years were mostly just folks: a bookkeeper, a schoolteacher, an art professor, a stage manager, a translator, an actor, a stray doctor or lawyer. Some of the grand brownstones were homes to families with young children. Others, like mine, had been chopped into tiny apartments. Old Sicilian women gossiped from the windows while their husbands gathered in folding chairs in the park around the corner. Dogs and their owners stopped to sniff and chat.

The highlight of our social calendar was the annual Blessing of the Animals at the Church of Saint Luke in the Fields around the corner. This was not a grand parade with camels, horses, and goats like the rites at the majestic Cathedral of Saint John the Divine uptown. This was a neighborhood affair. Mother Stacey, the rector, was herself a dog person. Augie and I often passed her walking Queenie, her Jack Russell. She was never without a smile for both of us.

Into the modest, whitewashed sanctuary of Saint Luke's, our neighbors and their children arrived with pet carriers containing all manner of cats, hamsters, snakes, frogs, turtles, and birds. And there were dogs, lots of dogs. They were remarkably well behaved (more so than many of the adults and children), as if they understood the sanctity of the occasion. Augie sat bolt upright in his pew, nodding hello to his friends. When the procession of the clergy began, he was mesmerized by the swinging thurible, his nose twitching at the incense. His ears perked up at the sound of the organ. When the assembled joined in "All Things Bright and Beautiful," I expected Augie to break out in song. We joined the procession in the nave for a sprig-and-sprinkle blessing on the altar. I took a pass but had Augie anointed. I was covering all bases for his soul.

After Augie died, I stopped going to the Blessing of the Animals. It's not as if I was not welcome. But being welcome is not the same as belonging.

In the wake of Augie's death, family, friends, and neighbors asked if there would be a memorial service or a celebration of life. No, I decided. Augie's life had been well celebrated. Before I met Collin, I threw modest birthday parties for Augie. Just a few neighbors and friends and their children. (Sorry, no dogs. There are limits for entertaining in a tiny New York City apartment.)

I vowed the birthday parties would never get too big, too cute, or too anthropomorphic. He would never wear a party hat or an outfit or even a kerchief. The closest I got to whimsy was buying Scooby-Doo paper cups, plates, and napkins. There were homemade finger sandwiches (crusts trimmed, of course), nibblies, a small grocery store sheet cake, coffee, and soft drinks. Out of concern for Augie's safety, there were never nuts, raisins, chocolates, or anything requiring toothpicks. Out of compassion, there was never a cheeseboard. The children were thrilled to bring gifts—toys, snacks, dog-themed books—and Augie was delighted to receive them. While I futzed in the kitchen, as if I were the help, he welcomed every guest at the door as if he were the host.

When Collin entered our lives, we "gayed-up" the parties a notch. Then another notch. And another. I vowed to keep it classy and never stumble into camp. We (mostly) succeeded.

The guest list broke twenty, then thirty. There was homemade punch for the kids and good wine for the grown-ups. To the finger sandwiches and nibblies, I added heat-and-serve hors d'oeuvres. We upgraded from a grocery store sheet cake to an inscribed buttercream round cake from Rocco's, the Italian bakery on Bleecker Street. We still used Scooby-Doo tableware for the children, but for the adults, I brought out my mother's wedding china and sterling flatware, all of which took a full day to clean and polish. We had the windows professionally washed. Any furniture with a flat surface was draped with a white tablecloth and used as a buffet or a bar. Any extraneous furniture was crammed into the bedroom. Augie received a menagerie of stuffed animals, enough treats for six months, and a growing library of books. There was story time with *Go, Dog. Go!* Our guests had a marvelous time, but we were too exhausted from polishing, prepping, serving, and replenishing to say much more than hello. It took us a week to put the apartment back together.

With each year, as our social circle and Augie's social circle expanded, so too did the guest list and the menu. I bought a chafing dish for cocktail hotdogs and meatballs. Collin, with his passion for mixology, designed a cocktail menu with Manhattans, Old Fashioneds, Martinis, and Vespers, as well as a selection of mocktails and wines. I loathed it when people served good booze out of cheap plastic cups, so I insisted we buy proper glasses to match each drink: highballs, tumblers, martini glasses, champagne flutes. Our bathtub was filled with ice to keep soft drinks, beer, and white wine chilled. We extended the party from two hours to four, hoping to thin the flow, but the strategy backfired: as opposed to coming in waves, people just arrived earlier and stayed longer and ate more and got drunker. It took us two weeks to put the apartment back together.

When the guest list hit forty, things got a little crazy. My mother's wedding china and flatware were no longer sufficient, so I retrieved her mother's wedding china and flatware from storage. We had the windows professionally washed again. We hired a musician-cater-waiter to polish, prep, serve, replenish, and clean up. Our landlord-white walls were embarrassingly dingy, but we couldn't afford to have them painted. Our solution was to buy peel-and-stick paw prints to create a pattern that looked like Augie had walked up and down the walls. Our apartment, which was cut from the parlor floor of a nineteenth-century row house, had twelve-foot-high ceilings. Collin spent all night on a ladder placing the pads and toes perfectly. The trompe l'oeil comedy succeeded in pulling focus from the tragedy of the walls. It was one of Collin's finest moments.

When Augie hit seventeen, we limited the invitations to forty but somehow the RSVPs hit fifty. We rented a U-Haul van the morning of the party and, with the help of two nephews, their friends, and the musician-cater-waiter, we loaded up every piece of furniture not essential for serving (including our entire bedroom set) and parked the van on the street. It was standing room only for food, drinks, cake, conversation, and laughter. There was that certain only-in-New-York party din redolent of Holly Golightly's soiree in *Breakfast at Tiffany's*. Afterward, my nephews and their friends and the musician-cater-waiter brought our furniture back into the apartment and we returned the U-Haul van. Augie now had a zoo's worth of animals, treats for a year, and Mary Oliver's *Dog Songs*. It took a month to put the apartment back together.

The paw prints stayed up until the next birthday. It was his eighteenth, and we felt he and we needed less commotion. We toned down the menu and the bar. We left the furniture as is. If it got too crowded, we didn't care. Indeed, it did get too crowded and nobody cared. People spilled into the hallway and sat on the stairs. There were childhood friends, college friends, work friends, old flames, neighbors who had dogs, neighbors who didn't, and shopkeepers. Among the guests were a psychiatrist, a rabbi, a pot dealer, a mathematician, an art curator, a film director, an actress, a tech guru, a photographer, a carpenter, college students, lawyers of every stripe, children of all ages, Augie's two water-yoga physical therapists, and his veterinarian.

It was not a party, I realized. It was a community. A community forged by the centripetal force of Augie's charisma. Our contribution was just the buttercream icing on the proverbial cake. No, when he died, there would not be a celebration of his life. His life had been well celebrated. The dishes and flatware and cocktail glasses went back into storage. The paw prints came down. The windows turned opaque. The community Augie forged, like him, became dust in the wind.

"We have all known the long loneliness and we have learned that the only solution is love and that love comes with community," the Catholic social activist Dorothy Day wrote in *The Long Loneliness*. It would be a long loneliness until I found my next community. Who knew it would be in a tiny Italian hamlet in the Alps?

Chapter 11

The Separation Tango

The blessing of the elders of Quarna was granted and, so honored, I stayed in Quarna for a month. I began the uncertain task of collecting facts and lore that I hoped to use as building blocks for a story I knew was there, even if I did not yet have a clear beginning, middle, or end. Absent the religion of a sociologist or anthropologist, I had no orthodox methodology. All I could do was ask, listen, and hope a story might coalesce.

Years ago, when I was a writer for *Symphony* magazine, I was surprised to learn that Montana—a state larger than Germany with one hundredth the population—boasted seven symphony orchestras. Amused and intrigued, I lobbied my publisher to fund an expedition. As I made my way from Billings to Bozeman to Missoula to Helena to Butte, even tiny Kalispell, I gathered lovely vignettes. Yet nothing coalesced until I met Mary Agnes "M.A." Roberts. A musician in the Great Falls Symphony, she was a founder of the orchestra and a central figure in the city's cultural life.

A few years before, at an unlikely age, M.A. had taken up the cello and quickly advanced in proficiency to play at the orchestra's high standards. For cello lessons with the nearest fine teacher, she drove three hours each way, every week, for several years—often in brutal weather. I wanted to ask "*Are you insane?*" Instead, I shaded my incredulity (not well, I'm sure) with a simple "Why?"

"Because the orchestra needed a cellist," she said. "And in Montana a three-hour drive is not a big deal."

What began as a quirky travelogue of small-town America became a story of indomitability—a story of musicians willing to do what it takes to make music—for themselves and for anyone willing to listen. The best stories, I find, come at you like a curveball. And I could feel a curveball with an Italian spin coming my way in Quarna.

I returned home from Quarna to find that Collin's affections had not rekindled. I was disappointed but not bereft. I did not beg or plead for reconciliation. Yes, I feared the void that would come with his absence, but I knew I could fill it with infatuations, romances, and faithful impressions of intimacy. I fall for men easily, usually the wrong kind, and there are always plenty of wrong men bobbing in the gay sea. Finding enduring companionship with a good guy, someone with whom I could cohabitate and navigate life, would require yet another miracle of chance. Absent a winsome dog, the odds decreased.

Collin had been such a miracle. Unusual by modern gay dating standards, we did not meet in a major city or gay resort town or at a circuit party. We did not meet in a bar, at a cocktail party, or on a dating app. We met at an old-fashioned backyard potluck dinner in Savannah, where I was spending time with family after my mother's death. (By happenstance, over the years my siblings and, toward the end of their lives, my parents, had migrated south from Ohio to Georgia.) Collin, having recently ended a long-term relationship, was licking his wounds while living with his parents in the Savannah suburbs.

Across a crowded backyard, I saw his face—a fair ginger with a dewy glow—and made a beeline. Our courtship was swift: an awkward lunch, a less awkward dinner, an excellent piano recital, a terrible movie, and finally, after several weeks and multiple dates, he all but moved in. Collin and I became a "we." And with Augie, our "we" was three.

Augie had never been shy when evaluating gentleman callers. If he approved, he stayed silent in a comfortable place. If he disapproved, his actions could be overt: a rude bark or jumping on the bed at inopportune moments.

Or he could be sly.

"Could you please tell your dog to stop staring at me?" a fellow once asked.

As if "stop staring" was in a dog's dictionary of commands.

"Can't you lock him in the bathroom?" another fellow asked.

Lock him *in* a bathroom? I could not even lock him *out* of a bathroom. He'd dig through the door.

Augie had seen me kiss a lot of frogs. He recognized a prince when he saw one. That he endorsed Collin at first hello with a happy bark and a jig was an unmistakable message.

"This is a good one! This is a good one!" he said. "Don't fuck it up!"

There were definitely fits and starts in the early days with Collin, the ordinary stuff of cultivating a relationship. It was clear from the beginning that he was the gardener and I was the garden, always in need of tending. To my relief, it was not a dealbreaker. He was congenitally programmed as a caretaker. He shared in taking care of Augie and never resented the time or money or logistics or priorities devoted to him.

Our catastrophes ended in laughter. Our fights resolved before bedtime. Our social life was quiet: the occasional movie or dinner with friends. Our domestic life was mundane: I shopped and cooked, he did the dishes and vacuumed. Our emotional bond was solid, until, after Augie died, it was not.

The march to finalizing the breakup was a tango: two steps forward, one step back, one step forward, two steps back. While I was away, he began dating and continued searching for an apartment, which turned out to be more complicated than he realized. Far from being annoyed that he was still hanging around, I took sadistic pleasure watching him go through the cruelest New York City rite of passage. Among the many reasons I have stayed in my tiny flat in the West Village for more than twenty-five years is not just the beauty, the location, and the cachet, but because finding an apartment in New York City is a pursuit for which Dante should have added another circle in hell. Collin quickly discovered that rental listings are bait-and-switch, all brokers lie, and there is always someone with more money competing for the same dump. He was working his way up as a lawyer, but his salary was insufficient to rent a studio apartment in a good neighborhood of Manhattan. He downgraded his search to studio apartments in bad neighborhoods of outer boroughs. He began to understand that a certain cliché was true: In New York City, unhappy couples don't stay together for the children; they stay together for the apartment. The quiet apartment in which we lived—with wonderful light and twelve-foot ceilings and a reasonable rent in a well-maintained building on a tree-lined West Village block—was an extraordinarily valuable asset to bring into a relationship. And the lease was in my name.

Just when it appeared Collin was destined to live in some dilapidated sixth-floor walk-up in Brooklyn, in conferring their blessing on me, the elders of Quarna indirectly conferred a reprieve for him. My work plan was to spend a full year in Quarna, with a linear narrative of the seasons, festivals, and musical life serving as structure for the story. Unfortunately, absent a special long-term visa, the maximum length of time that an American can stay in the Schengen Area—a collection of countries to which Italy is a party—is three out of every six months. Fortunately, Italy offered a special long-term visa for artists and writers. To buoy my finances, I could throw Collin out and sublet my apartment at a generous profit. Or I could show compassion for Collin, a man I still loved, whose journey I wanted to support as much as he was supporting mine, and who I knew would maintain the apartment and pay the rent and utilities in a timely manner. Of course, my compassion came with a price. I did not double the rent, as I would have for a stranger, but I did tack on a sufficient premium to cover a significant portion of my living expenses in Italy. He got a stay of eviction, and I got a one-year Breakup Fellowship.

I launched into the visa process with gusto. I registered for an interview at the Italian consulate and meticulously assembled the application. I showed up early in a suit, a crisp white shirt, my best tie, and my lucky cufflinks. After I spent what seemed like hours sitting in a cheap plastic chair, my name was called. I stepped up to the desk, presented my folder, and stood proudly awaiting yet another blessing. The consular officer licked a finger and flipped through the pages, closed the folder, and handed it back to me.

"No," he said.

No? What did he mean no? Surely there was a discussion, a process, a review, a waiting period.

"No," he said.

I asked to speak to a supervisor. A senior consular officer arrived shortly.

She licked a finger and flipped through the pages, closed the folder, and handed it back to me.

"No," she said.

No? Could she give me any reason why the visa was denied? *No*. Was there any other visa I could apply for? *No*. Was there any further appeal? *No*.

I consulted an attorney who confirmed that the Italian government, overwhelmed with immigration issues, was mercurial in their decision even when applications followed all necessary guidelines. The straight path unavailable, I listened to friends and to friends of friends for alternative routes. I followed internet threads from digital nomads. I could apply for a visa for creative professionals in Germany, or enroll in a language school in

Moldova, and skip Germany or Moldova and go straight to Italy. I read that I could claim right of descent from my Lithuanian and Polish ancestors and qualify for an EU passport. With each of these brilliant "alt" strategies came the same disclaimer: The savvy digital nomad who posted the advice on Reddit, or the friend or friend-of-a-friend who had heard about it, had not actually succeeded in obtaining a long-term visa or an EU passport in any such manner. And I had no interest in landing in a German or Moldavian jail.

Finally, I accepted I would have to design a suboptimal plan. I would reside in Quarna according to the constraints of the Schengen laws, breaking my visits into chunks and timing them with the changing seasons. I could complete my one-year plan in two years. The revised scenario complicated things on the home front—Collin and I would have to find a way to cohabitate amicably, but it was easier than expected. He was dating and often away for weekends. In his new bachelor life, he was building a circle of smart, funny, and supportive friends. What with me coming and going to Europe, Collin working long hours and spending time away, we managed to live together and live apart simultaneously. It was awkward. It was weird. It was New York City. It worked.

Chapter 12

Reprogramming

The interrogation by the elders was a lesson in humility. If, with Claudio as my moderator, I struggled to get meaningful replies from the elders—intelligent, educated, engaged community leaders—how could I expect to extract colorful stories of ordinary folks, even with a good translator? I was still a stranger in an insular world.

When I was able to arrange meetings and coordinate with a translator, instead of lyrical tales, I might get a shrug or a few words.

"Why do you do it this way?"

A shrug. "Ecco com'e." That is how we do things.

"When was this built?"

A shrug. "In tempi antichi." In olden times.

The elders, who I saw time and again over meals or coffee, were always delighted to confirm or deny the veracity of a story I had been told. They proved to be more eloquent individually than collectively, eager to share their vision of what could be as well as what was. I arranged meetings with municipal employees who shared details the mayors left out: revenues, expenses, procedures. Most meetings were over coffee or lunch at Circolo or Posta, but with successive trips I was invited into homes for meals or coffee and cake. I can see, in the jagged handwriting of my notes, those days when my hands were shaking from too much caffeine and sugar.

The band musicians were always ebullient, especially after weekly rehearsals. I joined them as they gathered at Circolo over beer and soft drinks. Adults talked about family and travels, boys played *scopa*, girls whispered to me secret nicknames for certain adults. Sometimes I would mention to a group of teenagers an interview I'd had with a schoolteacher just to see their response. I learned that teenagers' eyes roll the same in every culture.

At the other end of the age spectrum, I met the eldest citizens. Valerio arranged for me to meet his great-uncle Gino, known to all as Bis Zio Gino. A dapper man well into his nineties, I had often seen Bis Zio Gino driving slowly on quiet side roads, his well-fed chocolate lab walking beside the car. Gino was too old to walk Siria but wanted to be sure the lumbering old dog got proper exercise. In time, I would learn which dog owners were dedicated like Gino and which dog owners were lazy and kept their dogs behind fences—bored, lonely, detached from nature, barking incessantly. No less so than with pet owners anywhere, in Quarna the correlation of character to caring for an animal was clear.

My chat with Bis Zio Gino had Valerio enthralled. He had never heard many of the stories I provoked. Bis Zio Gino spoke of the various jobs he'd had over the decades, mostly low-paying, hourly piecework in small Quarna factories until, through a friend, he landed a position at the prestigious Allesi housewares factory down in Omegna. His wage was a multiple of what he earned in Quarna, but what he raved about most all these years later was the lunch they served, the likes of which he had never seen.

Why hadn't he pursued a job at Allesi sooner? I asked.

"I didn't want to go down and up the mountain," he said.

And then there was the all-purpose answer I heard every day:

"Chiede al Coppi Roberto!" Ask Roberto Coppi!

Most often referred to last name first, in the respectful formal Italian style, but also known fondly as Pupo by the many young people he had nurtured, Coppi Roberto was revered for his knowledge, respected for his leadership, and avoided for his long-winded soliloquies. He was a jaunty mustachioed man in his late seventies, and he was, by all estimations, the wisest man in Quarna. He was one of the first Quarnesi to attend university and went on to make a modest fortune as an executive with a global textile manufacturer, wealth he shared through generous contributions to various associations. He was, I was told, a polymath of history, archaeology, genealogy, and folklore, and a polyglot of numerous languages, including English. His passion was the history of Quarna. He researched civic and parochial archives throughout the region, curated museum exhibits, and taught at the village schools. And he was as elusive as a lynx.

When a translator was not at hand, I shifted to observing. Which younger children, in their adorable blue *grembiulini* smocks, took the village's bright yellow shuttle bus down to the kindergarten in Quarna Sotto, and which took the bus up to the grade school in Quarna Sopra? Which middle school and high school students rode the public bus down the mountain to Omegna, and which ones hitched rides with their parents?

I looked for nuances of behavior among teenagers that might indicate who were the leaders of the pack. I looked for nuances of clothing that might indicate who came from more affluent families. Shoes, particularly sneakers, were the tell.

I shopped slowly at the little grocery stores so I could watch the women kibitz. Going to Marisa the hairdresser for a haircut was a field study in itself: the woman on deck waiting, the woman in the chair getting her wash and set, the woman under the old-school hooded dryer. I could set an atomic clock by observing which men went to Giuseppe's bar up in Quarna Sopra or to Posta down in Quarna Sotto for their morning prosecco. Which men and women drove hastily down the mountain in the morning for office and factory jobs. Which blue-collar workers came up the mountain for day labor. I made notes on who drove an Audi and who drove a Fiat. I did head counts at concerts and processions and festivals and masses to assess how many villagers participated in community events. If children were walking about accompanied by their parents, I knew they were visitors. Quarnese children ran free. I mentally mapped direct connections and overlapping social circles like a television crime board.

As my presence and objective became known, the strategy reversed. The task at hand was no longer tracking people down but staying in one place as people sought me out. If I sat in Posta or Circolo or Giuseppe's bar nursing a coffee or a beer or lingering over a meal, eventually a genial Quarnesi would sit down next to me or insist on buying me another coffee or another beer. An older woman, perhaps with a child or grandchild in tow to translate, would pull out a family picture or tell me a story.

"Have you seen the…?"

"Do you know about…?"

"Have you met…?"

A man showed me the curtains his grandfather made from hemp and explained how the fabric was made. A young man eager to improve his English would update me regularly on his *liceo* studies. A thirtysomething couple from Milan eagerly showed me the renovations in process on their house. Avid hikers who had been searching for a weekend home in the region, they had never heard of Quarna until a real estate agent brought them here. They were instantly smitten. They arranged for their architect to give me a tour of the town. Her lesson in how to date a house by analyzing foundation stones was a fusion of sociology and geology.

"Come meet my daughter!" a Posta regular bid me time and again. I ducked and dodged. I pretended not to understand, I mimed an excuse, I checked my phone for an urgent message. I calculated that the man was well into his seventies and pictured the daughter he wanted me to meet as a plump spinster he was desperate to marry off. And I feared he saw me, a middle-aged American, possibly of good fortune and in want of a wife, as a prospect.

One night, unknowingly walking near his house, the man caught me by the arm and would not let go. He dragged me up the stairs and presented me to his wife and daughter like a prized kill. To my misogynistic shame, I had been wrong. Foolishly wrong. Their daughter, Matilde, who would become a wonderful friend, was a lively young woman with bright blue eyes, a sweet smile, and a lovely figure. A university student, her English was so naturally American—flawless to every vowel sound and idiom—I presumed she had lived in the United States.

"No," she said. "I just listen to a lot of Taylor Swift and Demi Lovato."

The father who had entrapped me, it turned out, was Valerio's uncle, twin to Valerio's mother and brother to Claudio's late mother. Matilde was thus a first cousin to Valerio and Claudio. My family ties were getting tighter.

Every society cultivates a vocabulary for differentiating themselves, writes the anthropologist Margaret Mead in her foreword to the book *Life Is With People*, the 1950s study of the pre-Holocaust shtetl life of eastern Europe. Some of these labels, Mead says, are self-approving, others self-deprecatory: "Each group proclaims its superiority in some respects and admits openly or covertly, inferiority to others."

This was true in Quarna too. A worldly, well-spoken man met me for coffee one morning and offered a sociology lesson. If I were to truly understand Quarna, he said, I first had to understand the caste system.

"It is not quite as strict as India," he said. "But it is close."

The lowest caste are the Fuorestieri.

"These are the foreigners who dwell among us. They could be from a village over the mountain or from a town on the other side of the lake. Or Milan or Turin. All the same. Maybe their grandfather bought a vacation home here a century ago. Or they met a Quarnese woman and married, settled here, and had children. Still, their entire lives, they are Fuorestieri. They may dedicate themselves to the community, but once a Fuorestiero, always a Fuorestiero."

Next up were the Villeggianti.

"They are a mixed bag. They may have been born to Quarnese parents, or they are the grandchildren or cousins of Quarnesi. Their roots may go back generations, but they were not raised here. They maintain the houses of their ancestors, but this is not their home. They come here for holidays and celebrations or a month in the summer. Some we welcome. Some we dread."

Quarnesi were the Brahmins.

"They are born of one Quarnese parent, better yet two. Their family lineage goes back more generations than they know. Some were delivered by a midwife in the same house where they live now. They have lived here their entire lives, perhaps even worked here their entire lives. They gossip and fight and swear at each other in dialetto. They will defend Quarna with their lives, though not necessarily their wallets; they fight every tax increase even when they have generous pensions and savings. They cherish the past, rage at change, and worry about the future of Quarna."

It didn't take long for me to recognize those Quarnesi, a hundred or so faces, who were ubiquitously engaged in community life. They went to church, concerts, festivals, processions, or town meetings. They were the women who chatted in front of the little grocery store or gathered at Posta in the morning for coffee. They were the men who chatted in front of the butcher shop or gathered at Posta in the morning for wine. They were the teenagers who played in the band or on the football team. They set up tables and served food at celebrations. What I could not yet see were young Quarnese couples with demanding jobs and family responsibilities. Or those who were totally disengaged from village life, who drove down the mountain each day for work, drove back up in the evening, watched television, and did nothing for the community.

"Vagnu ma duma per cagar," Valerio's father would say in *dialetto*, shaking his head with disdain. "They only come home to take a shit."

He could not imagine a life in Quarna without honoring the privileges and fulfilling the duties of being a Quarnesi.

Valerio inherited that ethic. He wasn't one to run for political office or sit on association committees or participate in every community event, but when he took on a civic responsibility—no matter how small—he committed fully. He sneered at visionaries who proposed grand ideas but never followed through, made promises they didn't keep, or took credit for the work of others. "Two-faced," he called them.

"You see my face?" he said. "I have only one."

I knew him well enough to know it was not cultivated arrogance. It was hereditary integrity.

There were still bugs in my operating system. Oftentimes I froze, mentally and physically, thinking there was something I forgot to do for Augie. On the first of each month, my inner calendar reminded me to give him his heartworm, flea, and tick preventatives. More than once on my way to the bathroom in the night, I stumbled on a pile of clothes on the floor and apologized, thinking it was Augie. I often had to remind myself that he did not need to be fed and walked.

In *The Grieving Brain*, her book on the neuroscience of grief, Mary-Frances O'Connor speaks of updating the "prediction algorithm" of the hippocampus, that part of the brain that controls memory, learning, and decision-making. Her mathematical metaphor fit my predicament precisely. Just as you cannot leap from arithmetic to calculus, she writes, you cannot force the hippocampus to learn overnight. "However," O'Connor writes, "you can allow your brain to have experiences, day after day, which will help to update that little gray computer." The return to Quarna for the blessing of the elders, and the subsequent visits over several years, allowed my brain to develop new prediction algorithms, to update my software.

In updating my software, I was vigilant not to erase memories. I struggled to retain Kodak moments and sense memories: the image of his paw prints in the sand or of him curled up like a croissant on the sofa; his soft-as-suede ears and thick winter coat; the maple scent of his chest and the taste of the bacon, egg, and cheese sandwiches we shared. The *tickety-tickety-tick* of his toenails on the hardwood floors. The *thumpity-thump* as he bopped around the apartment after losing his leg.

I missed the skills I had grown to depend on that I had not realized I depended on. I was born with a bum left ear and a not-so-good right ear. Without any formal training, Augie learned to give me visual cues to alarms, bells, and sirens. He nudged me or barked when, in a deep sleep, I did not hear the phone ring or a knock at the door.

When a new generation of digital hearing aids emerged, our roles switched. I began hearing sounds from him I never heard before: snoring, huffing, yawning. One evening, Collin and I were sitting around doing nothing, when I heard a series of squeaks. Ugh, I thought. A return of our friendly little houseguest.

"Was that the mouse?" I asked Collin.

He laughed.

"No," he said. "Augie farted."

I presumed he was blaming the dog for his own misdeed.

"No, no! It wasn't me!" Collin insisted. "You've never heard that before? He farts all the time!"

I was astonished. In all our years together, I had never heard Augie fart. Never.

"What on earth did you think that smell was?" Collin said.

I shrugged.

"New York."

In the West Village, I have never fully succeeded in reprogramming my brain—the possibility of Augie is always around the corner—but off the grid in Quarna, a new normal emerged. I developed a schedule to which I adhered: I awoke predawn, threw on layers against the morning chill, and hiked to the Belvedere to watch the sun rise over the Alps. My hometown of Toledo, and most of the cities where I have since lived, are flat, the sun merely a light bulb on a timer that switches on in the morning and switches off at night. Living in the West Village, I was too lazy to walk across town to the East River to watch the sunrise, but in the evening, walking along the Hudson River just three blocks away, we would often sit on a bench and watch the sunset. The towers of Jersey City were no match for the mountains or the beach, but sometimes, when the pollution was just right, an urban sunset could be a dazzling celestial event.

From Quarna's Belvedere, even on overcast days, the rising sun was a phoenix, its wings spreading color and light across the horizon. It took me a while to find a perch from which I could see the sunset. There was no west-facing marvel like the Belvedere, but there was Monte Matlucco, a modest hill above town where I could watch the sun fall behind the high peak of Monte Croce. The Alpenglow flooded the sky, accompanied by the *tramontana*, the flickering first breeze of evening. The sunrise and sunset panoramas soon proved insufficient; I became obsessed with the micro-degrees of dawn and dusk. I began setting my alarm earlier and earlier. The sunrise itself was no longer enough. I wanted to see the first light of day. Then first light was no longer enough. I wanted to watch the stars fade from darkness and the mountains emerge from the shadows. I was reawakened to the genius of astronomers who mapped the heavens and sailors who used those maps to discover new worlds. I was confounded by the skill with which great artists daub their palettes to light the worlds of their imagination. No Titian sky would ever be the same.

Quarna was slowly taking over Augie's job as my metronome, clock, and compass. It was restoring my link to the natural world. It was restoring my sense of community. Even though I was a detached observer, I was now a part of something. I was seen and I was known.

Waves of sorrow still washed over me. If someone asked me to tell an Augie story, I would draw a blank or have a mild panic attack. I could not remember our life together. All I could remember was his death. I could not see him racing along the shore. I could only see him dead on the floor. The despairing inner voice kept asking, *Why wasn't I there? What did I miss? Why hadn't I noticed he was so near the end?* How I wished that things ended differently. How I wished things hadn't ended at all. Remorse and regret were blocking memories.

And then I began to remember more and more.

There was the trip to Adirondacks when I ended up in the

emergency room after some mishap. Collin couldn't find a hotel nearby that would accept dogs, and I would not leave Augie in the car overnight, so I convinced the nurses to designate him as an assistance animal. He spent the night beside me, on the hospital floor curled up on a blanket.

There was the trip to Vermont when Collin and I rented a historic eighteenth-century farmhouse. I was absolutely sure the flue was open when I lit the fire. In a flash, flames shot out and smoke filled the house. I grabbed Augie and ran. Collin grabbed the fire extinguisher and with one good blast saved the house.

There was the weekend at the bed-and-breakfast in the Catskills. Collin and I found a wonderful restaurant with a grand, dog-friendly veranda. Later, we went to a drive-in movie theater. Augie stood between the bucket seats and watched the screen wide-eyed until he fell fast asleep in the back seat, just as I did in my childhood when we went to the local drive-in. Augie knew a B-movie when he saw one.

I could see him chasing a squirrel. I could see him posing among deer. I could see him completely ignoring a mouse as it scurried across the floor in front of his nose.

So many of the reawakened memories involved Collin and our idyllic days as a family of three. The longing for Augie made me appreciate Collin even more. Perhaps it was delusional, but part of me hoped that, as I was making progress in processing my grief over Augie, maybe there might be potential for reconciliation with Collin. Letting go is not my forte.

Chapter 13

Changing

As my mind and heart were recovering, so too was my body. With each visit to Quarna, I put on a few more pounds. My ribs no longer protruded. My second chin returned. My ass went back to sagging. I extended my hikes and quickened the pace. I did sit-ups and push-ups. But my valiant efforts were no defense against the usual Italian suspects: wine, beer, pasta, bread, and kindness. As opposed to typical shame associated with weight gain, I felt a bit of relief. I was giving up the ghost. I was getting back parts of myself (self-worth, self-esteem, self-confidence) that grief had stolen.

That Quarnese food was the antidote to what ailed me was unquestionable. On shorter visits, when I stayed at Valerio's inn, his overwhelming breakfasts could not be resisted: eggs, fruit, cakes, strudel, pudding, brioche, cheeses, salami. Alessio, the chef at Circolo, beguiled me with his intoxicating saffron risotto, lusty spaghetti puttanesca, gnocchi that popped on the tongue, tortellini with cacao and hazelnuts, tortelloni stuffed with fish. His basil and sage smelled as if harvested each morning. He waved chili oil over a dish like my Uncle Manny waved a bottle of vermouth over a martini, enough for the aroma but not so much that you spoiled good gin.

The secret, Alessio told me, was simplicity.

"Never more than three ingredients. If there are three you taste everything," he said. "Any more and you taste nothing."

If I was invited to a Quarnese home for coffee, the cookies and cakes were usually store-bought, fully hydrogenated and loaded with sugar. As with making fresh pasta, baking was uncommon among busy Quarnese women—except for bread pudding as dense as a brick. The hostess always wrapped an extra brick for the road.

If I was invited for dinner, it was the full monty: an aperitivo platter big enough for dinner, a pasta course big enough for dinner, a second helping of pasta big enough for dinner (it seemed rude to say no), and then an actual dinner of a breaded cutlet, potatoes, vegetables, a salad, and dessert, always topped with gelato. And bread and wine and bottles of grappa, génépi, limoncello, and some mystery hooch distilled according to some secret family recipe. I cringed when they brought out *zuccherini*, nasty little sugar cubes infused with 90 percent grain alcohol. They loved watching the American gasp for breath. Out of gratitude for a lovely meal, I was happy to suffer.

One afternoon I interviewed an insightful Quarnese woman at length. She spoke freely about the evolution of religious life and sexual mores over the decades, the decline in marriages and birthrates, and the educational and professional challenges facing young people. Our conversation ran into early evening, and she invited me to stay for dinner with her husband and children.

"Just pasta and salad," she said, apologetically.

"Thank God!" I wanted to say.

Compounding the restorative fats and carbohydrates, my smoking decreased, which slowed my metabolism. I wish I could say the decrease was from discipline or self-respect, but in truth, it was the result of a vicious cycle of American import restrictions, Quarna's geography, and my lung capacity. Gauloises, the rich French cigarettes to which my lungs had become accustomed, were no longer available in the United States, a victim of regulations and shame. When I returned to New York, I had to ration the two-carton duty-free allowance. When they ran out, I substituted American brands, but they smelled like formaldehyde, which diminished some of the fun.

Giuseppe's bar in Quarna Sopra was the only place in the village licensed to sell cigarettes, and it was a twenty-minute walk uphill. Even then, Giuseppe did not carry Gauloises. The European blends of Marlboro and Camel were earthier than their

American counterparts. They smelled like dung. Giuseppe suggested I try MS, the Italian brand made famous by the suave film star Marcello Mastroianni. How sophisticated! I thought. But instead of Mastroianni's sensual clouds of smoke, I got a wheezing, hacking cough. I was forced to cut down on cigarettes so that I might have the strength to walk up the mountain to buy them.

In their book *Our Towns*, a portrait of small-town economic reinvention in America, James and Deborah Fallows saw "mayor-driven transformation" as a primary catalyst for civic renewal. The same was true in Quarna. Carlo, the mayor of Quarna Sopra, was focused on ecotourism and had led the team that closed the deal with the Mandali center, which provided revenue to the municipality from nightly occupancy fees and good jobs for locals. Paolo, the mayor of Quarna Sotto, was shepherding the conversion of an abandoned woodwind factory into a cultural center. A long, two-story cinderblock structure perched on a hillside, the factory was built in the 1950s by Ida Maria Grassi, a Milanese woman admired for her business acumen and loathed for her imperious nature. Grassi employed dozens of artisans until the 1980s, when Chinese manufacturers flooded the woodwind market with cheaper instruments and Italian labor costs soared. She shuttered the factory, a blow to the local economy.

When I first visited the Grassi Center, it was still a wreck, a raw space littered with rusted tools, workbenches, an old pair of shoes, and crumpled newspapers. Project leaders were thrilled at the acoustical potential of the high ceilings, but unconcerned about sightlines obstructed by concrete pillars. They were not sure where a stage might go or how they might hang a lighting grid. As a music journalist, I have written countless stories about grandiose impresarios and celebrity architects meticulously reimagining dilapidated urban properties as arts centers. Never had I seen such optimism as I did from Quarna's grassroots community leaders. My every softball question was met with the same unworried answer: "We will figure it out."

The crowning glory of the Grassi Center was a soaring wall of windows that looked out over the village to the mountains, providing ample light for daytime events and a sunset cyclorama for evening concerts. Grassi would generate nominal revenues from ticket sales to help offset ongoing operating costs, Paolo told me, with modest trickle-down business to Circolo and Posta, but money was not the prime objective. "Our objective is survival," he said. The Grassi project was a bulwark against cultural extinction, a bet that music, in one form or another, could sustain the village's identity. It was not a financial gamble. It was an existential investment. Substantial funding was provided by a bank foundation and a regional development fund, but the villagers—the municipality, the music society, the museum—had to contribute a fair share too. Unlike Mandali, a shrine to mindfulness privately funded by millionaire Dutch outsiders, the Grassi Center, a shrine to music, was funded by small gifts of the pious, just like the churches of yore.

Carlo and Paolo were both committed to saving money by integrating redundant administrative resources between Quarna Sopra and Quarna Sotto, but it was not easy to win the approval of their respective constituents, even if the savings to both municipalities was clear. There was resistance from old-school separatists who feared that any consolidation endangered the respective identities that traced back centuries. The prevailing hope among progressives was that with the next generation of leadership—a generation that grew up after the schools, bands, and football teams had been consolidated—unification of the two municipalities would continue.

Despite the political challenges, the municipalities managed their resources well. Regional government allocations supported capital projects, and property taxes supported village operations. Expenses for the preschool and grade school—teachers' salaries, building maintenance, textbooks—were shared with regional authorities. But with young adults leaving Quarna for better jobs and economic pressures discouraging couples from starting families, enrollment in Quarna's schools was declining at a disturbing rate. Grade levels had been consolidated like old-fashioned one-room schoolhouses, but there wasn't much further they could go, and there was anxiety over what drastic actions might be required. Years before, the decision to combine the schools of upper and lower Quarna caused an uproar. "People were so enraged that they threatened to send their children to school in Omegna rather than up to Quarna Sopra or down to Quarna Sotto," a witness to the skirmish told me. Ultimately there was a Solomonic split: The preschool was placed in Quarna Sotto, the grade school in Quarna Sopra. The municipality purchased a van to shuttle the students to and from school.

The van solved another cultural crisis.

"How will the children eat lunch?" parents and grandparents fretted, when the schools were split. They could not imagine a world in which a child did not go home or to Nonna's house for pranzo. As part of the compromise, shuttle service was added at lunchtime.

Chapter 14

Crossing Over

With each return to Quarna, my days became richer in personal routines and in professional pursuits. There was the morning hike to the Belvedere for pre-sunrise, the evening hike to Matlucco for post-sunset last light of day. There were calm passeggiatas and the strenuous hikes in between.

Interviews multiplied. People were eager to tell their tales, and I was happy to listen, even when their stories were unremarkable. I recognized that what seemed mundane might come in handy at some point: Every piece of a jigsaw puzzle is equally essential, even if it does not reveal a primary element of the picture. After all, it was the seeming ordinariness of Quarna that beguiled me from the start. I was drawing scenes of a mountain village, not painting a sweeping Canaletto canvas of Venice.

Every town takes pride in hometown celebrities, and the Quarnesi were insistent that I recognize theirs. (That these celebrities were not born in Quarna but had discovered it and were bewitched validated that I was in good company.) Renato Beltrami, a modernist sculptor, was born in Omegna but made Quarna his home. His daughter Marie-Terese was delighted to show me his sculptures and reliefs around town and in her mother's home. Carlo Casanova, born in Crema, was an artist distinguished for his engravings and etchings. He too stumbled on Quarna and made it his home. His grandson, Dino, who inherited his grandfather's house, invited me for coffee and showed me Casanova's dusty studio, with an inspiring view of a small waterfall. The studio looked untouched by time.

Dino, tall and handsome with a mane of white hair, was an escapee from the wild days of 1980s Milan. He too was an exceptional artist, a craftsman of exquisite music box carousels with handcrafted figurines: human, animal, fantasy, and, occasionally, erotic. Sadly, his market—museums and private collectors—was limited, and the cost of the musical mechanisms had become exorbitant, so his workshop was mostly limited to souvenir key chains suitable for craft fairs.

Then there was a supernova, Enrico Cecchetti, one of the greatest dancers, choreographers, and teachers in the history of ballet. Balletomanes from around the world occasionally showed up to pay homage at his grave. Few Quarnesi were aware of who he was or that he lived there late in life and was buried there. Why he chose Quarna I can only surmise. In my experience, operaphiles can be obsessive to a fault, to put it politely, but balletomanes are certifiably pathological. It's no wonder a master like Cecchetti would escape to a tiny mountain village accessible only by a treacherous road.

Finally, with great veneration, there were the partisans who fought against the Italian and German fascists during World War II under the command of Filippo Maria Beltrami. Many Quarnesi risked their lives to provide food and shelter to the *partigiani*, hiding them in *baitas*, old shepherds' huts in the mountains. Others provided intelligence and weapons and fought alongside them. Even now, when updating an old *baita* into a family cottage, an antique rifle might be found hidden in the rafters.

Cultivating personal relationships was itself a form of research. If I were not a guest in someone's home for coffee, a drink, or dinner, or community celebration, I could be found at Circolo or Posta. Never in my life have I been a barfly, and I am a lightweight even with beer, but in Quarna, at all four drinking holes, everybody knew my name. I wish I could say my motives were pure, but eating and drinking in Italy was akin to a war reporter embedding himself with the infantry. Tipsy or hungover, I captured stories in my journal, even if I knew certain *in vino veritas* confessions would never see the light of a page. I never heard lurid tales of debauchery like those Truman Capote extracted from his social "Swans," but small details of private lives enriched my perspective: who was sleeping with whom, who was previously married to whom, who was on the road to divorce, who was a liar, and who was a crook. I felt no remorse listening to their secrets. From the very moment the elders gave me their blessing to tell the story of Quarna, it was clear I was a writer writing about their village. They may not have had the savvy to measure their words like practiced politicians, but they knew their words were building blocks for a story. Several people declined to speak with me. It was a choice I respected.

I embedded myself with equal fervor in every musical event, and not just public concerts. On Tuesday evenings, I went to band rehearsal and sat quietly in the back (making the occasional secret recording). Giorgio, the conductor, was stern but warm to the ensemble, not unlike the school band conductors of my childhood. I was surprised at the range of ages, from teens to elders, and in the range of abilities, from stumbling newbies to conservatory-trained musicians. I cringed at the occasional off-key *tutti* passages but was blown away by certain virtuoso solos. And I was amused by the repertoire. I expected Italiana. Instead, it was Americana: a Sousa march, Tijuana Brass, a Broadway medley. Puccini and Morricone were no match for Richard Rodgers, John Williams, and Andrew Lloyd Webber.

Over lunch one day, I asked Giorgio, known as "The Maestro of Maestros" for having founded numerous bands in the region, how he conducts auditions and sets standards. He smiled at the question.

"There are no auditions," he said. "Ability and talent are not the primary qualifications. Only a willingness to show up and do one's best. Artistic excellence is not the objective. The objective is that all may play."

I am rarely to be found in a synagogue back in New York but welcoming the Sabbath on Friday evening with a good meal and blessings over candles, wine, and bread is a tradition I uphold. It is how I honor my ancestors, how I pass on the tradition when others are present, and how, with the light of the Sabbath candles, I honor time itself. I did no less in Quarna. At Maria Grazia's grocery, there were *rosetti*, twisted rolls that resembled challah, and at least one decent red wine. Finding candles was a problem. For the Sabbath meals of my first visit, I could only pray the God of Moses would accept the Virgin Mary's flickering red *lumini*. On subsequent visits, I packed a bag of kosher votives.

The Sabbath also connected me with memories of Augie, who celebrated Friday evenings in his own way. He snoozed through the blessings over the candles and wine but snapped to attention for the blessing over the challah. After Collin and I ate our portions, we gave Augie his. Even now, when I greet the Sabbath, I set aside a small piece of challah for Augie. (If I am a guest in someone's home, I discreetly wrap a piece in a napkin and tuck it in my pocket.) The nuggets sit in a jar on the fireplace mantel. Every so often, Collin and I walk down to the Hudson River and toss the bread into the water, knowing the tides will carry Augie's Sabbath treats out to the sea where his spirit resides. In Quarna, I do no less. I save pieces of *rosetti* from my Friday dinners and toss them into a brook. Wherever there is wind and water and earth and sky, there is Augie.

In Quarna, I became a regular churchgoer. How could I understand village life without observing religious ceremonies and customs? How could I understand the centrality of lay music without hearing the liturgical music? My rules here were the same as those I adhered to when attending church anywhere. I stood or sat in the back, no kneeling, no praising Jesus or Mary, no dipping my fingers in holy water, and no crossing myself. A rabbi I admired once told me, "It's okay to go to someone else's birthday party, as long as you remember it's not your own." There were times when religious events were intoxicating—for the sense of community, if not a sense of piety—but I never forgot I was a Jew. I never forgot I was a guest.

Even if I had been a devout Catholic, it would have been

a challenge to join in liturgy and song: Every service was conducted by rote. Not a missal in sight. Where I could participate enthusiastically was with the "peace-be-with-you" handshake, an *offerta* of a few euros to the collection basket, and the after-church prosecco or coffee at Posta.

On any given day, the church bells summoned the faithful to a saint's day, a national holiday, or a festival day. There was Giornata dell'Unità nazionale, National Armed Forces Day, with a special mass at the big *chiesa* of Quarna Sotto, after which town officials, draped in colorful sashes, carried wreaths down to the piazza. The band, in neat uniforms of gray pants, sweaters, and ties with music motifs, played solemn anthems. After the ceremony was complete, the priest and the band members hurried up the mountain to repeat the ceremony in Quarna Sopra.

There was Giorno dei Morti, Day of the Dead, the all-too-grim title for All Souls' Day when ancestors were remembered. Families from every corner of the village walked solemnly to the cemetery, gathering beside the modest graves or ornate mausoleums of their ancestors as mass was held at the cemetery chapel. For these processions, there were no sashes or wreaths or music, just a stream of townsfolk quietly on their way to memory.

Each August, there was Festa di San Rocco, a tribute to the patron saint of Quarna, venerated as a healer during the plague. (Also, it should be noted, honored as the patron saint of dogs and bachelors.) The citizens of Quarna Sopra celebrated the occasion with a mass at the fourteenth-century Oratorio di

San Rocco, which once served as a *lazaretto*, a plague hospital. After mass, there was a community potluck in the adjoining piázza. The citizens of Quarna Sotto celebrated separately, with a hilltop mass and family feasts on Alpe Camasca, a high pasture above the village. Some Quarna Sotto families gathered for grand picnics on the grass, others gathered at their family *baitas*. On one summer visit, I was honored with an invitation for lunch at the *baita* of a village matriarch and her family. Among the guests was the visiting priest who had earlier celebrated the hilltop mass. He was an amiable young man, but in his presence all were on their best behavior. As soon as the priest left, the boys set up a table for poker and the girls switched on a boombox for line dancing.

For religious holidays or feasts, a procession through town might feature a precious terracotta Madonna hoisted by a team of men. A nighttime procession might be led by women dressed in traditional flowered peasant outfits, carrying candles. In these ceremonies, the faithful, led by a priest under a canopy held by four men, would wander through the streets and passageways.

The first time I saw a procession, I was confused: There were few, if any, villagers watching.

"If no one is watching, for whom is the procession?" I asked Ileana, a friend, neighbor, musician, churchgoer, and cherished source of facts and traditions.

She looked at me sweetly.

"For ourselves," she said.

All Saints' Day, Ognissanti, was celebrated with the secular fervor by which it is more universally known: Halloween. At Circolo, there was a festive dinner for families with young children, at Posta a bash for the young adult crowd, and at some secret cabin in the woods, a night of mischief for the teenagers. I signed up for the fete at Posta, but first, coaxed by the Pink Principessa, I made a guest appearance at Circolo for the "Hokey Pokey" and "Head, Shoulders, Knees, and Toes." Yes, it was shtick, but it was strategic shtick. I know that a good way to win the trust of parents is to win the laughter of their children, and the mothers and fathers at the Halloween celebration were a slice of Quarna I had not seen: the thirty- and fortysomethings with young children. Most of them worked down the mountain and made brief appearances at family-friendly events, but they had no time for kaffeeklatsches or prosecco eye-openers at Posta. Church or religious processions or band concerts were not their thing either. Several of the men wore witty costumes, but for most women, it was an evening to bring out the chic outfit, good handbag, jewelry, and heels. Valerio arrived in a tailored cutaway, his face painted as an Auguste clown. Tati was dressed as a Sexy Witch in a flaring tulle skirt, scandalous stockings, and stilettos. The Principessa arrived in a cloud of pink. I had a beer to steel my nerves, did my song and dance, knocked back the shots I was offered as kudos, and rolled downhill to Posta.

At Posta, the festivities were in full party mode, and there was yet another crowd I had not seen: the twentysomething women and men who worked down the mountain and were more likely to socialize at the clubs in Omegna than at the old folks' bars in Quarna. I chatted with a few whose English was proficient, but I was uncertain of the social protocol. The tables were set in multiple configurations for two, four, and large groups. Where and with whom was I to sit without seeming an intruder or a loner?

A cherubic young woman who spoke English well sensed my confusion and asked if I would like to join her and her friends for dinner. Indeed I would! In a blink, an extra chair and place setting were wedged into a rowdy table of more than a dozen young Quarnesi. Through no effort of my own (I swear!), I was seated among the dudes: a swarthy ambulance driver, a scruffy dental hygienist, a teddy-bear factory worker, and a burly cheese distributor. The rowdy jousting among the men and their flirtations with the women made me feel as if I had been seated at the cool guys' table in high school. Cool, yes, but not snobby. They had grown up together and there was a sense of peer parity, regardless of what family they may have come from or what they may have achieved professionally. They were puppies from the same litter, happy to be reunited in celebration. As best they could, they included me in the conversation, but simply watching them was entertainment enough.

The main course was *stinco*, pork shank stewed until the luscious meat fell off the bone. With bottles and bottles of wine passed around, I quickly got stinko too. When dessert arrived, along came spray cans of whipped cream, and as inevitable as a pistol appearing in the first act of a Chekhov play that will surely go off in the third act, they began decorating themselves and one another. As the cans moved toward my end of the table, an argument broke out. I could not follow the disputation, but the decision was clear: I was ambushed.

I had never belonged to a college fraternity. I had never been hazed. I never knew a rite of initiation could be such a joy.

At Circolo the next day, while having lunch with Quarnesi friends, I was approached by Mara, known to all as "Maestra." A retired teacher for the Quarna schools, Mara was the essence of kindness, her English modest but precise. She took out a piece of paper from which she read slowly.

"We have a request from the children of Quarna and their parents. Would you please accept an invitation to come to the school to teach the…"

Now she took a small breath as if to practice the enunciation of the letter *h*, otherwise silent in Italian.

"The '*Hhh*-okey Pokey' and the '*Hhh*-ead and Shoulders and Knees and Toes.'"

I was too frozen in the moment to laugh or cry, both of which I so much wanted to do.

Of course, I said. It would be my pleasure.

She beamed, as if a great artist had agreed to perform, then handed me a neatly prepared list of documentation that would be required before I could be allowed into the school: a copy of my passport, a copy of the words to the songs in English and translated into Italian, their origin and educational objective, my résumé, a letter of reference, and a signed agreement that there would be no photography or video recording. The documentation would then be presented to the teachers, the principal, and the regional authorities for approval.

Once again, I was too frozen in the moment to laugh or cry, both of which I so much wanted to do.

"The teachers are going to think I'm crazy," I told Valerio when I got back to the inn.

"Is okay," he said. "Teachers crazier than you."

The morning of my command performance for the children of Quarna, I was as nervous as I was for the blessing of the elders. Indeed, even more so. Children can be the harshest of audiences and their reactions would be the subject of dinner conversation in every home. Their mockery or withering silence could dredge up every childhood nightmare of humiliation.

When I arrived at the schoolhouse in Quarna Sopra, the children were gathered in the *palestra*, their little gymnasium. There were some twenty-five of them, from ages four to ten.

Some had caught my act at the Halloween party, others had heard about it and were eager to learn the new craze. The littlest ones were just full of beans, thrilled to have escaped the classroom for any reason. One teacher greeted me with a smile and kindness, relieved that I was providing a break. Another (presumably the crazy one Valerio warned me about) gave me the stink-eye of suspicion.

When I was introduced as an American from New York City, they roared as if I were a rock star.

I had them at "Ciao!" I owned the room.

For each song, I taught them the words in English, and they reciprocated by teaching me the words in Italian. They wiggled and jiggled and tapped and twirled. Two encores were all my ego, my body, and the teachers, now stuck with hyper-fueled children, could bear. I took a grand bow and raced as fast as I could to Giuseppe's bar for a beer to bring down my adrenaline.

Since that afternoon, rarely does a day go by in Quarna that I don't pass a child or a teenager—now a few young adults—who does not, as they greet me, smile and tap their head and shoulders. We all hope for a slice of immortality. Some seek it through art and literature or science or philanthropy, some through nurturing children who will carry on our traditions and values. As for me, whatever my accomplishments in life, deeds good or dastardly, I will always be remembered as The American Who Brought "Head, Shoulders, Knees, and Toes" and the "Hokey Pokey" to Quarna.

On my final night of that first fall visit, I was invited to dinner at the home of Valerio's parents. Their house, near the historic center of the village, was unusual for Quarna architecture. More of a mini-palazzo, it had an iron gate enclosing a U-shaped courtyard with a faded fresco of the Virgin adorning one wall. Balconies flanked the entrance. The doorways and ceilings of the house were low, consistent with the short stature of the Quarna Sotto heritage. The finishes on every door, doorframe, trim, and counter were impeccable and polished to a glow. There was not a nick or ding on any surface. Both of Valerio's parents had worked at the musical instrument factories. Their attention to detail was surely emblematic of their craft.

Valerio's sister was eager to tell me, in broken English, about her recent honeymoon in the United States. She was astonished at the beauty of the Grand Canyon, perplexed by hotels with windows that did not open, and shocked that Americans did not have bidets. At a subsequent family gathering, the Principessa's birthday, I would meet Valerio's brother. He spoke no English, but watching his ebullient chatter with Valerio was a precise reflection of the ebullient chatter I share with my brother. It was good to see Valerio among his own.

Valerio's mother was eager to show me her wedding album and pointed with pride at her stomach in the photos. "Valerio!" she said, without shame. Valerio's father was eager to show me photos of his past hunting companions—English setters in perfect poses—and to explain their bloodlines to Lola, the grinning setter following us around the house. I was eager to comb through a volume of their Childcraft set, the same juvenile encyclopedias on the reference shelf of my childhood home (albeit in Italian here). How universal is the desire of parents to expand their children's horizons, I thought. And how universal the capacity of an encyclopedia salesman to find his mark.

Dinner, prepared by Valerio's father, was *patate di cuccella*, the signature dish of Quarna. Bulging cotechino sausages were slow roasted in a Dutch oven over potatoes browned in lard with a fistful of bay leaves. It was a savory dream and a nutritional nightmare, truly a dish to die for. His father prepared polenta the old-school way, with a giant mound formed on the counter and then sliced in all directions with string. It was served in bowls with a combination of milk and cream. After dinner, instead of the usual limoncello or génépi, out came a creepy gourd with a medusa of spouts. It was a *grolla*, Valerio explained, a pitcher of friendship filled with a brew of coffee, cognac, and aromatics. One had to drink from a spout just so, tilting the head down and the bowl up. It was as intoxicating as any ritual I had known, the warmth of the brew an initiation into the warmth of the family, right up until the moment I lifted the *grolla* a bit too high and drenched my lap. There was a mad rush to get me out of my pants, but there were certain familial boundaries I was not willing to cross. I settled for a towel and laughter.

I had come to observe a community but now found myself a part of it. I had come to observe families but now found myself a part of one. I had come to tell a story but now found myself a part of that story.

Chapter 15

Coming Home

Home, for some people, is the town where they were born. Or the house where they live. Or a nightmare of memories from which they fled. Home for some is but a dream, for others a privilege. When you live alone, home is a quiet place where you drink out of the carton so you don't have to wash a glass, watch television and eat Chinese takeout in your underwear, and sleepwalk to the bathroom in the dark and not worry too much about your aim.

Coming home to Augie was always a serotonin surge. Whether returning from a quick trip to the bodega around the corner, a day at work, or a week away, the thrill—mutual—never ceased. As a puppy, he figured out how to leap up onto a windowsill. It appealed to his guarding instincts and served as his Nature Channel during the day. It was also a lookout post for my returns. I had the top carpeted for comfort. When he got older, I added a staircase. Always, he was there in the window to greet me, ears perked up, eyes bright. By the time I reached the apartment door, he would be there, tail wagging, politely awaiting a scratch on the head and a kiss on the snout.

Collin's returns were never sedate. When Augie spotted him coming up the street, he let out a fanfare of barking. When Collin came through the door he goaded Augie into a frenzy of play. The uproar infuriated me. I had trained Augie to greet guests quietly. The landlord was aware of Augie's presence, but it would not take more than a few noise complaints before his tolerance wore thin. I begged Collin to stop until *I* ended up in a frenzy. I'm sure my barking was more bothersome to the neighbors than Augie's.

Not a day goes by that I don't return to the apartment looking for Augie's face in the window, as if he were alive and alert, waiting for me to come home. Not a day goes by that I don't enter the apartment wishing he was sitting by the door. Not a day goes by that I don't miss the uproar when Collin comes home; I even miss the quarrels with Collin about the uproar. To hell with the neighbors and the landlord! What I wouldn't give to hear Augie's bark again. Hear it out loud, that is. I hear it in my head all the time.

Quarna added a new definition of home for me: Home is where someone picks you up at the airport. My parents, until they were too infirm, were always there to greet me, as close to the gate as security allowed. My every arrival was celebrated like Lindbergh landing in Paris. Over the years, friends or colleagues might provide pickup service, but it was rare and getting rarer. Generally, the first person to greet me at an airport or a train station was a taxi driver or rental car agent. From my first visit to Quarna, when Valerio picked me up in Stresa, to every arrival since—by plane, train, or bus—there has always been a Quarnese friend waiting for me with a warm handshake or a hug. It is the essence of hospitality, the essence of family, the essence of home.

My chief welcoming officer was Alberto, a well-traveled executive for a pharmaceutical company. He came to Quarna with his parents when he was a child, married a Quarnese woman, and raised two boys into fine young men. Alberto was always there at Malpensa Arrivals with a warm smile and a hearty handshake.

Alberto has an unbridled passion for American spy novels, mysteries, and thrillers. The walls of his home are lined with Italian editions of them. He is Stephen King's number one Italian fan. Now, giving carefully selected gifts is my hobby. I obsess to a fault. Sometimes I go overboard with something well-intentioned but too extravagant. Sometimes I hit a bullseye with a cheap doodad. Rarely have I seen such speechless joy as when, as a token of appreciation for his kindness, I gave Alberto a plastic souvenir keychain to Room 237 of the fictional Overlook Hotel. He looked as though he had seen the ghost that haunted that room in *The Shining*.

The descent into Milan Malpensa Airport is itself exhilarating, a thrill I rarely feel except when coming home to New York City. Flying into LaGuardia is a particular head rush. Your pulse quickens as the plane banks over New York Harbor—on a good day, the Statue of Liberty salutes you—and then the Manhattan metropolis. You grow giddy seeing the spires below, with Central Park as your welcome mat. You groan and sigh at the taxi queue, but as you lurch toward the city and the skyline rises before you, you cannot help but see the opening montage of Woody Allen's *Manhattan* and hear Gershwin's *Rhapsody in Blue*. The clamor of city traffic fades as the taxi turns onto my little West Village street. The trees quietly wave "Welcome home! Welcome home!" The high of coming home was even higher in the Augie Years, knowing he would be jubilant at my return.

The exhilaration I feel when I return to Quarna now differs from that of my arrival in New York only by topography. Instead of towers below, there are the mountains (on a good day, Mont Blanc). Instead of New York Harbor, there are the glistening lakes in the distance: Orta, Maggiore, Como, Lugano. Instead of Central Park, there are green-gold paddies of Arborio rice where risotto is born. There are the vineyards where Nebbiolo grapes mature. And at Malpensa Arrivals, there is Alberto and my first *caffè normale*. Nothing says "Benvenuto in Italia" like the first jolt of true Italian espresso.

I wish I could say that the meandering drive to Quarna has gotten less pukey. It has not. That Alberto drives a car with automatic transmission—the only one I have ever seen in Italy—helps. The switchback road, I fear, will never be easy. But as the nausea subsides and the terracotta roofs of Quarna rise before me, my stomach settles, and I am home.

For my first long summer visit to Quarna, a three-month sojourn, I asked Valerio to help find me an *appartamento* or *casa*. As much as I loved his inn, it seemed risky, in the interest of friendship, to stay there too long, and he agreed. I hoped he might find a place with two rooms, one in which to sleep, another in which to work and eat, preferably with good light, and ideally with an outdoor space—a courtyard, a garden, or a balcony.

"You want a unicorn with that?" he asked.

This became our shared jest for requests beyond normative standards. But Valerio was a unicorn hunter, forever chasing perfection for himself and for others. This unicorn—a short-term furnished rental apartment for the summer—was a head-scratching notion for the villagers. In the good old days, Quarna, like other mountain villages in the lake region, was populated with small resort hotels for middle-class families eager to escape the brutal heat of Milan or Turin. Like the Borscht Belt resort hotels in the Catskill Mountains once popular with New York Jews, Quarna's hotels offered mountain air, mountains of food, dancing to live music, and lively young men who entertained the adults and organized activities for the children (*animatori* they are called in Italian, *tummlers* in Yiddish). Like the Borscht Belt resorts, the golden age of Quarna's hotels faded in the 1960s as the declining costs of air travel lured families to more exotic destinations. One by one, the resort hotels of Quarna shut down.

Those Villeggianti who came to Quarna for summer would open up a house they had inherited for their own use, but even if they had multiple houses, which was often the case, they would not open one up for a stranger. If there was a vacant flat in one of the living, breathing, multistory family hives—perhaps a garret where a peculiar bachelor uncle lived and died—the idea of renting a room to a foreigner was creepy. Mandali had leased a few of the large houses for staff, and I was told there might be a room to rent, but I was uncomfortable sharing a group house with enlightened Europeans. Their lifestyle was built on community. Mine was built on privacy.

Valerio found—or more accurately, captured—a unicorn and, with Tati, groomed it to perfection. It was a half-floor of a house owned by an absentee Quarnese man who had inherited it from a great-aunt. It was built in the 1950s, new construction by Quarnesi standards, on a lot where a small factory once stood.

The factory had burned down decades before. ("Suspicious circumstances," old-timers would tell me with a wink.) On the bottom level of the house were four small garages the landlord rented out; dedicated parking spaces are as valued in Quarna as they are in New York City. The upper two floors had been chopped up into various apartments. The top floor was a long-time summer home for an elderly couple. The second floor became my home for three summers.

When I arrived, Valerio and Tati were putting the final touches on the apartment. He was installing a new shower curtain and putting a new slipcover on the tattered old sofa, she had planted a flower stand on the landing in front of the door and had stocked the kitchen with the necessities of life: olive oil, sugar, salt and pepper, a moka pot, a fresh box of Lavazza coffee. I occasionally saw the landlord and his wife, a lovely couple who lived in another town but held on to several family properties in Quarna. The rent was beyond fair, and while I did not ask who had done what to make the house a home for me, I am not sure the landlord would have considered the final touches with which I was greeted to be his responsibility. Valerio and Tati, virtuosos of hospitality, could not have imagined it any other way.

"Is one problem with apartment," Valerio said, apologetically. "Is no parabola." No satellite dish meant no television, no internet, and poor cellular phone service. For this "problem" I thanked him profusely. Being disconnected from the grid was a gift. Home was now a place where the phone did not ring, where

I did not feel compelled to check or return texts or emails, and where I did not fall prey to the news cycles of the day. Once a day, I walked up to Valerio's inn and stood in his garden or walked down to Posta for a connection to validate to family and friends and assignment editors that I was still alive.

The piazza my apartment faced was no Bernini masterpiece with a colonnade, an obelisk, or a fountain. Neither was it a true town square where markets and celebrations were held. It was not the main square or even the secondary square of Quarna. Down a steep, narrow road, around a blind curve where foreigners hesitated but locals accelerated, my piazza was more like an amorphous cul-de-sac, an egg-shaped convergence of time and space, of ancient footpaths erased by trees that seeded themselves in neglected patches of soil, of streams that once powered home workshops enclosed for sanitation, of dirt roads for donkey carts paved with asphalt for cars, of steep cobbled stairs leading to houses above, and of weed-covered pathways to shanties below. Cars were parked higgledy-piggledy like constellations of starfish.

This oval, officially named Piazza della Repubblica, was the convergence of four historic neighborhoods known to old-timers only by their *dialetto* names: Pyk, Cittadella, Visza, and Vongg. If an old Quarnese asked where I was living and I answered "Piazza della Repubblica," it would be like telling a tribal leader of New York's Indigenous Lenape people that I lived in Tribeca. If I described my location as Pyk, their eyes lit up. "Ah! Sì-sì! Pyk!" they would say and ramble on about some cousin who once lived above, below, or beside me, and invariably tell me about the Great Fire that destroyed the factory on the site where my house was built. But for every old soul who rhapsodized over the charming footbridge that once crossed the stream in the piazza, another spoke of the stench when, after a storm, dung from stables gathered into a cesspool in front of my house, or of the reeking fumes from the factory, or the constant noise from the lathes of home workshops.

To get to the apartment, one walked up a crumbling external stone staircase hewn a century before, still sooty from the fire decades earlier. With no railing, it was daunting in broad daylight, all the more so if carrying luggage or grocery bags while sidestepping lizards. With no external light, the staircase was a peril at night, all the more so if one was impaired by beer and wine and grappa. After a drizzle or sturdy rain or the occasional hailstorm, it was a stairway to hell. The staircase was originally shared with an adjacent hotel, a looming stone monolith long defunct. The rusted iron gate beside my front door led to a terrace that was the hotel's dance floor, now thick with weeds and wild shrubs. Eugenia, a nonagenarian neighbor I befriended, "mimed" that as a little girl, she and her friends would listen to the music and dance in the piazza as if they were guests of the hotel.

Valerio apologized for the "ancient" kitchen. He was amused when I explained that the apartment's 1980s modular kitchen, with its stainless-steel sink and cabinets, was state-of-the-art compared to my kitchen at home in New York, with its 1920s cast-iron farm sink and painted wood cabinets. He was further amused as I stared at elements he considered ordinary: a long, sturdy table in the middle of the kitchen, draped in red-checked oilcloth, which doubled as a prep station for the cook and a table for casual meals. On the far wall was a large oak hutch that housed a mash-up of cups, dishes, utensils, platters, and cookware. The feature of the kitchen I cherished most was the woodburning stove in the corner, functional for cooking and the main source of heat in winter. I imagined a frost-covered cord of wood just outside my door, a dry pile inside, me stoking a fresh log in the early morning, rubbing my hands in the warmth as my moka pot came to a boil. Sadly, it was not to be. On my winter visits, Valerio refused to allow me to stay there.

"You burn down building!" he said. After observing what he considered "disaster" in my every manual skill (he did not approve of the way I chopped vegetables or opened a wine bottle or washed a dish and was more traumatized by my driving than I was by his), he insisted that in colder months, when my visits were briefer, I stay at the inn, with its American-safe radiators.

The bedroom, off the kitchen, was huge and bright, with a wall of windows that suffused the air with quiet light in the morning and turned the room into an inferno in the afternoon. The landlord's lace sheers were no defense. I had to be sure to close the wheezing metal shutters well in advance of siesta time. Off to the side of the bedroom, French doors led to a Juliette balcony with a cabaret table perfect for writing, reading, eating, or dreaming. It was, I assumed, the only outdoor space that came with the unicorn. The one disappointment with the bedroom was the furniture. In my imagination, there would have been a *letto matrimoniale*, a grand marital bed carved from rich walnut (perhaps with a little gilding), and a mournful crucifix on the wall above my head. There would have been an antique chiffonier with a cloudy oval mirror and a matching wardrobe that smelled of potpourri collected from the pines and herbs of the hills. Alas, my pipe dream was quickly extinguished. An antiseptic Ikea bedroom set in brown melamine would have to do.

Beyond the tiny bathroom, the memory of which is best suppressed, was a formal dining room the likes of which I had never known in any home where I have lived. In my modest childhood home in Toledo, we "dined" around a Formica table in a kitchen nook. For special occasions, like Passover Seders or Thanksgiving dinners populated with a rotating crop of relatives and family friends, my father set up rickety Sears aluminum folding tables in the family room. Here in Quarna, I had a grand room designed for Sunday dinners and festive occasions, complete with a gleaming mahogany table and a matching breakfront filled with floral china, demitasse sets, cordial glasses, and crystal wine goblets. One could hear the uproar of laughter and arguments and joy and tears still bouncing off the walls. I made the dining table my secondary desk when my primary workspace on the terrace was rendered uninhabitable by the afternoon sun.

Only once in the years of renting the apartment did I raid the breakfront for the good china: the evening I prepared dinner for Valerio, Tati, and the Principessa. I took pictures in advance so I could be sure to put everything back precisely as it was the last time the landlord's late aunt served Sunday dinner.

Beyond the dining room was a fifteen-foot-wide terrace with beet-red herringbone tiles and a wrought iron railing perfect for flower boxes. Here was yet another big table for alfresco family meals and a small table for folding laundry. Once, just for fun, I had breakfast at the kitchen table, had lunch on the terrace table, folded my laundry at the laundry table, had aperitivo at the Juliette balcony table, and had dinner at the dining room table. Just because I could.

The terrace faced a sweeping landscape that I cherished each day. In the foreground was the piazza itself. With the outdoor table positioned just so, I could see the procession of daily life. There were men and women on their way to work, children on their way to school, old folks on their way to the market or Posta for coffee, cats on patrol. All of this was accompanied by a soundtrack of birds, barking, spats, and the occasional morning cry of sexual ecstasy. Across the piazza was a ravine that created an updraft upon which the swallows swirled in the evenings. In the middle ground, perfectly framed by trees and houses, was the jewel of Quarna: Oratorio del Saliente, a chapel completed in 1626, its stucco facade a dappled palette of pink, coral, and rose that changed throughout the day as the sun moved across the sky. In the evening, it was illuminated as if by a celestial cinematographer. In the background, high in the mountains, was a clearing in the pines, a pasture known as Alpe Sacchi. The terrace became the theater of my imagination. It was where I drank my coffee, ate my meals, worked, read, exercised, hung my laundry to dry, tended my flower boxes, and, through the changing hues of Saliente, clocked the time of day.

With Augie gone, Collin estranged, and my West Village community dispersed, my sense of home was shattered. In Quarna, I began to find a balm for the ache of feeling homeless. Later, I learned that the Italian language makes no distinction between "house" and "home"—both are *casa*. Telling Quarnesi friends that here in the piazza I felt "at home in my house" became a mind-teaser. This being Italy, it was easier to explain the difference with gestures. A "house" is a structure (draw a box with your hands). A "home" is a place in the heart (touch your hand to your chest). It needed no further translation.

Chapter 16

A New Order

In his ode to Turtle Bay Gardens, the enclave of row houses in New York City where he lived for decades, E. B. White wrote of the familiar faces he saw outside his window every day: "After a dozen years of gazing idly at the passing show, I have assembled, quite unbeknownst to them, a cast of characters that I depend on. They are the nameless actors who have a daily walk-on part in my play—the greatest of dramas."

Each morning, after returning from my sunrise hike to the Belvedere, I quickly brewed my moka pot of coffee and took a seat at the terrace desk, where the view of the mise-en-scène below was as perfect as a front mezzanine seat in a Broadway theater. The show, like a musical, began each day with an overture of birdsong. Then, as if a curtain went up, the daily drama began with a similar cast of characters on whom, like White, I came to depend. To the words assembled from interviews and the notes from observations, there was now the theater of my piazza.

The first actors with whom I exchanged a morning nod were the trash men in their neon jumpsuits, hopping on and off their wheezing miniature trucks for the day's catch, a rotating menu selected from the strictly enforced calendar of recyclables and compostables. The next face I saw each morning, at precisely six thirty, was a bittersweet reminder of the furry face I saw each morning for eighteen years. Snow, a lively black-and-white shepherd mix, was let out into his yard. Snow was followed a moment later by his best friend, Polpete, the family cat, who enjoyed her days sprawled atop the woodshed. If only Tennessee Williams were alive to see an actual cat on an actual hot tin roof.

A few minutes after Snow and Polpete made their morning entrance, a woman in a flowered housedress emerged from a house cantilevered above to water her window boxes, an uproar of cascading geraniums in a curated sequence of reds, whites, and pinks, and overflowing pots of petunias and begonias. To a serious gardener, these were common breeds, but she cared for them as if they were hothouse species. If the skies turned dark, she would rush out with netting to protect her pride against the villains of rain, hail, sleet, or snow.

At precisely six forty-five, a fortysomething man—always sporting a fresh buzz cut, always dressed in a gray polo shirt and black jeans, always carrying a matching gray backpack—exited from a weedy courtyard to my left and crossed to an old stable that had been converted into a garage. I got to know most of my piazza neighbors by name within a matter of weeks, but it would be two years before Backpack Man and I were introduced at a festival pop concert. He had never even noticed me. When in his morning zone, he said, he was on autopilot.

Just after Backpack Man drove out of the piazza, Snow's owner came down wearing the blue smock of a factory worker. I rarely saw her husband, a pensioner in poor health who spent his days at a computer doing something ill-defined. She smiled and waved and, typically blocked in by her son's pickup truck, backed out of their gravel lot in a complicated five-point maneuver. Watching her struggle each morning, I wanted to scold the son, a stylish playboy with a penchant for tilted fedoras. But I suppressed the urge, not just because I feared disrupting the space-time continuum, or because he and his sister were delightful members of the thirtysomething crowd, or because I knew that in an Italian mother's eyes a son could do no wrong. It was because she had a patch of land up above town with perfect sun, soil, and mountain water for growing blueberries. Her jam was the best in Quarna, and she had put me on her friends-and-family distribution list. No fit of pique was worth jeopardizing that. On one visit, she sent me back to America with a beautifully wrapped jar. I shielded it with every possible layer of clothing in my luggage, but Italian airport security discovered it.

"Marmellata di mia nonna!" I cried, hoping a sentimental appeal to my grandmother's blueberry marmalade might override the rules. The guard seized it anyway but did not chuck it in the trash with the other contraband. I have little doubt that my blueberry jam ended up on his kitchen table.

Precisely at seven, as the church bells tolled the hour, Carmen marched around the corner from her little row house, string sack in hand. Always dressed in a heavy wool skirt and sturdy short boots from another era (with which she wore signature red wool socks on chilly days), Carmen was a woman aged beyond her years, her face in a permanent scowl—owing to ailments, not bitterness, I was told. The reason for her determined morning march was to be first at Maria Grazia's grocery to get her daily bread, as if it were fresh from the wood-fired oven of the old village baker—gone many years, as was his bakery—instead of sourced from a chain grocery store in Omegna. So precise was Carmen's daily passage through the piazza, that on the rare occasion she was one or two minutes late, I would worry. One morning, when there was no sign of her by seven fifteen, I texted a neighbor out of concern. It turned out it was a national holiday and Maria Grazia's market was closed. There was no need for Carmen to leave home.

Just as the last morning dewdrop evaporated, an elderly woman in a small house up the hill had already hung a load of laundry on a double line that stretched the full length of her house. It was the first of many loads she hung throughout the day, every day, well out of proportion to any family that could fit into her small house. She was, in my imagination, a poor widow who took in washing to survive. She optimized every inch of line with swift movements, masterfully juggling clothespins with her hands and teeth. I would soon learn that she was no poor widow. My ignorance once again became comedy legend, no less than my assumption that the gilded *RC* on the gates of the saxophone factory had to do with the Roman Catholic Church or that the cell phone array on the Belvedere was an ancient Roman signal tower. The poor widow washerwoman was Dina, known as the "Nonna of Nonnas" for her warmth, wisdom, dedication to the community, feeder of all who entered her home, and keeper of the juiciest gossip. She was neither poor, nor a widow, nor a washerwoman. She and her husband, Bruno, enjoyed generous pensions from multiple jobs. The laundry I saw each day was for herself, her husband, her three adult children, and her five grandchildren.

When I first met Nonna Dina, she looked me up and down and spoke with sorrow and pity. Her teenage granddaughter translated.

"You don't have an iron?"

No, I said, the landlord had not provided one.

Nonna Dina let out a sigh of dismay and threw her hands in the air.

"How do you iron your sheets?" she wanted to know, as if my unironed T-shirt was not tragic enough.

Iron my sheets? It was not something most Americans do, I said. At least not any Americans I knew.

"Bring them to me!" she said.

I thanked her but declined the kind offer. I suspect that within the hour, the nonnas of Quarna knew the American slept on unironed sheets and they were collectively horrified. Being Jewish and gay would have been moral misdemeanors by comparison.

Nonna Dina was also rich in a way that was as important to the Quarnesi as money.

"She has good sun," more than one person said to me with a tone of envy. She could do so much laundry because it dried quickly. She could feed so many people because her vegetables grew quickly. She saved on fuel in winter because the sun heated her roof. She grew the most beautiful flowers because she could. Each morning, after she hung the second wash on the line, I watched as she clipped a bouquet of whatever was in season and bustled to the church to place it on the altar. (Like my grandmother, Nonna Dina neither walked nor strolled. She only bustled with intent.) Opening the church each day and refreshing the altar flowers was her religious duty. Long gone were daily masses, but still Nonna Dina opened and closed the church each day for prayer or offerings. It was Nonna Dina who emptied the *offerte* boxes with their coins of charity. It was Dina who made change for shopkeepers when they were running low on coins.

Shortly before Nonna Dina descended to open the church, her daughter Ileana, whose house was adjacent, scurried down to her car in the piazza, her three children scrambling to keep up. However mad the rush to drop the children at school and get to her job in Omegna, all four would pause to offer a quick "Giorno!" with a wave. Their smiles were the highlight of my morning.

By eight o'clock, the morning parade quieted down. Those who worked in the valley were gone, the children were in school, Carmen had marched back home from the market, and Nonna Dina was putting up her third wash. Eugenia, my nonagenarian neighbor, would come out in a housedress to sweep the pavement in front of her door. In my first days, she looked up at me on the terrace and glared with suspicion. After a week or so, and a good word from Nonna Dina, she looked up from her broom each morning with a wave and a smile.

That I might be looking through a one-way mirror was an illusion quickly dispelled. Just as my neighbors were a cast of characters in my morning show, I had become a character in their daily stories. I was the American on the terrace, tapping away at his laptop, drinking coffee, eating his meals, watering his flowers, hanging his laundry to dry, doing push-ups, or staring off into space. If I overslept and my shutters were closed or if I was late coming back from the Belvedere and they did not see me on the terrace, there would be concern. Someone might text Valerio, who would text me ("You are alive?"), to see if I was okay. If I went to Omegna on market day or to Turin or Milan for a weekend, I was sure to let my neighbors know in advance lest they worry. The piazza became my village within a village.

Chapter 17

The Menu

Two months into my first three-month sojourn in Quarna, my clothes began to hurt. My jeans were gouging my waist, my T-shirts tightening at the yoke, and my underwear was going places no underwear should go. I thought I could endure the rest of the visit, but the pain became too great. At first, I blamed the apartment's ramshackle washing machine with its mercurial temperatures and brutal spin cycles. Then I blamed the afternoon sun toasting and shrinking my cotton fibers on the clothesline. Finally, I accepted that the culprit was the slow retreat from acute grief. It had been eighteen months since Augie died, and while the sorrow was still palpable, the death had lost some of its sting. Absent the anorexia of depression and having eased off smoking and manic exercise, my former shape was returning. But the renewed shape was oddly different. I had developed what the French call an *embonpoint*, the pear-shaped paunch of a life well-lived.

I had done my best to maintain a healthy lifestyle in Quarna. There was the sunrise power-walk to the Belvedere followed by the colon cleanse of a full moka pot of coffee. For breakfast, I scrambled two eggs and limited myself to one crusty roll with a light touch of my neighbor Betty's blueberry jam. Then, after a solid four hours of writing on the terrace, I did my stretches, worked out with resistance bands, and took a brisk aerobic stroll through the village. I concluded my midmorning break at Posta with a cappuccino, stirred Italian style, with a brioche. It was a suitable reward, I thought, for a diligent morning of psychic, physical, and professional accomplishment. And while it was never my intention to take advantage of the native hospitality, inevitably a Quarnesi with a sleight of hand picked up my tab, which made the reward for hard work even sweeter.

After reviewing and editing my morning work, I put together a healthy salad, perhaps with lettuce from Nonna Dina, tomatoes from Valerio's father, and assorted produce from Davide, the jovial fruit-and-vegetable man who parked his truck in the main piazza twice a week. Some days I added a few slices of Luigi the Butcher's salami, a can of marinated tuna, or, courtesy of Valerio, thick slices of salmon cured in a backyard smoker he had assembled from an old woodburning stove and saxophone scraps. As a treat after my healthy lunch, I allowed myself a slab of Tomme or Taleggio cheese, offsetting the fat with an apple or pear picked from an abandoned grove in the hills. By the time I finished lunch, the sun was approaching an angle that rendered the terrace uninhabitable, so I retreated to the dark of the shuttered bedroom to read and nap. Then, a shot of espresso to revive my soul, maybe a yogurt, a few more hours of work at the dining table, and a walk up to Valerio's garden to tap into his Wi-Fi to file assignments and review emails. My workday done, the sun lower and cooler, I took an ambitious hike into the hills.

Dinner, if not at Circolo or Posta or a festival or someone's home, was a lazy Bachelor Stew: chicken *cubetti* from Luigi's butcher shop simmered with whatever vegetables from Davide were at hand: peppers, eggplant, zucchini, cherry tomatoes, carrots, leeks, and a fistful of fresh basil or oregano. For my Friday night Sabbath dinner, I upped the menu with fresh fish. Thursday was market day in Omegna, with stalls of clothing, linens, toys, candies, cheeses, and fishmongers hawking perch from Lake Maggiore, cod from Calabria, anchovies from Liguria, and tuna from Sicily. When planes, trains, and trucks were delayed or on strike, they sold frozen fish from the local supermarkets, gussied up like a corpse for a wake. As a means of contributing to family meals with Valerio and Tati, I often brought back a big blob of octopus, which they loved. Such fishing expeditions required a precision strike in the summer: the early bus down the mountain, a sprint to the stalls before the goods were picked over, and a swift retreat on the next return bus back up to Quarna before the sun rose high enough to fry the fish right through the shopping bag.

Aside from the crusty rolls, I showed remarkable restraint with carbs. I never made pasta. Why waste calories on boxed pasta and jarred sauce when I could bank the points on Alessio's fresh pasta at Circolo?

After dinner and my hike to Matlucco for the sunset over Monte Croce, I was the very model of moderation: no sugar in my evening tea and only four Nutella wafers. As a hedge against becoming a stay-at-home literary drunk, I allowed myself only one glass of wine or beer with dinner. If I was in the mood for more, it required a walk to Circolo or Posta, where there was always company.

It was impossible to decline an invitation from Valerio for aperitivo with salamis from Luigi's private reserve collection, cheeses from his friend's mountain goats, and museum-quality bruschetta. (Ordinary pizzettas were too mundane for Valerio.) I could not match him beer for beer, but I did my best to keep up. Often I would nod off on the sofa for a gentleman's booze snooze, only to awaken to the smell of Tati's mother's lasagna, which, having complimented enthusiastically on an early visit, was often prepared on my behalf. If I was lucky, the second course was one of Valerio's signature salads composed of peperoncini, pine nuts, radicchio, romaine, a fistful of fresh herbs, and his turmeric-vinaigrette house dressing. Or fresh trout from his latest catch in a mountain stream. There was no dismissing his semifreddo or apple cake, though nothing in his repertoire surpassed Tati's fresh summer peach torte.

I mock-groaned when he hauled out the cordial glasses and high-octane digestivi—génépi, Averna, and various grappas and mystery moonshine his father or his friends had distilled from herbs on the mountain—but the thrill of the wallop never ceased. How I drunkenly stumbled back to my apartment through the dark cobbled alleyways and perilous steps of Quarna unscathed when, sober in the light of day, I tripped on the sidewalks of New York City, I will never understand.

Equally odd, I never had a hangover in Quarna. Back home, I was a lightweight. Even with a good meal, a cocktail or a glass of wine left me with a sour stomach and a headache. Any more than that, and I had to call in sick to myself. In Quarna, poached the night before on beer, wine, and moonshine, I never missed a sunrise at the Belvedere.

I mentioned this to a veteran drinker-philosopher Italian friend and he explained that the dense proteins of the cured aperitivo meats, the absence of preservatives in domestic wines, and the pure waters used to ferment local digestifs all eased the symptoms.

"But what about beer?" I asked.

He laughed.

"Una bella pipì e via," he said. One good piss and it is gone.

Valentina and Alessio of Circolo were culinary felons whose

crimes of the stomach I could not escape. Ultimately, I imposed a twice-a-week Circolo pranzo limit, with its caveman-sized bowls of luscious pasta and mystery "meats" with lustful sauces and loaves of fresh bread and a semi-carafe of wine. But inevitably I would receive an invitation I could not refuse or I would host an out-of-town visitor for whom Circolo was part of the tour. At the risk of hurting Alessio's feelings, I wiped every platter clean with bread. At the risk of inciting Valentina's ire, I always went along with the full pranzo menu. It was excessive, unnecessary, irresistible, and cheap. Fortunately, dessert was not included. I was one tiramisu away from eternity in hell with the other sinful gluttons.

Dinner at Circolo was easier to avoid. Alessio elevated the menu—a perfect broiled branzino, pork loin in a red wine reduction, seafood risotto—but unlike the all-inclusive modest price of pranzo (ten euros, eleven if you added coffee, no tax or tip!), the dinner menu was à la carte and pricey. Dinner at Circolo was something I did only with visitors who wished to treat me out of gratitude for the grand tour. It was an offer I always accepted graciously.

I harbored no such resentment toward the proprietors of Posta for their Sunday pizza night. Yes, the pies were excessively large—an individual pizza the equivalent of an American large for two—but in my nutritional mathematics, there were plenty of vegetable toppings to justify the calories. And unlike Circolo, where Valentina would not serve the *secondi* until the *primi* platter was cleaned, at Posta, I was allowed to take leftovers to go. There was also a social obligation for pizza night at Posta. It was a see-and-be-seen affair. I felt professionally obligated to eat.

Chapter 18

Quarna Belly

One evening, while Tati was loading the dishwasher and Valerio was getting out the after-dinner bottles of hooch, I discreetly reached under the table to undo the top button of my jeans for a breather. The "pop" did not go unnoticed.

Valerio laughed too hard to speak.

"Quarna Belly," I said, and the label stuck.

I was well aware of the situation and had already planned a trip to Le Isole, a big shopping mall north of Omegna in the town of Gravellona Toce. There was an H&M and an OVS, its more stylish Italian cousin, where I could update my painful wardrobe. And it would be fun to roam the shops with teenage mall rats like those of my Toledo childhood, except I presumed the Italian *ragazzi* would be better dressed than we were.

"How you get to Le Isole?" Valerio asked.

I would take the morning bus down the mountain to Omegna and then transfer to the bus to Verbania, which stopped right in front of the mall. Then the reverse, allowing plenty of time to catch the last bus from Omegna to Quarna. It would only take an hour each way if I timed it right, with only one change. Low risk by Italian standards.

"Pazzo!" Valerio said. Crazy!

I would be fine, I insisted. It would be an adventure for me.

"You do what you want. But if you wait to Saturday, I drive you." He had to "polish" (his translation of "clean," which I found too amusing to correct) their rental house in Mergozzo for the next guests, then meet with a blacksmith who was replacing the house's iron gate, then go to Tati's mother's apartment to fix her dishwasher, then go to Verbania to get his phone repaired. On the way back, there was plenty of time to stop at Le Isole.

"But first, cappuccino e brioche!"

The day went something like this:

09:00

Valerio arrives my piazza. "Cappuccino e brioche!" he cried out like the Lone Ranger shouting "Hi-Yo! Silver!"—only Silver, instead of a thoroughbred, was his seventeen-year-old Fiat Panda and I was Tonto, the loyal sidekick. I explained the Lone Ranger character but also offered Batman and Robin (with the Batmobile) or Don Quixote and Sancho Panza (with the horse Rocinante) as alternatives. He chose the Cervantes metaphor. It needed no explanation. Valerio had attended a rigorous *liceo* high school and spent a year at university in Milan. He was no bookish intellectual, but he was no rube.

09:15

We arrived in Omegna and began circling the narrow streets to find a parking spot. The town was unusually crowded. Something was going on, but Valerio would not reveal the surprise. He wedged the Panda into a space, with millimeters to spare.

09:25

We reached a café on the lake. It was packed, but the proprietor, with whom Valerio exchanged a friendly greeting, parted the crowd and found us a table with a clear view of the lake. Our cappuccinos and brioche arrived. Hundreds of spectators lined the lake.

09:30

A starter pistol was fired, and a wall of swimmers dove into the water for the annual Oceanman Lago d'Orta, a swim marathon across the length of the lake. The most powerful swimmers instantly formed a chevron, like sailfish leaving guppies in their wake. Safety boats guarded the flanks to rescue those whose ambition did not match their ability.

10:15

We dodged the crowds back to the Panda and began the drive to Mergozzo.

10:45

We stopped at a tackle shop so Valerio could check out some new reels and lures. He kibitzed with the owner and another customer he knew. Between his job at the saxophone factory, running the inn, and his family obligations, the only hobby he had time for now was fishing. He leads up Quarna's Fishing Association, which consists of a large concrete holding tank for the regional water system that was stocked with trout and a pavilion with a small kitchen. The association exists as much for its members to drink beer as it does for fishing. For real fishing, Valerio disappears with Ryk for a few hours at a stream up in the mountains.

11:15

We stopped at a specialty cheese shop so he could get certain varieties that Tati loves. He chatted with the cheese ladies. When he explained that I was visiting from America, they insisted I sample several cheeses. I bought two. Valerio thinks it is crazy that I buy cheese from Maria Grazia's grocery in Quarna. Her cheeses are ordinary and overpriced. Tati calls Maria Grazia's shop "una gioielleria," a jewelry store.

11:45

We stopped at Lidl Market to pick up things for the inn, the holiday house, Tati's mother, and me. Lidl, and each store we go to, has specific things Valerio needed at the best price. By now, I have developed a few preferences too. Valerio knows Lidl is the only place to get the coffee creamer I can tolerate. It is the preserved type sold in tiny packets and not the fresh half-and-half I prefer back home, which cannot be found anywhere, but I accept that as one of those sacrifices one learns to make when living in a foreign culture, like decent toilet paper and Reese's peanut butter cups. Certain things have improved, however, since my earliest days touring Europe. You can get ice for a soft drink without a sneer.

12:15

We stopped at Penny Market, Valerio's preferred discount grocery chain. Again, an assortment of specific items for the inn, the holiday house, Tati's mother, and me: Valerio knows I prefer Penny's small *tarallini* crackers to the more common larger *taralli* crackers sold anywhere. And I am always on the hunt for good avocados at various stages of ripeness so they mature sequentially and not simultaneously. Valerio is fascinated by my avocado methodology and exasperated at the amount of time it takes. He shops as if it were an Olympic sport. I am always breathless trying to keep up.

12:45

We stopped at Tigros, a larger grocery store, to pick up things he couldn't get at Penny or Lidl. I continued my search for perfect avocados. Valerio shops like Shiva, the Hindu god, with six arms flying as he throws thing in his cart from both sides of every aisle. For me, grocery stores in foreign countries are like museums. I walk up and down the aisles pondering packaging as art. My favorite aisle is pet food. Mari's friend who works in pet food marketing explained to me that the packaging is branded by country. American cats, Italian cats, French cats, Asian cats, African cats, South American cats—not all cats look alike. I've often thought it would be interesting to collect pet food packages and hang them on a wall by side by side like an international cat and dog portrait gallery.

13:15

The Panda is now jammed with grocery bags, but there is one more stop: Aldi, which the Quarnesi love to hate for its high prices but Valerio likes because of discounts on certain bulk items. The Lidl, Penny, Tigros, Aldi circuit would become as familiar on our weekend adventures as the Stations of the Cross.

14:00

We arrived in Mergozzo, but before heading to the holiday house, we stopped for coffee at a café overlooking Lake Mergozzo. The lake is small, pristine, and ringed by thick woods, an Italian equivalent of Walden Pond. This was an odd moment: Valerio not in motion (or on the phone). Our adventures have never been about stillness. They have always been odysseys through which we see the world through the eyes of another.

14:30

Valerio does something shocking. He actually takes me to see a sight for no other reason than to see it: the Parish Church of the Beata Vergine Assunta, "Our Lady of the Assumption." It is around the corner from the café and I pop in for a moment. The church is the epitome of Romanesque splendor.

14:45

The holiday house, which Valerio named La Casina di Tati, is a bright yellow two-story cottage that had been Tati's home before they met. She adored it and could not bear to part with it when she moved to Quarna, so they decided to renovate it and rent it out. Unlike the Quarna inn, where guests typically stay for a few days at most, the Mergozzo casina was rented for longer stays: a week, a few weeks, a month. It too is a gem of interior design cut in the image of Valerio and Tati's impeccable taste. And it has something I have never seen in any house in Quarna—or in

Italy for that matter: an air conditioner. The clientele is mostly urban types from France, Germany, and Switzerland who come to Mergozzo for nature and hiking, but when they return to the casina they want the comforts of city life. Like a dervish, Valerio "polished" the house: changed the sheets, washed the dishes, scoured the kitchen and bathroom, swept, vacuumed, mopped, and primped the grounds. He stocked the kitchen with fruits, cheeses, snacks, and, of course, the essentials of Italian life: olive oil and coffee. For the casina, the kitchen is stocked but once. After that, guests are on their own.

15:15

The blacksmith and his teenage son arrived at the holiday house to take measurements for a new wrought iron gate for the fence surrounding the patio. Italians clearly have a thing about fences and gates. I have seen fences and gates in other European countries—granted, we Americans have our own emblematic white picket fence—but I have never seen them to the extent found in Italy, even surrounding the tiniest house in Quarna. I've heard all sorts of explanations: security, pride, keeping pets and children in, keeping predators and critters out. But after seeing so many fences and gates in cities and villages in Italy, I believe it is an extension of an innate Italian sense of artistry. No matter the size or genre, for an Italian, a picture isn't a picture without a frame.

The blacksmith's son was shy, but when he heard I was

an American, he perked up, eager to practice his English. His father radiated pride—*kvelling*, as we would say in Yiddish. I was reminded again that the ability to converse in English is an imprimatur of achievement for Italian parents. They smile watching their children speak with me. They see English as a door to greater opportunity no matter what career or profession their children choose. I am occasionally scolded with each visit to Quarna—particularly by older people—for not having mastered Italian beyond the niceties. The answers I give are multiple and true: I have never had the aptitude or self-discipline for languages; no matter how much money I throw at online courses, private tutors, and immersion programs, I would never be able to get up to the idiomatic speed at which all Italians speak, gestures included; for my work in Quarna, I have had sufficient access to those who can translate for me; and, most importantly, I believe I serve a better and higher social purpose by speaking good English to people who wish to learn—especially young people—than speaking bad Italian to appease those who wish to complain. *Non si può accontentare tutti* is among the Italian expressions I have mastered: "You can't please everyone." Even from the fiercest scolds, it provokes a laugh.

16:00

After the blacksmith and his son left, we walked over to say hello to a neighbor. The neighbor insisted we have a beer or a coffee. I decided on a beer. It was highly unusual for me to drink in the early afternoon, but I was hoping the alcohol would counteract the caffeine that was accumulating in my nervous system. I was having heart palpitations, and my jaw ached from grinding my teeth.

16:45

We arrived at his mother-in-law's apartment, a short drive away. Her cherubic smile matched her daughter's, and on this and every occasion, she greeted me with family warmth. She lived on a modest pension in an apartment beside a lumberyard and railroad tracks. Tati's brother lived with her. Her husband had left many years ago and moved to South America. On a subsequent visit I would meet Tati's father. Tati and Valerio had a cordial relationship with him, and Valerio and I once joined him for an afternoon at a pub in Omegna. What relationship he had with Tati's mother or brother I had no idea—I respected certain boundaries with regard to family matters—but I had a strong sense that Valerio had long since taken on the role of the man of the house for Tati's mother.

While Valerio set to work tinkering with the broken dishwasher, Tati's mother and her son were glued to the kitchen television. A *Gilmore Girls* marathon was underway. Astonished and delighted, I sat right down and glued myself beside them. In the first months after Augie's death, except for going to the gym and going out for cigarettes, I spent most of my time bingeing in bed. How I stumbled onto *Gilmore Girls* I have no memory—its original run on television had ended a decade earlier, and I had never even heard of it (Augie and I were more *Law & Order* types), but the magic of Netflix pulled me through a looking glass to the fictional Connecticut town of Stars Hollow for all seven seasons and 153 episodes, plus the four-episode reboot.

Gilmore Girls was a magical escape—my Quarna before Quarna—filled with characters who worked hard, celebrated community, squabbled, and ate and drank coffee all the time. Here in a kitchen in a small town in Italy, I was seeing my old friends again. I was amused to hear how well the folks of Stars Hollow spoke Italian. Valerio tinkered and fiddled and pulled apart the dishwasher but was not able to fix it, a frustration for a man who takes pride in the ingenuity of his hands. He went on to do several other manly chores around the apartment while I stayed in the kitchen with Tati's mother watching Lorelai battle with her mother, Luke battle with Taylor, and Rory juggle suitors.

17:45

We drove to Verbania to the repair shop for Valerio to get his phone fixed, but the repairman was backed up with other customers. Valerio dropped the phone off and the repairman said to return in an hour. He had to get a part from another store. I glanced at the time. "Not to worry!" Valerio said. The Le Isole mall stores were open until nine. Plenty of time. We walked around Verbania. He showed me where he once worked in an insurance office. It was one of several jobs along the path after his year at university in Milan—he loved animals and might have pursued a degree in a related field, but he did not like big city life. Since university he had worked in manufacturing, insurance, and the auto dealership before finally settling into the family saxophone factory. He had an introspective side, and we often spoke the buddy language of life choices and dreams, but there were personal boundaries we never pushed. I was open about the lingering rift with Collin, sparing him any unnecessary details. Only once did he mention a previous marriage. The woman had ended it cruelly and was difficult about divorcing. I did not probe. It was painful, he said, but he was grateful too. If she had not left, he would not have met Tati, undeniably his true love. I explained the Jewish concept of *bashert,* the soulmate preordained by God. He liked the word. "Sì-sì! Tati is my bashert!" he said.

18:00

We ran into an old friend of Valerio's, a trim, handsome, silver-haired man in vibrant biking clothes. He and Valerio had lots of catching up to do. Aperitivo was required! We found a bar not far from the phone repair shop. Our Aperol spritzes arrived with a jumbo-size platter of noshes. The friend had British grandparents and he had spent time in England, so the three of us were able to converse in English, without Valerio having to translate to keep me in the loop. It was already a given that Valerio would meet a friend everywhere we went, but what became increasingly compelling was the diversity of his friendships, from men of the earth to urbanites. Uncommon friendships were common for Valerio.

19:00

I checked the time. Valerio laughed. "Plenty of time for jeans! Le Isole open until nine!" Another round of drinks, another monster platter of noshes.

19:30

The phone is repaired! We depart Verbania for Gravellona Toce.

19:45

We entered the mall at Le Isole through the massive IperCoop "hypermarket," yet another stop on his Stations of the Cross grocery stores, but altogether different. In my adult life I have always lived in big cities with human-scale grocery stores. This IperCoop is on par with a mega-Walmart. It resembles an airplane hangar. Valerio needed a few items he could not find, or at least, not at the right price, at Penny or Lidl or Tigros or Aldi, which was fine because there was an enormous pharmacy section and I was out of sunblock and mosquito repellent. I asked the pharmacist for recommendations and directions. Valerio scowled.

"Why you ask pharmacist? I show you where! I show you best!"

We argued for five minutes over sunblock. He said the spray-on was better, but I preferred the lotion. He threw up his hands. We argued for five minutes over mosquito repellant. I started to read the labels and compare the ingredients to find the least toxic brand. Finally, Valerio took his preferred bug spray off the shelf and threw it in the cart. I conceded he knew the bugs of Quarna better than I, so I did not argue. Laundry detergent was in a nearby aisle, and I was running low. We argued for five minutes over which was best. He preferred the low-suds lavender. I wanted something scent-free. We opened the caps of the various brands and sniffed them like connoisseurs smelling the "nose" of a fine wine. We could not find anything truly scent-free. I put the low-suds lavender in the cart. I realized now we have found the reciprocal taunts of friendships. We have learned the buttons to push for fun. He likes to watch me flinch when he is driving, so every now and then, just for kicks, he makes a sudden turn. I like to see his exasperation when I take my time shopping, so every now and then I stop to smell the roses. Or in this case, the detergent.

20:00

We walked two New York City blocks to the grocery side of the store. He sprinted up and down the aisles, grabbing what he needed while I did my gallery tour of the pet food and produce. I found a few good avocados and then searched for broccoli. I could not find it. Valerio thought I must be blind. He ran up and down every produce aisle. There was indeed no broccoli. He was incensed. "Impossible!" he said. He hunted down the produce man.

"Mattina," the produce man said dismissively. In the morning he would put out the broccoli. It was too late now. Valerio was outraged. There was shouting. Hands were flying. Valerio won the war of wills. The produce man stormed off and returned with a head of broccoli. He tossed it to Valerio like a basketball. En route to the checkout, I made a strategic error. I glanced ever so slightly at the olive oil. Valerio caught my eye.

"You need olive oil?" he said, throwing his hands in the air. "You need olive oil."

This becomes a dispute of Talmudic proportions. Which varietal? Which brand? And, most vehemently, which size? I preferred the medium-sized bottle because it is easier to manipulate and would last me the rest of the summer. He insisted I get the huge can because it was cheaper. I would not use that much in a year, I explained, and I could barely lift it. An agreement was reached: I would allow him to replenish my bottle from his jumbo-sized can. I would barter something. Avocados, I decided. I had prepared guacamole when they came for dinner and it had become a favorite of the Pink Principessa.

20:25

We arrived at H&M with thirty-five minutes to spare, only to find that the employees were locking up. Valerio smacked his forehead. The mall did indeed stay open until nine, but only for the IperCoop and food court. The shops closed at eight-thirty. We looked at each other. We threw our hands in the air. We shrugged. We laughed.

20:45

We stopped in Omegna at his favorite gelato shop. Anticipating a potential mess from the twisting ride up to Quarna, I ordered a single scoop in a cup. Valerio ordered a double scoop in a cone. I presumed we would sit on a bench. I was wrong. To his driving repertoire—the swerving, the passing, the phone calls, the texting, the shifting, and steering with his knees—Valerio now added the feat of eating a double gelato on a cone down to the last crunch without spilling a drop. My shirt looked like a Jackson Pollock before the first curve.

21:00

He dropped me off at my apartment. Twelve hours. No jeans. Still, it was a good day.

Interlude

Cappuccino e Brioche

Cappuccino e brioche!" became Valerio's rallying cry for adventure. In Quarna, he was usually too busy to chat over a beer or a meal, but on road trips, he delighted in conversation. If I was silent too long, he got worried. He was amused by what I found amusing and confused by what I found confusing. We had taken to the road as buddies. Now we had become each other's teachers.

Sometimes I would be informed of the day's *cappuccino e brioche* objective, but often the explanation was vague. I quickly learned that with Valerio's adventures, there was no such thing as informed consent. If I got into his car in the morning, I waived all rights for the day. Any other plans I might have were conditional.

Ordinary errands with Valerio became a soothing reminder of my weekend "milk run" chores with Augie back in New York: to the post office for stamps, to the laundry for shirts, to the pet shop for kibble, to the little grocery store for fresh produce, to the big grocery store for other essentials, to the cheesemonger, to the fishmonger, to the butcher, to the bakery, and always a stop along the way for a coffee and a snack and a sit in a park. Some people may think it rude to compare a human to a dog, but a dog person will tell you there is no higher compliment. Valerio, with his boundless energy and intelligence and humor and curiosity and mischief and character and integrity, was very much the personification of Augie. He was not just a friend. Valerio had become a transitional figure on my path to healing, a guide from grief over a dog back to life with people.

And, like Augie, he was just damn fun.

"Cappuccino e brioche!"

We drive an hour north to Domodossola to a repair shop for scales. As president of Quarna's Fishing Association, it is Valerio's responsibility to ensure that the fishermen weigh their catch and pay accordingly. The repair shop boasts a vast collection of scales, modern and antique, a veritable museum of weights and measures. I tell the elderly repairman—likely the last of his species—that I am from Toledo, famous for its scales, and he lights up as if I were a violinist who arrived from Cremona. He has a classic Toledo scale in his collection, "Una vera bellezza!"

a real beauty, but he has lent it to a shop in town for a window display. He gives us directions. Valerio finds the shop and I pose for a picture for my siblings and the few friends and relatives I still have back in Ohio.

On the way home, we stop at a bakery to buy a loaf of black bread that Valerio loves. The baker offers me a sample, warm and rich and earthy. I cannot wait to slather butter or jam on it. I buy two loaves. The following week, when we return to pick up the fish scale, we stop at the bakery again. I buy seven loaves—two for myself, the others for friends and neighbors who have invited me for meals. Bringing a bottle of wine as a hostess gift in Quarna would be like bringing a bottle of water to a hostess in Evian. Flowers? Everyone had them in their garden. A good bakery black bread ensured a repeat invitation.

"Cappuccino e brioche!"

Valerio arrives at my door with Tati and the Pink Principessa onboard. We drive the main road toward Mergozzo, then a side road, then a dirt lane leading through the woods to a clearing. There, on a portable landing pad, is a bright yellow Barbie-sized sightseeing helicopter. Valerio has arranged for us to fly over the mountains and circle Quarna. I am thrilled and terrified. I have never flown in a helicopter, and a tiny chopper in a remote field in the Italian Alps does not inspire confidence, but if Valerio trusts the pilot with the lives of his wife and daughter, then I trust Valerio. The owner of the sightseeing company and the pilot come out to greet us.

I insist on paying for all of us—it is less expensive than dinner in New York—and offer the owner my credit card.

"No, no," he says. "You pay when you return."

The pilot delivers the punch line.

"*If* we return," he says.

The rotors whir and we rise as if floating in a dream. The sun lights the glistening mountain caps, the lakes, and the rivers wriggling through the Ossola valley. We pass through a missing tooth of a jagged mountain ridge and swoop down to the rolling hills that lead to Quarna. From above, I can see that Quarna is bigger than I realized. I see roads and hollers and houses and meadows and *baitas* and waterfalls and streams beyond the familiar boundaries. The pilot dips lower and I hold every blink so as not to miss a moment. Saliente! My piazza! Valerio's house! Every church and chapel steeple! The Lilliputian Quarnesi look up and wave. They have been expecting us. Everyone in Quarna, it seems, knows that Valerio's family and the American were going for a helicopter tour that morning.

"Cappuccino e brioche!"

Valerio, Tati, the Principessa, and I trek to Alpe Sacchi, a working farm and restaurant high above the village. By day, it is a slice of green on a mountain I can see in the distance from my terrace. By night, its farmhouse lamp flickers like a distant star. We hike over hills and through pastures (me, as always, the breathless caboose) until we reach our destination. Cows and goats greet us like a bell choir, pigs snort and loll in their pens, chickens wander freely, all blissfully unaware of their fate at the farmhouse kitchen not far beyond. We reach the restaurant and, with the binoculars Valerio has brought, my daily view is reversed. Instead of seeing Alpe Sacchi as a distance farmhouse, I see my laundry flapping on my terrace.

We arrive at this distant outpost to find the restaurant is filled with familiar Quarnesi. The menu is the usual country fare to which I have become accustomed—antipasti, grilled vegetables, a lettuce-and-tomato salad, polenta, mystery stew—but the flavors are elevated by the fact that every morsel—animal, vegetable, grain, herb—has been raised, grown, churned, and cured within five hundred meters. "Farm-to-table" is not a concept here. It is reality to which we can point. Farm *there*, table *here*.

"Cappuccino e brioche!"

We hike up to Valerio's *baita* in the hills for a family lunch. It is my first visit and I feel honored, yet another step in being drawn into the community. Valerio's mother and father join us, as well as Tati and the Principessa and a gaggle of her friends. Ryk dashes about. Teresa, the expat California attorney who sparked the journey to Stresa and thence to Quarna, is visiting with her husband, and they have been invited too. When we arrive, I instantly understand why the *baita* is Valerio's happy place. A light-year from civilization, it is a simple log cabin set into the hillside, surrounded by trees and a meadow. The first floor is one room, to the left a rustic kitchen and to the right a rough-hewn dining table. The kitchen is anchored by a woodburning stove (how it was hauled up the path I cannot imagine), ample for preparing an elaborate meal and warming the cabin on the coldest days. A single bulb, powered by a solar panel, lights the room. Mismatched pots and pans adorn the walls. Shelves are crammed with essentials of life: sugar, coffee, olive oil, vinegar, and the usual array of digestifs. A rickety staircase leads to a sleeping loft. A sturdy outbuilding houses supplies, equipment, and a bathroom with a toilet powered by a bucket of water.

Valerio immediately sets to work firing up the stove. He and Tati unpack the ingredients for the meal that had been distributed among our backpacks: bread, polenta, vegetables, salad, stew, fruit, cake, wine, beer. They cook and fuss as the rest of us chat and drink and nosh around the outdoor table. Ryk, exhausted from frolicking with the girls, takes refuge at our feet. We sit down to eat, a repast of Italian realism worthy of Norman Rockwell.

Teresa, her husband, and I have nothing to do but wonder, "How are we so blessed to be here?"

"Cappuccino e brioche!"

Valerio informs me that the next day's adventure will begin at their home. He advises me not to eat. When I arrive, there is indeed cappuccino and brioche, but "Surprise!" there is a "full American breakfast," complete with bacon, eggs, and pancakes. I marvel at the authenticity. I demonstrate how to make a New York deli–style bacon, egg, and cheese sandwich. I explain how much Augie loved them and how we would sit on a stoop each morning and share one. I demonstrate by making a small version for Ryk, and he gobbles it down.

It is the week of Ferragosto celebrations, music and dancing and food in the piazza every night, and Valerio enlists me to tend a wine bar he has created out of an old storage room in the piazza. He has curated it with works by local artists, built a bar, and stocked it with a selection of his favorite wines from Carlo Costa, a small family vineyard in the fertile region between Alba and Asti. As always, Valerio's creation is a level of sophistication above conventional Quarnese tastes.

"Anything Valerio does he does to perfection," his cousin Claudio once told me. "Biking, hunting, fishing, the inn. Nothing short of perfection." No less with a festival wine bar.

The night before the last night of Ferragosto celebrations, Valerio goes into shock when he sees that the stock of Nebbiolo, the most popular of the reds, is dangerously low. Normally, Carlo Costa, the eponymous vintner, would deliver, but this final day of Ferragosto is a national holiday so a truck and driver are not available.

"Why not just let them drink the other reds?" I ask. Valerio looks appalled. "Why not just buy a case of Nebbiolo from a store down the mountain?" Finding Nebbiolo in Piemonte is as easy as finding Coca-Cola in Georgia. Valerio shakes his head with disgust. He would not think of substituting grocery store garbage at his *vinoteca*!

"Cappuccino e brioche!"

We drive two hours to the heart of Italian wine country. Carlo walks us through the winery, inviting us to sample from his stainless-steel tanks. No pretentious swirling or spitting here. *Salute!* We drink like real men! While they chat and transact and load up the car with Nebbiolo and other specialties, I sit quietly watching Carlo's aged mother sitting under a gnarled olive tree peeling carrots with a gnarled wood-handled knife.

Carlo invites us in for a coffee. Out of curiosity, I ask how Carlo's mother will cook the carrots. He translates and she bids me close. She will teach me. She turns on the stove and shows me the precise dice, the right amount of heat, the right amount of oil and salt, and the right pinch of sugar to bring out the natural sweetness. Of course, now I must sit down and eat them. With some bread. And salami. And cheese. Thank God, the undulating hills of wine country are soft, allowing my stomach to settle before the ascent to Quarna. I take a good long siesta and wake up in time for my *vinoteca* shift. I am appalled and impressed with myself that evening: For the first time in my life, I drink an entire bottle of wine by myself. Nebbiolo, of course. I feel only bliss.

"Cappuccino e brioche!"

Valerio, Tati, the Principessa, and I head north through the Strona Valley, up a mountain road treacherous even by Valerio's standards. The road narrows to one lane, twisting around blind curves, plunges on either side. In certain places there are no guardrails. I know it is serious because Valerio has both hands on the steering wheel.

After an hour's ascent, we break through the tree line and a vast landscape emerges. We have arrived at Campello Monti, a Walser settlement dating back centuries. In the foreground, stone houses sit on the hillside beside a little baroque chapel. Goats freely graze. In the background is a godly intersection of the Italian, Swiss, and French Alps, towering confections dwarfed by an achingly blue summer sky. In the distance, cows are descending a trail, coming down from their breakfast in a high meadow. Hikers dot the hillsides. The village has been a rest stop for nomads and travelers since ancient times. Recently, a family from a nearby village reopened a long-defunct inn, the Albergo Nigritella. The inn has a few guest rooms and a destination restaurant.

Elvira, the proprietress, greets Valerio and Tati as old friends. I have stopped wondering if Valerio and Tati are actually friends with every proprietor in the galaxy of villages and towns surrounding Quarna. Or perhaps effortless hospitality is just the way things are done in this corner of the world. Perhaps next time I come, Elvira will greet me as an old friend.

Elvira's husband runs the kitchen and her son does the serving, while she goes from table to table chatting and fussing. The menu yet again is Piemontese country food, but just as the farmhouse food at Alpe Sacchi is elevated from the rustic food of Quarna, the food here is elevated two steps closer to paradise. Zucchini sliced to transparency is served with slices of salty parmesan. Pesto-stuffed cherry tomatoes are so ripe you have to cover your mouth to keep them from exploding outward. A medley of marinated beans—just beans!—are seasoned into an improbable delicacy. A ricotta, garnished with charred red pepper fibers, is so fluffy it's like eating a cloud. I want to thank the goat. A steaming platter of gnocchi in a light marinara arrives, accompanied by a bowl of spiced ground beef and a creamy polenta. Dessert is panna cotta (a dish born in Piemonte, I learn this day) served old school: from a jam jar, the layers of cooked cream and chocolate mixed and eaten with a demitasse spoon.

Beside us is a family as familiar as if sent from central casting: a young mother with a baby on her knee, her husband trying to contain a spirited toddler, an aunt and uncle, Nonna and Nonno. Behind us, an elderly couple dines wordlessly. In the corner, a distinguished man of a certain age holds hands across the table with a beautiful young woman (a woman other than his wife, I imagine). And, of course, there is us: a joyful young couple, their pink little girl, and a peculiar American who asks a lot of questions.

Later, when I visit the restroom, the young mother is changing the baby's diaper in the anteroom. She sings a sweet song as the baby coos. I am captivated and ask Tati if she might ask the woman the name of the song. When the woman replies, there is laughter all around. "Il topo con gli occhiali" is a song known to every Italian, and they are amused that it should be a novelty for anyone. It tells the story of a bespectacled mouse with a passion for reading, who hides in a bookstore and comes out at night. As a courtesy to the American, the assembled sing:

I libri sono ali che aiutano a volare
Books are wings that lift us to the skies

I libri sono vele che fanno navigare
Books are sails that take us to the seas

I libri sono inviti a straordinari viaggi
Books are invitations to extraordinary journeys

Con mille personaggi l'incontro sempre c'è
With a thousand characters to meet along the way

I express my appreciation like a true Italian man. I weep.

"Cappuccino e brioche!"

A short trip down the mountain, Valerio says, just to Tigros and a nearby garden center. The garden center doesn't have the species of plants he and Tati are looking for—black-eyed Susans and a rose bush, I think—but he is so focused on his mission I do not ask questions, so we drive ten minutes to another garden center. It has the plants he wants but they don't look healthy, so we drive another twenty minutes to another garden center. It has one of the plants but not both, and something is wrong with the one it has. The color is wrong, the shape is wrong. We drive half an hour to another garden center.

Finally, nearly two hours after we leave Quarna, we arrive at a garden center so astonishing I can only think this was Valerio's destination all along and the others were just to tease me. Huge and immaculate, the center has acres and acres of annuals and perennials and bulbs and shrubs and seeds and herbs and seedlings and Japanese maples and ornamental olive trees and fruit trees and succulents and houseplants under a canopy and irrigation system suitable for a small nation. There are tools and ornaments and planters and fountains and outdoor furniture and barbecue grills and candles and incense and soaps. It is so huge that Valerio, even though he has been here many times, does something I have never seen him do in a store: He asks for assistance. It is all too much for me. To avoid sensory overload, I find a chaise in the outdoor furniture department and snooze.

On the way home from the garden center, we stop at an

ordinary café for aperitivo. To one side is a cluster of sullen young adults, inked and pierced. In the back is a birthday party where little kids, high on cake and soft drinks, are running amok. At the bar are the usual suspects: old men drinking wine and flipping through the day's newspaper. And there in the middle are Valerio and I, two guys drinking beer and eating an ordinary aperitivo of salami, cheese, mystery sandwiches, and microwaved pizza slices.

With *cappuccino e brioche*, Valerio has become not just a transitional figure in my journey out of grief but a transformational figure in my professional journey too. His friendship and our adventures transformed a modest story of a magical village into a book with wings and sails, a book of extraordinary journeys, with a thousand characters to meet along the way.

Chapter 19

Bastone I

Outside Quarna, Valerio was an irrepressible buddy in adventure. Inside Quarna, he had no time to give tours or explore historical sites, so I was on my own. Many Quarnesi were neither particularly knowledgeable nor curious about the history of Quarna, ancient or modern, or the origin of its celebrations, religious or secular. If I were to ask them, "Why do Quarnesi do things this way?" their answer would be: "Because this is the way we do things!" Like Americans who scratch their heads at the origin of Labor Day or Catholics who don't know who was present at the Last Supper or Jews who don't know why we eat matzoh on Passover, whatever grade-school knowledge the Quarnesi had of their heritage had long since evaporated. A Quarnese cared less about the meaning of an event than about the associated logistics. Why do we celebrate this saint, this mountain, or this victory? Who cares! More important was who would post the announcement on Facebook, promote the event on the WhatsApp group chat, arrange for a priest, sell the tickets, tend the bar, set up the tables, stir the polenta, slice the gorgonzola, make the *miacce* sweet crepes, serve the meal, clean up, and plan and prepare the celebratory dinner for those who had volunteered for the celebration? Then the cycle began again for the next event.

At one celebration, when the young people clearing the tables were overwhelmed, I jumped up to help. Nothing special, just gathering empty wine bottles and bussing dirty glasses. I wish I could say it was magnanimity, but it was more a matter of instinct. In my youth, I had paid my dues as a restaurant busboy. I had the skills and the humility. It was also a matter of guilt. I felt like a heel standing around while people I had come to consider friends were running around in a panic. I had no idea that such a small effort—a few minutes at most—would become an inflection point in my acceptance into the community. That the American should clean tables? Without an apron or a Pro Loco team T-shirt? I was instantly advanced in social stature. The following week, at the luncheon tribute to San Rocco up on Alpe Camasca, I was given the honor of stirring the giant vat of polenta. I felt as if I had been given an *aliyah*, the honor of ascending to the altar of a synagogue to bless the Torah. At a subsequent event where I helped out, one of the young leaders took off his Quarna Pro Loco T-shirt and handed it to me (with a sworn promise to wash it first before I wore it). It is no metaphor: A Quarnese will give you the shirt off his back.

However the Quarnesi viewed me, I still considered myself an objective storyteller. But my objectivity was crumbling. I was crossing into the frame. I was no longer just telling the story of Quarna, but the story of myself in Quarna too.

"Ask Coppi Roberto," I kept hearing in response to questions of history and tradition. The sage of Quarna, Coppi Roberto appeared at every event I attended—the kindergarten graduation (he was president of the school association and handed out the diplomas), a holy day procession (he carried a banner), a memorial day march (he served in the Alpini mountain corps and wore the signature green hat), a town meeting, a band concert, but when I approached, he would disappear in a puff of smoke. Cigarette smoke to be precise. That he was a vigorous man nearing eighty who chain-smoked Camels reinforced his Yoda-esque reputation.

When we were finally introduced, I nodded my head as a sign of respect and asked when we might find time to speak.

"Very busy now," he said. "In one month, please." Meanwhile, he suggested I meet with my friend Alberto's son Edoardo, a university student whom he praised for his intelligence and involvement in the community. At first, I thought Roberto was just blowing me off. I was wrong. Edo was a go-to guy: His blog of village life was a must-read, he was editor of the village's annual report, and remarkable for such a young man, he served as the vice-mayor of Quarna Sopra.

Tall and lean, Edo was an unusual amalgam of ebullient youth and outsized maturity. On his breaks from Bocconi University, the distinguished private college in Milan where he was pursuing a degree in international economics, Edo could be found in Quarna playing trumpet with the band (alongside his mother on the saxophone and his brother on the clarinet), monitoring the polling site during an election, hanging out with his childhood buddies at Circolo, taking communion at Sunday mass, serving dinner at a community event, or bounding up the steps of city hall with the determined look of a reformer. But he was far from Quarna-centric. His parents had passed down to their two sons not just a fine education and a dedication to Quarna, but also a passion for international travel. Each summer, and often again in winter, they loaded up their camper and drove to the far corners of Europe, or went on safari to Africa, or visited the big cities and national parks of the United States and Canada.

In addition to his educational, civic, social, and family obligations, Edo became my enthusiastic guide. Far from shrugging off my curiosities, any question he could not answer he wrote down to research later. On the first of our many walks, he took me to the original center of Quarna Sotto, a fifteenth-century mini-piazza, where the early footpaths to and from distant villages converged. As we stood in the middle of the piazza, he explained how Quarna's unusual location made it an ideal crossroads for words as well as goods. Because it was nestled in the Province of Verbano-Cusio-Ossola in the north of the Piemonte region and tucked into the intersection of France and Switzerland, those going to market in any direction had to be able to buy, sell, and haggle in multiple languages and dialects for centuries.

On my hikes with Edo, there was always a destination: up a steep footpath to the Castellaccio, the ruins of a Roman encampment; down a ravine to the *lavatoio*, a pool on a sunny slope where the women once gathered to do laundry and gossip; up to Monte Gioco, a circular plateau above Quarna Sopra believed to have been a pre-Christian Celtic worship site. Edo's narration of the religious, historical, military, or social importance of each site was informed and inspiring. It was not provincial boasting. It was a clear-eyed sense of history as identity.

Some days we just ambled. I would ask about shuttered factories, dilapidated houses, unusual ornaments, symbols, and odd bits of architecture.

"How strange that you find the familiar exotic," Edo said. "For us, the familiar is invisible. *You* are the exotic!"

He did his best to translate the faded tributes to the Virgin Mary on wayside shrines that dotted the roads. He knew which of the public water fountains were originally for humans, which were for animals, and which were for washing. He guided me through the cemeteries, explaining symbols for war heroes, distinguished citizens, and children. He knew which houses were occupied and which were vacant, not by familiarity with the owners but by the telltale signs of life: a cat, a flower box, a table and chairs in the courtyard.

He was cautious in discussing politics—mindful of his civic leadership role, he was impeccably diplomatic and averse to gossip—but he was open about issues that other Quarnesi were reluctant to discuss, such as religion. He attended Sunday mass, but he acknowledged that piety was filtered with each generation.

"My grandmother is a true believer, my mother is what I would call a spiritual rationalist, my father I'm not sure," he said. "I like being part of the community. To not go to church in Quarna would be strange."

Most Quarnese children, whether their families were devout or lapsed, he explained, went through the standard rites of passage: baptism, first communion, confirmation, the full catechism. Most Quarnese adults had church weddings. Civil marriages were rare. Even the least devout Quarnese could not imagine a wedding without the eyes of God upon them.

It saddened Edo that the religious life of the community had diminished since his youth. As recently as twenty years before, there were separate, full-time resident priests, one for the Church of Saint Stefano in Quarna Sopra and one for the Church of Saint Nicolao in Quarna Sotto. With declining attendance and shrinking budgets—Vatican financial scandals and sex-abuse settlements depleted the coffers of the church—the diocese reduced the staffing to one priest for both parishes. Father Casemiro, the priest of Edo's childhood, was greeted with skepticism at first—he was South Asian—but was quickly embraced.

"He was a wonderful listener for the old people and a wonderful youth counselor for us," Edo said. He led weekly activities and summer programs. There was a bit of religion from time to time, but he was never dogmatic.

Father Casemiro was eventually transferred to a larger parish. No full-time successor was appointed. A kindly older priest from Omegna came up to celebrate mass on Sundays and to lead processions and commemorations. For special masses in the mountains requiring arduous climbs, or when the main priest had conflicting engagements, young seminarians were sent by the diocese. They were vibrant and intelligent, but they were at best special guest stars. They were not an integral part of Quarna's spiritual life.

There was one philosophical conflict that Edo and I never fully resolved. He was orthodox with regard to property lines. If I passed through an open gate or into a courtyard to get a closer look at a house or a garden—even a ruin clearly unoccupied for decades—Edo would not put a toe over the line. Without the owner's consent, Edo considered it disrespectful. He was too polite to admonish me, but I could read his disapproval.

I shrugged and taught him a maxim I had learned long ago: "It is easier to beg for forgiveness than to ask for permission."

The maxim soon became a meme among the young people of Quarna. It did not always go over well. When, at Nonna Dina's Sunday after-church lunch table, I coached her grandson on the adage in an attempt to avoid punishment for a teenage crime (he had invited too many friends to a holiday pranzo at the family *baita* without asking), Nonna Dina held one pitcher of water over his head and another pitcher over mine.

"Now who will beg for forgiveness?" she said, with her loving laugh.

Chapter 20

Bastone II

When the sun was high and sightseeing in the heat too brutal, Edo and I would sit and have a cold drink at Circolo or Posta.

"I do love Quarna, but I am not naive to its limits," he said. "The more I see of the world, the smaller Quarna gets."

"What would you miss most if you left?" I asked.

"Family and community," he said. "Knowing that in good times there are people to share the happiness and in bad times there are people who will be there to help. Knowing that if you ask your neighbor for a cup of milk, she will bring you her cow."

Edo introduced me to many people on our walks, explaining their familial or social relationships, the nature of their work or sport, their eccentricities, their nicknames. He colored his commentary well but always stayed within the lines of discretion. He introduced me to his chums, most of whom were desperate to avoid speaking English—it was a form of torture they associated with rigid schoolmarms. Some, recognizing I was not the enemy, overcame their fears and asked me about life in New York City and sports. They were fascinated by basketball and knew the major teams and players. (Not that I had much to add to their knowledge.) They had no interest in American football. Baseball they found inscrutable.

Edo's most important introduction was to Guido, a spirited octogenarian who often wandered about town sporting a broad-brimmed straw hat like those I had seen in vintage photos at the village museum.

"Finally I meet the legendary American!" were Guido's first words.

He paused to correct himself.

"No. Not a legend yet. An attraction. Eventually, a legend."

Guido's English was rough-hewn, learned in the school of working-class life, much of it lived in the United States. He immigrated to America in his twenties, but his recollections of his childhood in Quarna were many and specific: dates, events, images, and sensory experiences. Guido's digressions could be maddening—on our walks, he would often stop suddenly for a lengthy aside—but each walk was like a journey into a storybook, with him as author, illustrator, and narrator.

In her foreword to the book *Life Is With People*, Margaret Mead wrote of anthropology as developing "a capacity to listen to the broken accents of the present and reconstitute the whole which was the immediate past." Guido, with his shards of English, Italian, and *dialetto*, and with his verbal ellipses, parentheticals, and footnotes, was the voice from the past I had been seeking. He embodied the collective memory of Quarna. He and his wife split their time between Los Angeles, where the winds of work had taken him, and Quarna, where the soil firmly rooted him. His nonlinear stories needed real-time editing, but I quickly learned how to follow his digressions. His facts and figures would have required a time machine to fact-check, but he was so meticulous in his recollections that I had no reason to believe he spoke anything other than the truth.

This was Guido, unfiltered:

> I was born on December 4, 1935, a Wednesday, in a little house seven meters down the hill from your apartment. You know your apartment is on the site where a factory burned down. A "suspicious fire" we say. Business was not good. Valerio's uncle Gino—I mean his mother's uncle—he could tell you more. He is older than me. He was born 1928. Next to the factory near the house where I was born was a cow that gave the sweetest cream. We always wondered what the woman put in the hay. A midwife delivered me. She was the grandmother

of Valentina, the girl who works at Circolo. Valentina's father used to be the chef at Circolo. That is why their garden is so big. Below the house where I was born is a big stone basin where my mother did the laundry and would bathe me every Saturday. It was carved by Valerio's grandfather, a stone mason. It took two donkeys to move it. One gray, one roan.

Five years of school was all that was offered in Quarna when Guido was a boy. Guido's father asked the teacher—who had received his degree through correspondence school—to fail Guido so he could stay in school one more year, but he had already passed the final exams so that was that. He then worked various menial jobs in Quarna until, at age nineteen, he was drafted into the mountain corps for his military service. When he returned to Quarna, he expected that he would settle there for life with a factory job like his father and most of the men he knew. But one day he received a letter from a childhood friend who had a job carving ice sculptures for Italy's Home Lines cruise ships. He invited Guido to apply for a job with the company. It was an elaborate process—health exams, a passport, applications. The greatest obstacle, he said, was that he was not a "man of the sea."

"I was a mountain boy. I did not know how to swim or row a boat!"

He succeeded in jumping through every hoop and was hired

for the lowest kitchen scut work, but he was thrilled. Life on a ship was a revelation.

"We lived and worked several decks below. I never saw so much food! We were permitted above deck only in certain places at certain times during the day. I had never seen such furnishings! One evening I looked through the door at the dancing. I had never seen such elegance!"

Life among his shipmates was equally fascinating to him. The kitchen staff was Italian, the officers British, the laundry staff Chinese, the service staff German. He could not legally disembark outside of Italy, but when he saw the skyline of New York City, this son of Quarna, with a fifth-grade education, no English, no visa, but with insatiable curiosity and a work ethic to match, decided to stay.

"I crossed Tenth Avenue with a little suitcase and did not look back," he said. A shipmate had given him the name of an Italian man who owned a restaurant. He hailed a taxi, something he had seen only in a movie. The restaurant owner, admiring his moxie, gave him a job washing dishes, a cot in a storage room, and a little money each week. After a few years, through a series of "connections" in the Italian community, as he put it, he was able to get better restaurant jobs, then a work visa, then a green card, and then a union job at an airline kitchen at JFK Airport. Later he was transferred to Chicago and then Los Angeles, where, riding a city bus to work one day, he met Mercedes, a young woman from Mexico who would become his wife. Of equal poverty, humility, and determination, Mercedes had crossed the border and found work first as a housekeeper in Beverly Hills and then as a hotel maid. With Guido's union airline benefits and her union hotel benefits, they traveled the world. When he retired, he restored the family house in Quarna, where they spent their summers.

Between their union pensions, his Italian pension, and owning houses outright in Los Angeles and Quarna, these simple people were comfortable. Still, Guido was defiantly frugal. Outraged at the price of admission to eat and drink at village celebrations, he watched from a distance. At Circolo or Posta, after long walks in the midday sun, he refused to allow me to buy him anything more than a tonic water. He much preferred we drink and eat at his home. And he insisted I bring along any visiting guest. Coffee and cake with Guido and Mercedes became a regular stop on the tour. Now and then I was invited for lunch. Mercedes's Mexican food was a refreshing change. Never had I been so happy to eat a tamale.

Guido was not a siesta man. After an ample lunch prepared by Mercedes, he would jump up and grab his hat and expected me to rouse myself as well. He was tireless and fearless in any weather. He was most eager to take me to scenes of his childhood: a secret passageway where he and his friends escaped their parents, an old firepit where they roasted chestnuts, an overgrown arboretum (he could still name the various species), a well where boys hid from conscription by the fascists, remote *baitas* where partisans hid from the Germans. Just outside the village, beside the most powerful mountain stream, lay the remnants of the stone structure that once housed the village's first power plant, a small hydroelectric generator that allowed for one lightbulb per home for two hours each night. We hiked to Causello, a former summertime osteria that once brimmed with life but was now a ruin. Untouched for decades, its roof had collapsed on the refreshment stand, the playground equipment was a pile of rusted bones, the tennis court net was a sagging cobweb, and the tile dance floor was hidden under a forest of weeds. Each time I walked by Causello, I expected Norma Desmond, the reclusive silent movie star of *Sunset Boulevard*, to emerge from the rubble.

Guido told me of the day in 1944 when he saw an airplane for the first time. The Allies were dropping supplies to Italian partisans hidden in the mountains.

"We heard this strange sound and then we saw the airplanes, low over the mountains. We had only seen pictures of airplanes in newspapers. We could smell the fumes. We could see the faces of the pilots. Then down came crates tied to parachutes of different colors. Colors and patterns the likes of which we had never seen! For years after the war, men and women were still dressing in clothes they made from parachute fabrics. They used the nylon cords to secure their woodpiles."

He took me to a steep staircase not far from my apartment, where, on a day some eighty years before, he and his friends were entertained for an afternoon by three young partisans who offered a five-lira prize to the boy who could race up and down the stairs fastest.

"We thought they were so handsome and heroic!" he said. "We only knew them for an afternoon, but we idolized them." He smiled at the memory of watching them chatting and laughing as he and his friends raced.

The day after the race on the staircase, the three men were found dead, executed by Germans patrolling the mountains. The snitch was presumed to be a local Fascist sympathizer eager for a reward.

Guido looked down at the staircase as if it was hallowed ground and recited their names in the traditional Italian manner, last name first:

"Rossetti Livio, Savona Pietro, Busalacchi Stefano," he said, then looked up at me. "When you write the story of Quarna, will you please include their names?"

Guido cherished the memories of his childhood but did not wallow in the past. He was fascinated by how Quarna had changed and welcomed its evolution.

"The air is much fresher now," he said. In the old days, the air was acrid with smoke from woodburning stoves. The hillsides, barren for centuries after trees were harvested for firewood and woodcrafts or cleared for grazing, were now blanketed with trees that filled the air with oxygen and the scent of pine. The water tasted better, he said. In the old days, factory solvents and animal waste got into the streams.

The most significant catalyst for change, he believed, was the Marshall Plan. "The Italian communist party was very big in Italy, and the Americans did not want us to fall in with the Russians," he explained. "The Americans threw money at us. There was free land down in Omegna if you had money to invest, and free money if you had land to build on. The new factories created jobs with wages as we had never seen. If you were willing to go down the mountain and work hard, you could make more money in an hour than in a day in Quarna."

Plastics and heating oil further changed the economy. There was less wood needed from the mountains for crafts and heat, so the logging jobs went away. Factory jobs meant no time for cows and chickens. Televisions and cars took people away from community life. Bocce courts became parking lots.

The most difficult change for Guido was the loss of so many friends he had outlived. He was not a barfly or a cardplayer or a hunter or a fisherman. He did not play in the band or serve on festival committees. His primary hobby was walking about and chatting with old-timers, newcomers, friends, and strangers. He was a collector of people and stories, mine included. He peppered me with questions about my family, from my great-grandparents' shtetl roots in eastern Europe to my siblings and their families. He was delighted to meet my visitors. He remembered every name and asked for updates on everyone each time I visited. Just as Guido became a part of my story of Quarna, he was making me a part of Quarna's story too.

Hikers on rugged trails often use *bastoni*, walking sticks, for balance and endurance. Edo and Guido became my *bastone*. Intelligent and engaging, each in his own way, they guided me on journeys to the past, the present, and the future.

Chapter 21

The Blue and the Red

Rare is the travel memoirist who addresses the messier aspects of the human condition. Their journeys tend toward aspirational fantasies whitewashed of the untidy facts of life. We are invited to laugh at the foibles of provincial locals, but in travelogues, unlike sweeping novels, there isn't always time for more than a simple snapshot. Individuals become stock characters for color or humor or pathos. We meet shamans, peddlers, buffoons, impudent workmen, beggars, and intellectuals, but we don't often meet two-income, two-children, two-car, working-class families. We don't see the schizophrenic man wandering in a medicated trance, the teenage alcoholic in a fog, the elderly woman with dementia, the young father with multiple sclerosis, the woman who lost a son to a drug overdose, the children and adults with profound physical and developmental disabilities. We don't hear about the spiteful who demean others in public or the greedy who derail projects that would serve the common good. In Quarna, the afflicted and the selfish are not marginalized or institutionalized or pitied or shunned. You see them every day, playing, stumbling, wandering, fighting, drinking, smoking, celebrating, praying, scowling, and smiling. Angels or bastards, they nod "Buongiorno!" to all. Even to the peculiar middle-aged American man who asks a lot of questions.

Also cleansed from most travel narratives are the unpleasant discomforts of life. Bon vivants gobble down fruits, vegetables, meat, and fish prepared in questionably hygienic conditions and never suffer gastrointestinal distress. Richard Halliburton swam the length of the Panama Canal in 1928. One can only imagine the consequences to his bowels. In the collected letters of journalist Martha Gellhorn, editor Caroline Moorehead presents a classic Gellhornism: "Laxatives and travel are one and the same." Jonathan Swift makes us feel the giant Gulliver's poop-shame as he holds back the urge to "disburden" himself in Lilliput. I once danced a tarantella at an Italian train station while waiting for a stoic bathroom attendant to write out a receipt for the one-euro fee for the privilege to pee.

Matters of the heart are exposed in various shades of gray. In *Under the Tuscan Sun* and *Eat, Pray, Love*, Frances Mayes and Elizabeth Gilbert are open about divorce as a catalyst for reinvention. In *A Year in Provence*, Peter Mayle, twice divorced and the author of two books on divorce, somehow swims in calm marital seas while renovating a house with his third wife. Collin and I barely survived choosing window treatments for our rental apartment. Where among the dappled days of Mr. and Mrs. Mayle are the raging fights over blinds, shades, curtains, drapes, and shutters?

We often read of the thrill of exotic romance but rarely the consequences of sex. Kudos to Gilbert, who bravely gives us a glimpse of real life when, after a period of abstinence, she has a passionate affair with a Brazilian man in Bali.

"After all those nights of not sleeping and all those days of too much lovemaking," she writes, "my body struck back and I got attacked by a nasty infection in my bladder. A typical affliction of the overly sexed, especially likely to strike when you're not used to being overly sexed anymore. It came up as fast as any tragedy can strike." She eschewed Western antibiotics in favor of a Balinese healer's poultices and potions. Within hours, she was cured.

Despite my sexual adventures in Europe over the decades, only once were there consequences. On a visit to Paris in my twenties, a few days after a night in a garret with a scruffy poet-lawyer, I woke to an uncomfortable itch. Instead of consulting a smiling Balinese medicine woman, I had to appeal to a scowling Parisian pharmacist. When my every attempt at translation failed, I was forced to draw a childlike picture of a crab.

Collin and I remained estranged during my early visits to Quarna, but my sadness was mitigated by a bit of glee. Some people loathe dating. I never have. Getting a date is the hard part, but the date itself is like the prize in a box of Cracker Jack. When the lights dim at the movies or the curtain goes up at the theater, you never know what you are going to get. Good? Bad? Or so bad, it's good?

I anticipated that my prospects would be limited now that I was in the speculative era of middle age. I was wrong. Now that—courtesy of grief—I had lost weight, gotten in shape, and entered the "Daddy" category, men not yet born when I was coming out were now coming on to me. It was thrilling even when it was ridiculous. Their May–December fantasies faded when they discovered that the virile, cuddly "Daddy" of their dreams was a gassy snorer. Meanwhile, Daddy's fantasy of spooning an adoring youth quickly faded with the umpteenth "it's like, you know" or "super" in every sentence.

During my stays in Quarna, I occasionally escaped to Milan or Turin or Bologna to recharge the human spirit. I was single and might as well enjoy it without inhibition. There were fleeting encounters and there were substantive dates. In Milan I had aperitivo with a nerdy-handsome architect, who took me on a tour of Piazza Gae Aulenti and narrated the contemporary Italian architecture. In Bologna, I had gelato with a buff art historian from the ministry of culture who took me to the Oratorio di Santa Cecilia and narrated the sixteenth-century frescoes. In Turin, an adorable young government bureaucrat I met in a bar professed undying love within the hour. Clearly insane, he was incredibly handsome, charming, and talented in the ways one dreams an Italian man to be. On our second date, he asked that I stay in Turin and marry him. On our third date, he unleashed a crazed interrogation. What was I doing all day while he was at work? He did not believe I could spend so much time in museums. He accused me of cheating on him, as if our bond was already sanctified. Wisely, I had not given him (or any man I met) the specifics of Quarna. I did not need a stalker in my story.

As for romantic attractions to men in Quarna, I never felt a *zing*. If I had, I would never have acted on it. Even with the increasingly wobbly boundaries in the narrative of my story, there were limits. As for men who might have had a thing for me, I never sensed it. Were there latent desires among the many old bachelors? Were there devoted husbands who had trysts with men when they traveled? Young men on the down-low yearning to breathe free? Likely on all counts, but not evident to me.

I had the occasional crush, to be sure, based more on charm than looks. The shallow truth is that pale Northern Italian mountain men are not in the same league as swarthy Southern Italian men. Even when Quarna hosted a regional soccer tournament, with a hundred sweaty men from across the province gathered in a shirtless mass of pulsing, drunken energy, there were no fireworks. These men preferred pasta, beer, and camaraderie to egg-white omelets, protein shakes, and the gym.

Only once, at a soccer tournament, was I gobsmacked by an Adonis: tall, muscled, black ringlets, aqua eyes, fair-skinned. When he approached to say hello—he had heard me speaking English and was eager to talk—I was speechless. (An unusual affliction for me.) He turned out to be sensitive, intelligent, keen on American culture, open about his fractured childhood and ongoing emotional troubles, and unquestionably straight. When a surge of drunken players and fans nearly toppled me over, he put a chivalrous arm around my waist to steady me; I nearly swooned like a damsel on the cover of a romance novel. Sadly, he was not even Italian. He was a German friend-of-a-friend-of-a-friend recruited as a ringer. The Italian of my dreams was from Dusseldorf.

There were bumps in the road of another kind. In my natural environment, I have a mercurial temperament. I shuttle between peaks of boundless energy and troughs of sleepy sadness. Years of therapy have tempered the frequency and amplitude of the peaks and troughs, but whatever the biological or psychological roots, they cannot be eliminated. Sometimes my moods manifest in witty quips, sometimes in cruel barbs. A distinguished psychoanalyst, now a professor at a prestigious medical school, cites me in his lectures as the only patient ever to have made him cry. I am very, very good at being very, very bad.

Augie was a potent mood stabilizer. Had I known the powers of a dog for alleviating depression and anxiety, I would have adopted one years earlier and saved a fortune on psychotherapy and pharmaceuticals. With Augie, depression and anxiety were luxuries I could not afford. I could not stay in bed staring at the ceiling or escape to a multiplex for triple features with tubs of self-pity popcorn. With a dog, whatever the weather of my mind, I was obligated to go out and walk multiple times a day. It is a cliché but true: Augie walked me.

Short walks would suffice for quick relief ("saluting a tree" as Steinbeck would say of Charley, his poodle), but depriving Augie of at least one long walk a day would be inhumane. It wasn't just about waste removal. Any dog can do that. A robust daily walk for a dog of Augie's sentience was as much a necessity as food or water or air. No matter how far I descended in the diving bell, I had to come up for air for him, even if I just took him to the dog park, where I could wallow on a bench while he romped with his playmates. Heat waves, cold snaps, hurricanes, blizzards, Augie had to go out. He could sprawl on pavement superheated by the sun. He could leap for joy in snow drifts up to his neck. A designer jacket? *Bosh!* His natural double-ply fur coat was all he needed. He allowed boots only when freezing slush made the city sidewalks unbearable for his toes.

Only one form of weather perturbed him: rain. The sound

of a single drop and he refused to go out. With remarkable force, he glued his ass to the floor and refused to move. Twelve hours, sixteen hours were nothing for him. Eighteen hours was the breaking point for me. Against his will, I would carry him several blocks in a downpour, putting him down and pressing on his bladder until he surrendered. His revenge was explicit. When we returned home, before I could reach for a towel, he would jump on the sofa and shake off the water with the force of a monsoon. Augie's emotions were not limited to love. Resentment was among the others.

In Quarna, absent Augie, the powers of fresh air, consistent exercise, sound sleep, comfort food, and socialization were a tonic. The mood swings ebbed, but never to zero. There were mornings I awoke in deep sadness. Sometimes the sadness was triggered by a troubling dream, a jag of grief, the frustration of a writing assignment, homesickness, melancholy over Collin, or nothing at all, which is the worst shade of the blues. On those mornings, I skipped my sunrise walk to the Belvedere and canceled my appearance on the balcony. I warmed up just enough day-old moka coffee to ward off a caffeine-deprivation headache. Otherwise, I drank and ate nothing. I slept all day, with occasional breaks to stare at the shadows on the ceiling.

At home in New York, the blues can last a fortnight or a month. In Quarna, the clouds dissipated within a day, two at most. Sometimes the sadness lifted on its own, sometimes the reawakening was triggered by an event, often a concert. What good was sitting alone in my apartment when I could hear the village band play a *My Fair Lady* medley at Saliente? Or attend an international gathering of alpenhorn on the Belvedere? Or join a Sunday afternoon music "crawl" following a woodwind soloist–organist duo performing repertoire from five centuries on three different instruments—a Renaissance coronet, a traditional clarinet, and a modern saxophone—in three different Quarnese churches? Or have pizza with a gaggle of visiting teenage pianists and their teacher after their masterclass recital? The great English playwright William Congreve's most famous verse is generally misquoted. He did not write "Music soothes the savage beast." He wrote "Music hath charms to soothe the savage breast. To soften rocks or bend the knotted oak." How often the musical charms of Quarna soothed my savage breast and unbent my knotted brain.

At the other end of the spectrum were, to borrow from Holly Golightly in *Breakfast at Tiffany's*, the "mean reds." The outbursts were rare, and some arguably justified. Like my tirades at bicyclists weaving among pedestrians on the sidewalk in New York, in Quarna I screamed unadulterated profanities at summer Villeggianti with their big, fat, stupid BMWs speeding down narrow streets with no regard for human life. My rage was well within the range of what Italians would consider acceptable, even normal. Still, I felt no glory in my outbursts, only remorse at the loss of control. I wanted the Quarnesi to see only the whitewashed version of me. The polite, curious, and amusing version of me. I often failed.

Time and again, I was told, if I wanted to learn more about the history of Quarna, I must speak with Coppi Roberto. Time and again, he rebuffed me.

"Very busy now, in one month please," he had said when he directed me to Edo. Roberto's excuse was legitimate, Edo assured me. He was curating an exhibit for the museum, and it was truly all-consuming. He was combing village and parish archives for photos and documents, writing exhibition text and captions, and working with designers to create displays. The exhibit opened to great fanfare, with a musical performance, speeches by civic leaders, and a ribbon-cutting ceremony. Indeed, it was a remarkable display of words, pictures, and objects tuned just right. Scholarly, but not pedantic, it was a testament to Quarna's resilience that never slipped into sentiment.

A few days after the opening, I saw Roberto at Posta. I stopped by his table, praised the exhibit, and once again asked for a time to meet.

"Yes, of course. Two more weeks, please." There was no clear explanation, but I surmised there might be a backlog of things postponed by the exhibit.

I frequently saw him having a morning coffee at Posta, but I politely kept my distance until two weeks had passed.

"Just two more weeks, please," he said, again. His daughter was in town.

Two weeks later, I saw him on the terrace of Giuseppe's bar. When he saw me, he ran off.

"Must go! Soon we talk!" he said.

Another two weeks, and still Roberto continued to evade me. One day, I was having pranzo at Circolo with a group of elders and confessed my disappointment at not yet having met with Roberto. I had tried repeatedly, I told them, but he had always been too busy. As if on cue, he appeared a few feet away at the bar, and the elders summoned him over. In the company of his peers, it was hard to elude me. He agreed to meet me on the Circolo terrace after pranzo.

I waited an hour. He was a no-show.

I was furious. I ordered a beer and vented to Valentina and Alessio, who were relaxing after the pranzo rush.

"Coppi Roberto has been avoiding me for three months! What an *asshole*!"

They smiled and nodded in what I interpreted as a combination of assent (Roberto was known to be difficult) and amusement (the polite American was now a hot-headed Quarnesi). I finished my beer, and there was Roberto in the distance, chatting in the piazza. I marched down the hill, approached and waited, arms crossed, steam coming out of my ears, until his guests departed. I let loose in a way I regret.

"What is the problem, Roberto? Is the problem me or is the problem you? Everyone in Quarna tells me, 'You must meet Coppi Roberto! Coppi Roberto knows all! Coppi Roberto can answer your questions!' And time and again you refuse to meet me. You say, 'So busy! No time! Two weeks!' *Bullshit*. Everywhere I go I see you talking, talking, talking. But you have no time to talk to me?"

His face fell. He was not angry. He was not insulted. He was contrite.

"I fear my English is not good enough for you," he said.

I wanted a sinkhole to open in the cobbles beneath me and to plunge deep into the boiling core of the earth. He had avoided me not out of arrogance but out of humility. And here, instead of showing patience, I had caused him to feel shame. Worse, an untimely breeze carried my tirade up the hillsides like an oration in a Roman amphitheater. Later, a friend who had heard about the incident assured me that taking Roberto down a peg was no crime. He was not always so humble.

(That evening, at a village event, a lovely woman of a certain age—a woman I had never met—offered to buy me a coffee. As with all such offers, I accepted. The kindness was observed by those sitting nearby with a mixture of amusement and respect. The kind woman, I was told, was Coppi Roberto's wife. It was not clear if she was presenting me with an olive branch or a medal of honor.)

I suggested a solution to Roberto. As I had done with other Quarnesi with limited or no English, I would use my phone to translate my questions into Italian. He could answer freely in Italian or English as he wished and I would record them. I would later have the recordings transcribed. He smiled and agreed. Our first conversation, on the terrace of Circolo, lasted two hours. The more he spoke, the more he switched to English. As his confidence grew, the need for translation shrank. It was an experience I often encountered with Italians who had studied English or used English for their work but had become rusty and were reluctant to speak. Once the wheels were greased, their language skills kicked in. Roberto was the source I had hoped for. His insights were sophisticated. He was now generous with his time.

Sometimes generous to a fault. The following day, we met at the Saliente chapel so he could tell me the story of the frescoes and the terracotta Virgin and the mystery of a masterpiece that had disappeared. As I turned a page in my notebook, I got a paper cut that bled profusely. I tore out several sheets of paper to form a compress, but still I was dripping blood onto the seventeenth-century stones of the nave like a martyr with stigmata. I tried time and again to excuse myself but my pleas went nowhere. His lecture lasted two hours. The next day, he asked me to meet him at the museum. Another two hours. The day after that, when I saw him at Posta having his morning coffee, I fled.

Chapter 22

Good Dog/Bad Dog

As predicted by Bill Berloni, the matchmaker of the Humane Society, Augie adapted well to city life. He engaged dogs and people politely and trained easily. He was housebroken within weeks and was an excellent student at obedience school. He received his diploma with a gold star.

When I showed the diploma to a friend's precocious six-year-old, there was a curious look on his face.

"Where do they find the teachers?" he asked.

I was about to give the obvious answer—a professional trainer—but after a pause I realized his question rose to a higher plane of logic. His assumption, brilliant and beautiful, was that the teachers themselves would be dogs. He was disappointed to hear that Augie's teacher was a mere human.

As for learning party tricks, I'm sure Augie would have excelled, but neither he nor I were interested. The first time I threw a ball for him to fetch, he didn't budge. Instead, he gave me a withering look.

"You want the ball?" he asked. "Go get it yourself."

Even when he reached full maturity, Augie never outgrew his Fawn Dog look. He never grew into his ridiculously long legs and big ears. But his gait was far from gangly. Nose high, tail high, he developed a noble prance worthy of a Lipizzaner stallion. An elderly neighbor, a Viennese woman with an old-world accent, would say, "Such an aristocrat!" every time we passed. I didn't have the heart to tell her he was a Brooklyn mutt.

In *Travels with Charley*, John Steinbeck heaps scorn on dog lovers who project their own "sloppy characteristics" onto a dog until he becomes their alter ego. Steinbeck will have none of it. Nor will Charley: "For Charley is not a human; he's a dog, and he likes it that way. He feels he is a first-rate dog and has no wish to be a second-rate human."

I never anthropomorphized Augie. I never saw him as a child substitute. I never spoke to him in high-pitched baby talk. His affectionate nicknames were few. I respected him as an intelligent, curious, contemplative representative of his species, not as an adjunct to my own. The respect, I am fairly sure, was mutual. Aside from a fine Italian collar and leash, black leather with saffron stitching, his wardrobe was limited to the necessities: a reflective vest for nighttime walks in the country and a red cable-knit sweater in his later years after a swim on a chilly day.

Only once did I succumb to an elaborate outfit. Our neighborhood block association was conducting a dog pageant as part of its annual festival. So many of our friends and their dogs were participating that I would have seemed a party pooper to bow out. My friend Mitch, a costumer for the Metropolitan Opera, created a bespoke white-tie outfit complete with a wing collar and top hat. Augie was unquestionably the most distinguished gentleman in the parade. Sadly, the judges, led by a C-list television personality, went for a pedigreed snoot in a designer confection. Some people just don't know what real class looks like, and Augie had class.

Augie was by no means perfect. He had his Marmaduke moments: seizing mattress real estate by eminent domain; twisting and turning during the night until he forged us into pretzels; refusing to relinquish a favorite chair; inserting his way into intimate situations. He learned that Collin was an easier touch than me for a middle-of-the-night walk for any reason or no reason.

He had Lassie's heroic instincts. Augie, Collin, and I were on a hike in the hills of North Carolina, a rhapsody until we heard the unmistakable roar of a bear. The fur on Augie's back rose to a massive mohawk, puffing up as if to intimidate any monster. His ears and eyes went on full alert. Collin and I were not Boy Scout material. We didn't know the behavioral differences between a black bear and a brown bear. We didn't know whether to be silent or make noise. We made an educated guess. We sang "The Other Day I Met a Bear," the classic campfire song. I am sure it was Augie's defensive mettle rather than the campfire song that saved us.

He had his Marley moments too. His "thunderphobia" was off the charts. I would have to stay home or rearrange plans or hire a dogsitter according to the weather forecast. The panting and shivering and bulging eyes began well in advance of the first flash of lightning. If I was home, he would sit on my chest, shivering and whimpering and panting, eyes bulging. There was no sleep for anyone during nighttime storms. If I was out and could not get home fast enough, there was damage. He pulled up carpet. He chewed window ledges. He clawed hardwood floors.

I once came home and the doorknob came off in my hand. He had bent the brass escutcheon plate that secured the lock and the knob from the inside.

He bent metal designed to ward off thieves. He bent it ninety degrees until the screws popped. He bent it with his claws and teeth.

I didn't give a damn about the doorknob. All I cared about were his paws and teeth. Miraculously, nothing was broken. Not even a drop of blood.

Valium and behavior modification and a hokey thunder vest did nothing. To this day, my nerves go on high alert when the sky darkens and the smell of electricity is in the air. At the first flash of lightning, I feel the urge to race home and comfort Augie.

When he was seventeen, we came home to find something we had never seen: kitchen garbage strewn throughout the apartment. He was down to three legs by then, but still he had figured out how to push the pedal on the heavy-duty flip-top can with one front paw, use the other paw to tip the can over, and then use his teeth to pull out the heavy plastic liner and the trash bag. This was not just some old dog who had learned a new trick. This was the same dog with strategic capacities I saw snatch a squeaky toy from an alpha dog at the Humane Society when he was two months old. He hadn't lost his wiles. After all these years with a dog who never went dumpster diving, if Collin and I went out, we had to put every trash can in the bathtub and lock the bathroom door.

Augie was an astonishing escape artist. Left alone in an unfenced yard, he never went beyond the nearest shade tree. But fence him in, and the challenge began. No barrier could stop him. Chain-link fences, picket fences, brick walls were a cinch. He leapt over or crawled under or pried open any enclosure. In Springs, he dug a tunnel under the cinderblock foundation of my house, slithered the width of the house on his belly, and then dug a tunnel on the other side to escape.

Once, while in a conference room in Cleveland, I received a terrifying call. Augie was fine, the woman said, but he had been found off leash at the corner of Hudson and West Fourth streets, a busy intersection nearly half a mile from home. Later I learned from witnesses that he had caused quite an uproar. He ran up Hudson past the local grade school as classes were ending for the day. The children screamed, driving him into the street. Cars screeched to a halt, traffic stopped for blocks, cars honked in a classic New York cacophony. Dozens of people, including two police officers, tried to grab him. He eluded them all. Finally, the woman who called me captured him and brought him to a local pet store. I called a friend, who retrieved him and brought him home. She found my housekeeper weeping. Augie had slipped out the door when she arrived and raced down the stairs where, coincidentally, the building super had propped the front door open while taking out the garbage. Augie took a hard right to the corner and then made a beeline north. There was no doubt of his destination: He was heading to his dogsitter Lauren's apartment. He adored her. Lauren's scruffy terrier, Mabel, was his best city friend, a pal with whom he walked for years and with whom he had slumber parties when I was away.

In Springs, I once attempted to board Augie with a woman who boasted of having constructed an escape-proof yard for her own Houdini dog. She had built two tall, concentric chain-link fences anchored in cement footings that formed a kind of moat. In between and around the fences were shrubs and pines. As an extra interior line of defense, there was a wall of mature bamboo. The entrance was double-gated.

In the midst of explaining her inescapable Alcatraz, we heard a rustle and turned to watch the Great Escape, as if in slow motion but already too far along to thwart. Augie had scoped out the perimeter, discovered a pliable section of bamboo, pushed and pawed at it to form a ramp, and then ran up and flew over the double moat. The woman was apoplectic. I shrugged.

"That's my dog," I said.

My gap years at the beach with Augie came to an end when I was offered a management job in publishing that I could not refuse. I dreaded the return to the corporate world, but it was time to get back on the treadmill. Even with the profit from subletting my apartment in the West Village and renting out a room in the Springs house at the summer peak and taking on freelance writing gigs, the life of a beach bohemian was expensive. My health insurance premiums were skyrocketing and the old Ford Wagon was nearing the end of its life. The salary and benefits of the corporate job offer were exceptional, until I was told I had to begin at a satellite office in southern Ohio for the first year. I hesitated, but to close the deal, they threw in a leased car. I negotiated for a small SUV so there was room for Augie's travel crate. It is no exaggeration to say I took the job for Augie as much as myself: Now we had new wheels for road trips.

Unfortunately, the job required travel. A lot of travel: to San

Francisco, Toronto, New York, and London to visit operating locations; to remote towns to visit printing plants and paper mills; to team-building retreats conducted by an imperious boss at luxury resorts. Had I not been concerned for Augie's welfare, I would have enjoyed the travel. But I resented each trip. I flew out at the last minute and flew home at the first chance.

Fortunately, there were two superb boarding options. My parents, aging but spry, were still in Toledo, three hours away, and were thrilled to take Augie for any length of time. They would guard him safely. Even if he did escape, their yard was unfenced so, true to form, he never went farther than the nearest shade tree.

When my parents were not available, there was a second option: Miss Judith's, a sixteen-acre dog retreat with a barn and a stream and a pond. She limited her guests to six or seven dogs, plus her own. Each evening for dinner she prepared chicken tenders or sirloin tips to go with their kibble. There were dog beds throughout the house and her bed was a free-for-all. A doggie door allowed for relief as needed. And since there was no fence and Augie was in the company of a pack, I felt confident he would be safe.

I expected that Augie would warm to Miss Judith's bed. Or hang out on a warm dog bed playing poker with the boys. I was surprised at his choice, as was Miss Judith. He spent each night in the open barn, curled up beside a large German shepherd, with whom he had bonded. It seemed Augie had a passion for sleeping outdoors in cold weather, which I never knew. If the temperature plummeted to dangerous levels, she had to bribe Augie and his buddy to come inside.

When I dropped Augie off at Miss Judith's, he was hysterical with glee. When I arrived to pick him up, he would run away at the sound of my car coming up the long drive. Miss Judith and I laughed. He was a happy camper. His coat thickened from the outdoors, and with unlimited exercise and indulgent meals, he was several pounds heavier—all muscle. After a week at Miss Judith's, his wolf heritage emerged. He was as dashing as White Fang. When he came back to our boring apartment, he slept for three days.

After each stay at Miss Judith's, he received a handwritten report card on behavior and play and eating. He was a straight-A student right up until I got her phone call that he was expelled. Miss Judith asked that I return from my business trip as soon as possible. There had been an incident. On one of their daily group hikes, Augie wandered off to a neighbor's property and began to herd the owner's llamas. Augie meant no harm, but the farmer shot Augie in the ass with a pellet gun. Miss Judith had to rush him to an emergency vet. He was fine, she said, but she was not. The anxiety was too much for her. She loved Augie, she said, but he had broken a cardinal rule: He had defied a voice command and wandered off. He had endangered his own life and the peaceable relationship with her neighbor. He was no longer welcome. Not even for a day visit with my presence.

There was nothing I could do but thank her for having given Augie a happy place.

I often wonder what dream Augie was dreaming in his final moments on the floor in his sunbeam. I assumed he was racing along the shore or hiking a trail in the mountains with me. But camping at Miss Judith's was surely a possibility. Eating and sleeping and hiking and running and playing with a pack of his own kind. Bracing cold. Meat with his kibble. Coming and going and peeing and pooping as he wished. Unleashed and free. A dog's life.

Chapter 23

Folly and Fear

"Are you the kind of person who shit happens to every day?" Collin asked early in our courtship. In our first ten days dating in Savannah, there were at least a dozen assorted dramas. Collin took me to the emergency room (a cornea scratched by an innocent rambunctious Augie), rescued me and my father from a restaurant during a torrential thunderstorm (my car was parked too far away for an elderly man in a wheelchair), helped me move three times (a gas leak in the first apartment, a neighbor with a ferocious pit bull at the second, a hotel stay in between). When, at Collin's insistence, we made New York City our home, there began a litany of woes, from the daily hysteria of finding my reading glasses, keys, wallet, and phone to all manner of medical maladies.

I was no less needy in Quarna. Edo's proverb about the community—that if you asked your neighbor for a glass of milk, she would lend you her cow—proved true. I needed a lot of milk, and a lot of kindly cows came a-calling. One could say it was just carryover from my ordinary life. One could also say I was assimilating into a community. One could say I was a needy person who, sly as a dog, was good at getting others to take care of me.

On a lovely summer day, the clouds suddenly turned black. Like a biblical plague, the heavens unleashed a violent hailstorm that shattered my bedroom windows. While the landlord arranged for repair, a neighbor raced over to sweep up the mess below the window. Another brought a vacuum cleaner to hoover up the shards in my bedroom.

My friend and neighbor Ileana and her children often came to my rescue. While on deadline with a magazine story one summer, my laptop adapter died. Just at that moment, Ileana's son was walking through the piazza. I shouted down to ask if he might have an extra adapter. He did not, but five minutes later he returned with his own laptop, for which no adapter was required. There was no rush to return it, he said. He and his sisters could share their other computer.

Returning from a church cake auction, I arrived home to find that the chocolate bread pudding I won had fallen out of my backpack. I retraced my steps only to find it on the street, run over and flattened like roadkill. Ileana witnessed the catastrophe, invited me up for a coffee, and sent me home with a plate of cookies. Her little girls, fearful the klutzy American would drop the plate, carried the cookies for me.

One morning, the drainage hose from my washing machine dislodged and the apartment flooded. Ileana, a petite woman, came running with a tower of towels twice her height. She insisted on helping me mop up the mess. Then she invited me over for coffee.

One summer day the washing machine died altogether. I texted my landlady.

"I will call Nonna Dina," she replied. "She will be there as soon as possible."

Nonna Dina? My neighbor, the little old lady with the "good sun" who did laundry for her children and grandchildren every day? Okay, perhaps a woman who did so much laundry for so many years could diagnose and repair an uppity machine. It made sense. A short while later, Nonna Dina arrived, not with a toolbox but with a basket. My landlady had not called Nonna Dina to fix my machine. She sent her to pick up my clothes for washing.

I took out my phone to translate for Nonna Dina.

"Thank you," I typed. "But I cannot accept this kindness. I can wash things by hand in the sink until the machine is repaired."

Her reaction was somewhere between befuddled and insulted.

"I do laundry for twelve people. What is one more?" she said.

Later, when I told Valerio, he was already aware of the situation. He had heard from the landlady who had heard from Nonna Dina that the American was being stubborn.

"You bring laundry here," Valerio said. "We do it."

I thanked him but repeated what I had said to Nonna Dina. I would wait for the machine to be repaired and, in the meantime, I could wash what I needed by hand.

His reaction was somewhere between exasperated and angry.

"Why you like this? We everybody family. Why you not let us help you?"

To keep the peace, I relented and agreed to distribute the tasks. Nonna Dina would launder my jeans and towels because they would dry more quickly with her "good sun." Valerio and Tati would launder the rest. The landlady brought two sets of fresh sheets. Ironed to a crisp, of course.

I was often asked, by Quarnese and American friends alike, if I considered turning my story into a novel. My answer was immediate and unambiguous: I didn't have the imagination to invent Quarna. A five-hundred-year-old Italian Alpine village with a saxophone factory? I could not make that up. I could not have invented Valerio, my guide and co-adventurer, Guido, custodian of the past, or Edo, leader of the future. I could not have invented Tati's heart or the Principessa's smile or Nonna Dina's generosity or Ileana's friendship. I could not have invented Renato the policeman or Gabry the rock-obsessed train conductor or Claudio of Rampone & Cazzani or Coppi Roberto the Sage or Valentina and Alessio of Circolo. The reality of Quarna was far better than my capacity for invention. These were not characters. These were real people, full-blooded and three-dimensional.

What did trouble me was the lack of an antagonist to my story. I did not need a villain in a black hat, but certainly there were people averse to my presence, suspicious of my motives, or who plain didn't like me. Richard Halliburton navigated dictators and dodged armed tribesmen. John Berendt stumbled into a Grand Guignol murder. Martha Gellhorn was among the bravest war correspondents in history. Her motto in covering the Spanish Civil War was "Follow the smoke."

Eventually, I found my Black Hat: Stefano, or as he was known to all, Stefano the Bad Boy Who Lives with His Mother and Has No Job. He was a brute in his thirties with a history of drugs, alcohol, and violence. His rages had long since passed the stage of youthful offenses. He had hit a girlfriend, but the matter was resolved by the families. His mother blamed her frequent injuries on household accidents and refused offers of help. The drugs and drinking became more violent and out of control. Often a posse had to be summoned to subdue him at Posta or Circolo and drive him home. Still, absent formal complaints, there was nothing the local or regional authorities could do. And since the authorities might take forever investigating the complaints, the potential of Stefano's retribution was great.

My first encounter with Stefano was comical. One evening at Posta, nursing a beer—standing at the bar, Italian style—I looked down briefly to check my phone, and when I looked up my beer was gone. A few steps away, Stefano was chugging. I already knew his reputation; I didn't want to start a fight. So I just asked the bartender to pull me another and put the first one on my bill. A short while later a friend walked in, and I stepped over to greet him. When I returned to the bar, my beer was gone again. A few steps away, Stefano was chugging. The better part of wisdom, I thought, was to avoid conflict, so I paid the tab and left.

The next encounter was not so funny. I was sitting at a table at Posta quietly enjoying a pizza with friends when Stefano sat down across from me and snatched a slice. And another. He was drunk and stoned and in a rage. He launched into a manic monologue. The only word I could understand was *finocchio*, the Italian slang equivalent of "faggot." I was not sure if it was generic tirade against all mankind or a specific insult directed at me, but I was less concerned with his politics than his actions. As his tirade escalated, good citizens gathered round and escorted him out. This was not some village drunk. This was not some television bully one could dismiss with a quip. This was a man capable of indiscriminate violence. After that evening, if I saw him drinking at Posta or Giuseppe's or Circolo, I paid my tab and left. If I saw him stumbling in the street, I kept my distance.

The last time I saw Stefano was again at Posta. I had gone to meet a young student eager to practice his English over a soft drink. Stefano was sitting at a table indoors, mumbling to himself, as pathetic an ogre as one could imagine. The student and I took a table on the terrace, where, in the light of day, I felt safe. A short while later, Stefano came out and placed a modest plate of aperitivo on my table.

He pointed to the plate and encouraged me to eat.

"Americano, sì?" he said as if it were the first time we'd met.

"Sì," I said.

"America," he said, with an echo of longing. America, he seemed to say, a place far away where he could start over. America, where he could put Quarna behind him.

"Mangiare," he said, and then left.

On a visit two years later, I did not see him. Not that I missed him, but his absence, and the absence of fear in the air, was noticeable.

"Where's Stefano?" I asked Valerio.

"Which Stefano?" he said. There were several. His tone was evasive.

"Stefano the Bad Boy Who Lives with His Mother and Has No Job," I said.

"Gone," he said. His tone went from evasive to eerie.

A few months previously, I was told by others, there had

been an incident at Circolo with a guest from Valerio's inn. The visitor was dining quietly when Stefano walked over, took a piece of bread from the man's bread basket, and walked away. The man yelled at him, Valentina and Alessio yelled at him, and Stefano retreated to the bar. Moments later, he returned to the man's table and took more bread. The visitor yelled at him again. This time Stefano punched him. The other diners tackled Stefano and dragged him out.

The visitor, enraged, threatened to sue Circolo and Valerio's inn, ignite flames on tourist review websites, and file criminal charges against Stefano. There were effusive apologies and earnest assurances that Stefano would be dealt with, that such an incident would never happen again. There were pleas not to punish two small businesses in a peaceable village because of a bad act by one person. The visitor was never heard from again.

Nor was Stefano the Bad Boy Who Lived with His Mother and Had No Job heard from again. What happened, I am not sure.

"Gone," was all Valerio would say.

"Gone," in the same eerie tone, was all I heard from others.

I had hoped that with such a public act of violence and so many witnesses the authorities had commenced slow legal proceedings against Stefano. But his departure, by all accounts, was immediate. It seemed improbable that any Italian legal process could be that swift and his exile so complete.

For a moment, I considered the possibility that Stefano went the way of a wayward *cinghiale*: dispatched and conveyed in a wheelbarrow down the hill to Luigi the Butcher and turned into sausage. But that would be a theatrical fiction. The sad truth was that no less than the Quarnesi who embraced me with kindness, Stefano, malice and all, was a full-blooded, three-dimensional Quarnese too.

Chapter 24

Going Up

"You come for UTLO? You come for UTLO!" Valerio said by text, as if it were a cross-Atlantic *cappuccino e brioche* adventure.

Ultra Trail Lago d'Orta—the rugged mountain race in which my stunning Russian inn-mate from a previous visit had participated—was approaching, and the Quarnesi were organizing teams of volunteers to serve refreshments at stations along the way for the fifteen hundred or so runners who would sprint, jog, and trudge up and down the treacherous mountain paths in any weather. Some would run a modest twelve-kilometer route, some a full one hundred forty kilometers, with others running various distances in between. (Or to exhaustion, whichever came first.) Valerio was the volunteer in charge of the station at Monte Croce, the apex of the race. It was a source of great excitement and pride. And he wanted me to share it with him.

My plate was full with work that autumn, but I could squeeze in a three-day weekend trip. Extravagant, yes. Exhausting, absolutely. But off-season airfares were cheap and Valerio's adrenaline was contagious. He would arrange for pickup and drop-off at the airport. I would stay at the inn. We would have dinner with his parents on Friday night, featuring *patate di cuccella*, the slow-cooked potato-and-cotechino dish that was the pride of the Quarnesi. We would helicopter up to the peak of Monte Croce on Saturday morning with a gondola of supplies for the racers, set up camp, prepare a bonfire, and sleep in a tent. We would rise before dawn to serve the early diehards and cheer the other troupers all day. When the race was over, we would pack up the gondola and hike down, Tati's mother's lasagna waiting for us. Our collective spirit of "bro-venture" overcame common sense. It was October in the Alps. No matter how much I trained or how much money I spent at Patagonia and L. L. Bean and REI, I was an amateur hiker, easily winded and vulnerable to conditions that could shift from sunny skies to thunderstorms to a micro-blizzard in a moment.

There were cracks in the plan from the beginning, lapses I would have dismissed for an ordinary host, but ominous for an event planned by a perfectionist like Valerio. There was no room at his inn and the rooms at Posta were booked. There were not even friends with a spare sofa. The best he could do was a musty room with a well-worn mattress at an old schoolhouse converted into a hostel, but it was free and warm and more than adequate for such a brief visit. When I woke up famished after my post-arrival nap, thrilled for pranzo at Circolo, I discovered it was closed. Alessio and Valentina were on holiday. Posta, for no clear reason, was also closed. The little markets in Quarna Sotto and Quarna Sopra were both on siesta. I had no recourse but to pull the emergency cord. I dropped in on Nonna Dina unannounced, knowing there would be something on the stove. When she saw me coming up from the piazza, she could read my stomach. She stopped hanging her laundry, and in a New York minute, there was bread, cheese, salami, salad, and a bowl of pasta before me.

As soon as I was fed and served coffee and grappa, she went back to hanging her wash. Nonna Dina, who could read clouds better than a meteorologist with advanced technology, explained with simple words and gestures that there would be two more hours of sun, enough to dry the load she was hanging, then the skies would go from hazy to overcast, then there would be drizzle, and then rain for several days. When I told her excitedly that I would be going up by helicopter with Valerio the next morning with the gondola of supplies for UTLO, she shook her head and pointed up, twirling her fingers. Because of the deteriorating weather, the helicopter and gondola had already gone up.

The next omen came at dinner. The mood at Valerio's

parents' house was absent its usual mirth. Everyone in the family had some task for UTLO, it seemed, and there was anxiety in the air. The Principessa, deprived of the attention to which she was accustomed, was hyperactive to the point of obnoxiousness. She refused to take off her wheelie shoes, which riled up Lola, her grandparents' English setter. Even Nonno, who adored his granddaughter, was losing his patience.

"Calma, calma," he kept saying to no avail.

The Principessa was unresponsive to any Uncle Matt distractions or computer games or television. Nonno and Nonna were cooking. Tati was on her phone organizing food and staffing for the UTLO refreshment stop on Alpe Camasca. Valerio was glued to the weather forecast on his phone. Instead of *patate di cuccella*, with potatoes I could easily digest, his father made *spezzatino*, a thick *cinghiale* stew served with polenta, and it was their custom to eat polenta with a mixture of whole milk and cream. Ordinarily, the change in the menu would have been amusing, but the older I get, the more temperamental my stomach gets. Stoking me with huge portions of fat and lactose was going to keep me sleepless all night.

Halfway through dinner, Valerio's face turned grim. The weather forecast was looking worse.

"Now too difficult for you," he said. "You stay on Alpe Camasca and help Tati and Pro Loco serve food."

Too difficult?

I took offense. Okay, so there would be a hike instead of a

helicopter, and while I was not exactly a Quarnese goat, I had climbed most Quarna peaks, often in crappy weather. Twice I had reached the summit of Monte Mazzoccone, a smaller sibling to Monte Croce but still a challenge, once on a day so clear I could see five lakes, once under clouds so dense I could not see beyond an arm's length. Monte Croce seemed a reasonable challenge. At sixteen hundred meters, it is an anthill to audacious climbers, a bunny slope to experienced day hikers, a Sunday *passeggiata* for the Quarnesi. And we would be driving up in the Panda on old mountain logging roads as far as she would go, so the actual climb was more modest.

By "difficult," did he mean too uncomfortable for a citified American? I had worked my ass off to prepare. I stopped smoking a month in advance and pushed my limit on every piece of aerobic and strength-training equipment at the gym. I spent more money on manly outdoor gear than on my airfare: Gore-Tex boots with sturdy treads, layers of synthetics for warmth, lined waterproof pants, arctic-grade hat and gloves, and a day-glow waterproof jacket perfect for summit-conquest photos. In the windmills of my mind, I was prepared for a bold ascent above the tree line. And I did not come all this way and spend all this money to hang out with the Pro Loco gang slinging pasta on lowly Alpe Camasca. I came for a Halliburtonesque adventure with Valerio on Monte Croce.

"I am not a fair-weather friend," I said, and I preferred he not treat me like one either. The idiom translated well into Italian.

"Okay," he said, with a resigned shrug.

Neither of us realized what was lost in translation. He had said "too difficult." What he meant was "too dangerous."

The revised plan was that Valerio and a sturdy mountaineer sent by the UTLO organizers would carry additional supplies up to Monte Croce in the morning and then come back down to get me. I would have breakfast at the inn and lunch at his mother's house. He would fetch me at two o'clock, allowing us plenty of time to set up camp while there was good light.

At two, he texted me. There were delays, so we would leave at three. By the time we loaded up the Panda, it was four. He discouraged me from bringing my phone. It would be useless. Even in good weather, cellular signals were intermittent on the mountain. High-powered walkie-talkies were the only means of communication and there was no point risking my phone getting lost or damaged. Instead, he strapped his dog Ryk's GPS collar to my belt, so if we got separated he could track me. It was ingenious. And it was touching. There are few higher compliments than when a man treats you with the same concern he treats his dog.

The weather was holding steady, the sky overcast but the trail clear. The mood was cheerful in the Panda as we drove the logging roads as far as we could. When we switched to the foot trail for the final seven-hundred-meter ascent, the climb turned more vertical than I expected, and even with the traditional painted trail markings supplemented with UTLO flags, the path still required instinctive navigation. In a matter of minutes, Valerio and the guide were out of sight, and I was on my own, increasingly breathless, increasingly disoriented by the twists and turns. One moment the iron cross on the peak of Monte Croce was in view, the next it vanished. When I finally arrived at the summit, Valerio's signature smile was a beacon in the fog, but beyond that, there was nothing more to see. The revered panorama, a grand convergence of three valleys, was hidden by clouds. Not even Monte Rosa, second only in Alpine glory to Mont Blanc, was visible. Also hidden behind our smiling summit pictures was Valerio's anxiety. He later told me that from the way he saw me lagging behind at the outset, he realized it had been a mistake to allow me to come, and he wished he could have taken me back immediately. But with the fog thickening and dusk approaching, we had reached the point of no return. Even with headlamps, it was too late to get me down safely and for him to get back up to do his job.

It was too cold and too wet to camp outdoors, so the alternative was to descend two hundred meters to a cabin where Valerio, anticipating the change in the weather earlier in the day, had carried our sleeping bags and food. (It was that task that had delayed our departure.) There was no firm trail from the peak of Monte Croce down to the cabin, just limp, wet grass shrouded in the fog and dark. Valerio's headlamp kept moving out of my visual range. I had to shout for him to slow down. He had to shout out each step to me. The tension was getting as thick as the fog. There were tones of voice we had never exchanged. I was annoyed at him for leaving me behind; he was annoyed at me for failing to keep up. By the time we arrived at the cabin, the temperature had plummeted. He and the guide hurriedly gathered wood to get the stove going, smashing old apple crates into kindling. There was no electricity, but by the light of candles and flashlights hung from the rafters, Valerio put out a spread of salami and cheese and bread and beer he had carried up that morning. To his delight, a previous visitor had left a box of pasta and cans of tuna and there was running water. It took a while for the water to boil on the woodstove, but soon we sat down for a hearty meal. The heat kicked in, the food kicked in, the beer kicked in, and the mirth kicked in. This was the bonding experience for which Valerio invited me. Tipsy but full, we went up to the loft, where the sleeping bags had been warmed by the rising heat. The hard part was over, I thought. I had scaled Monte Croce.

Chapter 25

Going Down

A few hours later, with a minimum of sleep—Valerio was glued to his phone for updates on the race and weather—it was time to return to the summit to put up the tent, start the fire, and set up the refreshments. The fog had lifted slightly in the dawn's early light, enough so I could find my footing on the wet, grassy path, but once again, Valerio and the guide were soon far ahead and once again I lagged, huffing. By the time I arrived at the summit, the bonfire was roaring and the refreshments were ready. Soon a headlamp appeared in the dark and the first runner whizzed by.

"Allez! Allez! Allez!" we shouted. "Go! Go! Go!"

He was blind to our presence and deaf to our cheers.

"He not human," Valerio said. "He cyborg."

The fog became a drizzle, and the drizzle became light rain, but the runners came in unceasing waves. Some were muscled, some toned, some emaciated. Some men looked like they had stepped off the cover of *Men's Journal*. Some women looked like they had stepped off the cover of *Vogue Italia*. Most looked like they had been dipped in mud and regret. Now and then, a runner less focused on time and more focused on survival stopped to warm up or hydrate with water or hot tea or a shot of grappa or a piece of cake, or to relieve themselves in the designated areas on the slope behind us. There were no porta-potties or any form of privacy, just reminders to aim downhill.

Valerio and I cheered them on with gusto.

"*Allez! Allez! Allez!*"

We hawked our refreshments like vendors.

"Acqua! Te caldo! Biere! Vin Brulé! Grappa!"

It was fun as hell right up until the moment it became miserable. The light drizzle and cold rain were unrelenting. Not a ray of midday sun breached the fog to temper the chill. I cheered with gusto until I was hoarse and served the runners dutifully, but jet lag, sleep deprivation, exhaustion from the climb, and a touch of altitude sickness kicked in. Valerio was right. It was too difficult for me.

Valerio could see I was withering and was eager to get me down the mountain—if not all the way to Alpe Camasca, where I could hitch a ride back to town, then at least to the Panda where I could cocoon.

"You get to Panda, you start engine, you turn on heat, and you wait," he ordered. After he and the UTLO guide extinguished the fire and closed up the campsite, they would meet me there.

But there was a hitch. I could not descend until the last runners came up lest I risk a collision. The herd was thinning, but Valerio had to wait to receive a signal from a checkpoint below that the last runners were on the way up and the Scopa, the official "sweep" guide, was walking the path to be sure there were no runners lingering in distress. After the signal, I was to start down.

That I might have to go down a steep, rocky, mud-slicked trail alone in the rain with no form of communication other than a dog's GPS collar, with twilight approaching, was not a scenario for which I had prepared.

"You'll be coming down behind me, right?" I asked. No doubt Valerio could hear the concern in my voice. I could hear it in his too.

"Yes, but we must wait for last runner."

The plan was for me to start down at three when there was still plenty of light, but because of the conditions, there were still runners en route. The green light didn't come until four.

"Now you go," he said, the look on his face stern. "You get in Panda, you turn on engine, you stay warm, okay?"

It would be at most a twenty-minute descent for me, he calculated, so neither of us thought provisions for food or water were necessary. With no spare walkie-talkie and no cell phone, I could not summon help, but he would monitor Ryk's GPS strapped to me. If I was moving, he would know I was okay. If I was not moving, he would know I was not okay.

I knew with the first step going down that I was in trouble. Serious trouble. Even above the tree line, where the slope was mild, and with a firm grip on my *bastone*, I was slipping. Every rock and pebble on the trail had been polished to a shine by the treads of fifteen hundred runners coming up. Between and over the rocks ran a stream of mud as viscous as crude oil. Each step, each placement of the heel and toe, each shift of my weight required methodical plotting. Every few yards where the trail became too steep and too slick, I sat on my ass and slid. Now and then I lurched, lost my balance, and tumbled forward or backward. Each time I slipped and fell, spatchcocked like a chicken, soaked in mud, my right leg going one way, my left the other, my *bastone* bent, a rock up my ass, I contemplated grievous injury or prolonged death. I checked for fractures and wondered, *How many strikes before I was out? When would I break an ankle or an arm or hit my head? How long before the wild boars smelled their dinner?*

As the situation grew more dire, a mental switch flipped from selfishness to selflessness, as if altruism were some primitive survival mechanism or a bargaining tool for safe passage to a better place in the next world. I began worrying less about my own life and more about the lives of others—most of all Valerio and his fellow Quarnesi who would surely form a search party if I did not return soon. I knew these mountains had claimed the lives of the heroic helping the inept. Guido once told me that a few decades before, an elderly man from Omegna did not return from a hike. A search party was formed, led by a forest ranger who had moved to Quarna with his wife and young son. During the search, the ranger lost his footing, fell into a ravine, and died of a head injury. The elderly man from Omegna was never found.

I had imagined myself a modern-day Richard Halliburton, an audacious writer-adventurer-dandy. I had imagined myself an intrepid Martha Gellhorn dodging bullets. I had imagined myself a sturdy Quarnese mountain goat, agile and unafraid. Instead, I was a mud-drenched schmuck who oversold his abilities and didn't listen to reason, without considering the danger to others.

My knees turned to jelly from muscle contractions. My shoulders locked from the pressure I was putting on the *bastone* to keep my balance. My torso shivered. My brain went on autopilot. My so-called waterproof jacket and pants were soaked. It was getting darker. I was thirsty. I was losing strength. Now and then, I took refuge under a rock, hoping Valerio would appear from above or the Scopa would arrive from below and someone would help me down safely.

I have superstitions, but I'm not much for good luck charms. For some reason, impulsively, I felt the need for one on this journey. Before I left my wallet at Valerio's house for safekeeping, I took out a laminated picture of Augie that I carry with me always. I put it in the secure chest pocket of my obscenely expensive Patagonia jacket, right next my heart. At my most terrified moments, I'd touch it as an amulet. Augie was not a totemic embodiment of God. I wasn't an animist. Whether I ended up safe in the Panda or dead in a ditch, I knew I would have Augie's spirit beside me.

Finally, the Scopa arrived.

He didn't even stop.

"Please, I need help," I said.

"Non parlo inglese," he said.

Seriously? A guide who was a safety official for an international mountain trail race didn't understand the English word *help*?

"Aiuto," I said. Help. The urgency in my tone was unmistakable.

"Calma, calma," was all he said, before walking on.

My brain was trapped in a fugue of rage and fear. The entire trip was a mistake. Going to the summit instead of joining Tati and the Pro Loco gang on Alpe Camasca was a mistake. I was furious at Valerio for sending me down alone. And I was even more furious at my arrogance, for taking umbrage at Valerio's warning instead of heeding his good judgment. He had a job to do. He was responsible for a station in a major race that was months in the planning and a source of community pride. We had hiked enough that he knew my limitations better than I knew them. And instead of a friend in deed, I had become a friend in need.

Finally, down below, some fifty meters in the distance, I could see him. He and the guide had taken an alternate route—faster but more difficult—and arrived before me.

He was smiling. Even from a distance, through the trees, he could see I was not.

"What is wrong? I wait for you half hour at Panda. I follow you on Ryk's collar. You move and stop and move and stop. So slow. But you okay?"

"I am not okay."

"Why you not okay?"

"Please don't talk," I said. Even the last ten meters I was still focused on every step, every rock, every placement of the *bastone*. I was undeniably in shock and did not have the capacity to explain or complain or discuss.

We got in the Panda. I was shivering beyond control. I was mute.

"Why you no talk? Why you not okay?"

"Just take me to the hostel."

"Why you angry?"

"Please don't talk," I said again. I was beginning to thaw out, and I was afraid I might pop my cork. I just wanted to strip off my clothes and stand under a hot shower for eternity.

We drove in silence. He dropped me off at the hostel in silence. I showered as long as the hot water lasted and then threw my clothes in the shower behind me. There was mud everywhere, like blood in a war zone. I put on my jeans and what dry clothes I had and wrapped myself in the bed blanket like a burrito. I dozed briefly. When I awoke, I was famished. If I had my druthers, I would have avoided Valerio, but Circolo and Posta were closed and I could not very well walk up to Nonna Dina yet again wide-eyed with hunger.

Umbrella in hand, I walked to Valerio's house and rang the bell. Regardless of my anger, if I wanted dinner, I knew I might have to eat humble pie first.

There was no answer. I could see lights on and shadows moving in the window.

I rang again.

Finally, the intercom crackled.

"You not welcome here," Valerio said.

It was a tone I had never heard from him: pure anger.

Maybe I was wrong. Maybe it was *ironia* or *sarcasmo* or *scherzando*.

"But you said on the schedule that tonight is lasagna night!" I said, hoping a little levity might defuse the hostility.

"No lasagna for you," he said. "You too rude."

Now I was confused. If anyone should be aggrieved and worthy of compassion, and at least deserving of a hot meal, it was me. There was a long pause. I buzzed again.

“Okay, but how will I eat?”

“You stay at gate. I bring you salami and cheese and bread. If not enough for you, go ask other friends in Quarna for dinner. You have many friends. We are no more friends.”

After a few minutes, he came out with a sack. He opened the gate only so far as to hand it to me and closed it.

“Thank you,” I said.

“I say, ‘You welcome,’ but you tell me ‘Shut up.’”

I hadn’t a clue what he was talking about.

“Shut up? I would never tell you to shut up.”

“You do. You come down mountain. I ask, ‘You okay?’ You say to me, ‘Shut up!’”

I had to rewind to the moment.

“I did not say ‘Shut up.’ I said, ‘Please don’t talk.’”

“Same thing,” he said.

“It is not the same thing. I was terrified for two hours. I was in shock. I was watching every step. I could not talk at the same time. I am sorry if I sounded rude.”

Tears welled up in his eyes.

“I am sorry you in shock. I am sorry you terrified for two hours. I worry every minute the day before we climb. I worry every minute the day we climb. I worry every minute you go down alone. You terrified two hours? I terrified three days! What else I do? How I do different?”

“What else could you have done? Instead of ‘too difficult,’ you should have said ‘too dangerous.’ Instead of ‘okay’ you should have said 'no.' I would have been disappointed, but I would have respected your decision. You never told me I might come down alone in rain and mud and fog. And where were you? I was expecting you to follow behind me after you closed the camp."

"I camc down other way. I think you are okay in Panda!"

His face scrunched and he began to cry. I could not be sure of the emotion. Was it anger? Was it resentment? Or was it contrition? Either way, this was not the time or place for armchair psychotherapy. There were no words that could help in a situation where emotions were so fraught. Now I teared up. There we were, two men with wounded pride, standing in the rain, crying.

I apologized for my harsh words.

"Perhaps someday we will be able to repair the friendship," I said.

"No," he said. "Friendship is over. It cannot be repaired. Impossible."

I hadn't the strength to argue. I accepted his decision. But I asked one favor. Would he allow me to say goodbye to Tati and the Principessa? I did not want them to think I had left in anger without saying goodbye.

That he would allow, he said, and opened the gate.

I wish I could say my motives at that point were pure. They were not. It is true that out of great affection for Tati and the Principessa, I did not wish to compound injury to Valerio by insulting them, but there was also strategic opportunism. The thought of losing Valerio's friendship would be the true catastrophe of the weekend. If repair was possible, then I had to move fast. The way to a man's heart may be through his stomach, but the digestive system is slow compared to the circulatory system. The mainline to a man's heart is through kindness to his wife and children.

Tati kissed me on both cheeks warmly. Either he had not told her the extent of the conflict, or she was being diplomatic.

"Now you okay?" she said. Her voice reflected concern more than anger.

"Yes," I said. "Now I am okay."

The Principessa was sitting on the floor with a toy xylophone struggling to make music out of nonsense. Reaching into Uncle Matt's kit bag, I sat beside her and demonstrated "Twinkle, Twinkle Little Star." She hesitated. I placed the mallet in her small hand, put my hand on top, and showed her how to sing a melody and match the notes and the colors. Again. And again. Then "Frère Jacques." Again. And again. Then "Mary Had a Little Lamb." Again. And again. As with the "Hokey Pokey" and "Head, Shoulders, Knees, and Toes," I had made new magic in a dusty world.

Out of the corner of my eye, I saw Tati setting the table. I knew it was a moment of truth. If she set the table for three, I was persona non grata and would take my leave graciously with my sack of salami and cheese. If she set the table for four, there was hope.

She set the table for four.

"Solo lasagna e insalata. Benne?" Tati said. They were all too weary for anything other than a simple family meal.

"Benne," I said.

The Principessa ate quickly and went back to her xylophone. Valerio and I were unusually quiet at dinner. The silence was not lost on Tati.

"Che silenzio," she said. She was accustomed to us yammering away.

"Esausto," he said. Exhausted.

Dinner was the first stitch in the wound. The second stitch came after.

"You want génépi? You want génépi!"

We knocked back our shots silently and he walked me to the gate.

The rain had stopped. Our tears had stopped. We said goodbye with a handshake but no words.

By the time I got to the hostel, there was a text message from Valerio on my phone.

"You my friend in good weather or bad."

"Anche tu, mi amico," I replied. "Anche tu."

At no risk of hyperbole, that I survived the descent from Monte Croce was a miracle. That my friendship with Valerio survived was equally miraculous.

Chapter 26

A Place for Healing

The story of Quarna I had intended to tell—a story of cultural survival—continued to evolve from professional to personal, from journalist to memoirist, from audience to actor. The metaphor of crossing the proscenium occasionally became literal. When an itinerant two-man circus came to town, I was pulled on stage by the clown to have my hand chopped off with a (fake) guillotine. When a commedia dell'arte troupe came to town, I was pulled on stage to dance Offenbach's cancan while playing thumb cymbals. I suspect these were not random events, that I had been marked as a stooge in advance. Seeing the American humiliated was a guaranteed laugh. I was happy to play the fool as a community service.

I continued to interview and observe diligently, but when I took off my reporter's hat, Quarna became a place of self-discovery, a place where, absent labels (gay, Jewish, someone's son, someone's brother, someone's boyfriend) and imprimaturs of status (education, affluence), I could find my authentic self. Quarna was a space where I was not judged by my accomplishments or measured against my potential. I could take a hike or gaze at the sky and drink a beer without wondering if there was a better or higher use of my time.

Quarna also became an asylum from emotional shocks. One summer, reeling from a catastrophe, I went completely off the grid. I left my laptop in New York and arrived in Quarna for the summer armed only with a box of pens and a stack of old-school composition notebooks. Rather than traveling a digital pathway from brain to computer, my writing went analog from heart to hand.

The catastrophe's name was Adam. He was handsome and intelligent and charming, with hazel eyes and a naughty, come-hither smile. He was younger, but not in an unseemly way. He was from a good family, well educated, and had a successful business. He had a sweet singing voice. He cooked. He had a dog. He loved classic films. In bed he was the perfect cocktail, equal parts wild and warm. I fell fast and hard.

Adam wasn't perfect by any means. He was an emotional windsock, one moment affectionate and kind, the next withholding and critical. He was maddening and he was exhilarating.

Each day our bond grew deeper, each night we spooned tighter. So certain was I of a committed relationship with Adam that I decided to end the polite coexistence with Collin, whatever the emotional or financial consequences. I was a day away from asking Collin to move out when a disagreement with Adam over *Mulholland Drive* (I did not revere it as he did) led to an exchange of insults that quickly escalated. He went mean. I went vicious. Like a magician's flash paper, the timeless relationship burned fast and bright and went up in smoke.

I fled to Quarna with my pens and notebooks, and on the terrace of my apartment in the piazza overlooking Saliente, I feverishly wrote and rewrote pleas for forgiveness, offers of amends, appeals for reconciliation, and odes of love, fully aware that every paragraph and verse was delusional. My every word was met with silence. The "complicated grief" I was still experiencing from the loss of Augie was now compounded by what is known in the literature of counseling as "cumulative grief." With each new loss, traumas of the past come crashing forward like train cars that accordion into twisted metal when a locomotive derails. Adam was the latest in a series of irreparable losses. With each plea to Adam, I might as well have been asking Augie to return from the dead and forgive me for not being there at the end.

Finally, Adam sent a terse email asking me to stop, which I did. Even I knew I was getting too close to the line between penitent poet and crazy ex. My heart broke, and not just metaphorically. A few weeks later, it took a team of cardiologists to put my heart back together with stents, balloons, and a mouthful of pills I will take every day for the rest of my life. As soon as I was physically well and emotionally stronger, I went to Quarna.

Loss, grief, Quarna, recovery. Repeat. It was becoming a habit.

To my healing experiences in Quarna, I added another: an immersive three-day program at the Mandali center. I usually groan aloud when I hear words like *mindfulness*, but despite my prejudices, I vowed to keep my mind open. Peter, a Scottish meditation coach for the Mandali center I'd met at Giuseppe's bar, had become a good friend. Precisely my age, a tall, burly man with a hypnotic brogue, he had worked in the corporate world before embracing a spiritual life but had never abandoned his pub camaraderie. He never proselytized spirituality. He explained rather than lectured. And for a disciple of mindfulness, he was refreshingly human. Now and then, he lost his temper at some outrage—a selfish human, a barking dog—and popped his cork. It was enlightening to see an enlightened man pissed off.

When I was considering the Mandali experience, I was concerned that, as a jittery New Yorker with a cynical mind and stiff spine, I might not adapt to a program of meditation and yoga. I asked Peter for guidance.

"The result generally matches the expectation," he said. "What is the feeling you desire from this adventure? Use your imagination to invoke it into every cell of your body right here and right now!"

"I hope I will find tools to quiet my unquiet mind," I said.

In addition to my personal quest, I also felt a professional obligation to get inside Mandali. The specifics of Mandali's financial contribution to Quarna and its long-term plans were a black box, but I was assured by community leaders that the Mandali-Quarna relationship continued to be mutually beneficial. Rampone & Cazzani would always have pride of place in Quarna, but there is a limited market for handmade saxophones. Mandali tapped into the fast-growing international demand for upscale meditation retreats. There is lemonade to be made from the Lululemon market, and it was trickling down to the Quarnesi in the form of good jobs with good wages.

The Mandali experience exceeded my expectations. The yoga instructor treated me with no less respect than the reed-thin Degas ballerinas surrounding me. The qigong instructor pushed me to reach for the sky and touch the ground without a twinge. The meditation leaders mixed wit, empathy, and breathing to create a dome of silence that, for a brief, blessed moment in time, quieted my unquiet mind. For the first time in my life, I heard nothing. My dorm mates (the private rooms were beyond my budget) were two amiable men in their twenties, a Canadian music promoter and a Belgian landscape designer. They tolerated my snoring and multiple nighttime trips to the bathroom, and I tolerated their painful youth and beauty. I walked the lawns barefoot and passed through a tunnel of crystals. I switched from coffee to ginger tea. I snoozed in a hammock. Some guests sought silence. Some guests sought fellowship. I sampled a little of both. Mandali was not life-altering, and I cannot say I will make a habit of such spirituality retreats but simply knowing that I am capable of finding a moment of inner peace is as inspiring as having found it.

There was only one major flaw in my Mandali experience. As a newbie to meditation and yoga, I was unaware that every class was conducted barefoot. I had arrived after ten days of traveling and my feet were a disaster. My toenails were longer than an armadillo's, my heels looked like a horse's hooves in need of reshoeing, my soles were shedding skin like a reptile. At the first break, I raced to the Mandali spa desk to schedule an emergency pedicure, only to find it was a service not offered. I was incredulous. How could a luxury spirituality resort that celebrates bare feet not have a pedicure on the spa menu? Fortunately, Quarna saved me: I busted out of the compound and ran downhill to Valentina's Farmacia just past the piazza of Quarna Sopra. I told her my nightmare and—*whoosh!*—like a Salon Superhero, she came to my rescue with nail clippers, a pumice sponge, and moisturizer. I raced back uphill, locked myself in the shower, and clipped, boiled, scrubbed, and moisturized. I had arrived at Mandali as a man still searching for a path out of sorrow. Now I was walking that path with feet as smooth and pink as a newborn's.

Chapter 27

The Chapter I Wish I Didn't Have to Write

When Augie was ten, he and I were trapped in a log cabin in a raging blizzard in the mountains. I was in the final stretch of a major writing assignment and, as I often did, escaped the city to tune out distractions. The midwinter snowstorm was not a surprise, except in degree. Dubbed "Snowmageddon" by television weather wags, it dropped two-foot drifts around us. We had plenty of food and firewood and batteries for a lamp and a radio, so we were fine. More than fine. It seemed yet another of our intrepid adventures together. Until, snug in front of a roaring fire, petting Augie nose to toes, I felt a lump on his thigh.

A snowbound cabin in the mountains is ideal for writing,

but not ideal when waiting for a tractor to dig us out so I could get Augie to a vet. My concern was that, while dashing through the snow, he had nicked his leg on a twig and an unnoticeable wound had festered. All he required was antibiotics, I thought. I did not imagine the lump would require a biopsy. Or that the biopsy would reveal a malignant tumor that required surgery. Or that the surgeon could not achieve clean margins and radiation would be required to prevent recurrence. I did not imagine, could not imagine, the cries of pain from the brutal radiation burns. I was told that once the wounds healed, he would have no memory of the pain. I wasn't told that I would never forget.

Required is a fuzzy word when one goes down the rabbit hole of modern veterinary medicine. The distinction between what is best for the animal and what is best for the owner gets blurry. The decision tree sprouts all manner of medical, ethical, and financial branches with diagnoses and prognoses and price tags. Calling each step of canine cancer treatment "required" allows one to rationalize a selfish truth: These were choices I made, seemingly for him, but ultimately for myself. Augie was not an ordinary man who wanted to see his children grow up, or an extraordinary woman who might one day cure cancer. He was not some metaphorical knight bravely battling a malicious invader. This was a vivacious ten-year-old dog who loved to walk city streets and sniff garbage and run along the shore, whose joy gave me joy and whose presence defined my world. Within reason—and with cancer, the scrimmage line of reason moves quickly—I wanted every year, every month, every day, and every hour that medical science and money could buy.

After six joyful, cancer-free years, he suffered a spontaneous fracture at the radiation site. I presumed it was the end. The time we bought had far exceeded every medical forecast. I was devastated, but I was ready to let go.

Augie was not. Nor was his vet.

"Aside from the fracture, there is nothing systemically wrong," he said. "It would be unethical for me to euthanize him and I doubt you'd find a veterinarian who would."

He referred me to an orthopedic surgeon.

The orthopedic surgeon looked perplexed.

"This is an unusual animal," he said. That he was a sixteen-year-old dog otherwise healthy and robust six years after surgery and radiation for a soft-tissue sarcoma on his leg was remarkable. Pinning the bone was an option and might save the leg, he said, but it was a complicated procedure with uncertain results, and the bone might fracture again. Amputation was his recommendation. He had no doubt Augie would quickly adapt.

Adapt he did. Indoors he was remarkably agile. He thumped and bopped around the apartment with complete independence. Outdoors he struggled for balance, but the artisans at The Leather Man, the West Village's renowned bondage lifestyle store (the co-owner's dog Dylan was a friend of Augie's), helped us custom design a body sling that, when attached to his leash, gave him extra lift to do his business, stroll, and even sprint with assistance. He had to be carried up and down the stairs to the apartment, but just as with our first encounter at the Humane Society, he relaxed without a struggle. Collin came to cherish the moments cradling Augie in his arms. The feeling was mutual, I am sure.

His sociability with people and dogs was undiminished. He invited kindness from adults and curiosity from children.

"Hey, mister, where do you buy a three-legged dog?" a little boy asked me.

"Will it grow back?" asked another.

Our friend Felix, a gifted mathematician with an alternate view of the universe, gave Augie a stuffed animal with its right hind leg removed so that he might see a creature in his image and know he was not alone.

What Augie could not do was pursue his favorite adventures in the natural world. We took him to the beach, and he still loved the sea air and digging in the sand, but he no longer had the stability to run along the shore or into the dunes. We bought a wagon to take him to parks so he could lounge in the grass and savor the smell of leaves, but he could no longer amble on trails or dunk himself in a stream. We rented a cabin up in the Catskills now and then, a retreat for ourselves as well as him, and brought along carpet runners so he could navigate hardwood floors. We spent a day in Woodstock, where, nearly fifty years since the gathering that symbolized the counterculture of the 1960s, there were still enough oddball hippies on the streets that the sight of two gay men wheeling an eighteen-year-old, three-legged dog in a red Radio Flyer wagon went completely unnoticed.

What never changed was Augie's curiosity, his affection, his sense of mischief, and his capacity for engagement. He was always at the door to greet us, always welcomed guests, always at my feet when I was writing or reading, always ready for a cuddle, always chasing a sunbeam, always underfoot in the kitchen. There was only one consequence of the surgery that none of his doctors could explain: He never barked again.

When, eighteen months later, in my grief after his sudden death, furious that denial had blinded me and I had not seen the end was near, that I had abandoned him in his final hours and he had died alone, friends would try to comfort me by saying, "Look at all you did for him!"

For *him*? I wanted to say. For *me*! All that seemed "required," all those "choices," all those grandiose treatments in retrospect seemed selfish and cruel. And greedy: The extravagant sums we spent could have helped care for so many animals needing homes. (Let alone human beings needing food.) I could have forgone the radiation for the tumor and put him down if and when it recurred. I could have vetoed the vet and the orthopedic surgeon and put him down when his leg fractured. Instead, I had put him through immense pain and stolen his greatest pleasure—running along the shore—so I could have my greatest pleasure: his companionship.

In fairness, there were treatments in his last year that brought him joy. After he lost the leg, we took him for twice-weekly hydrotherapy at an animal rehabilitation center in Tribeca. In a heated pool designed for dogs, a veterinary physical therapist in a wetsuit would guide him through swimming, stretching, and aquatic yoga, the buoyancy of the water giving him the freedom of movement he once had on solid ground. It was obscenely expensive, but to see the bliss on his face with each upward- and downward-dog pose was beyond any measure of value.

My friend Karen, highly accomplished in finance, a CPA with an MBA, a disciplined athlete, a sensitive woman not prone to excessive sentimentality, came to watch a session out of curiosity. She cried. She had long since abandoned her Catholic upbringing, she said, but this was a religious experience. Augie floating in repose was beatific.

His last session in the pool was the day before he died. The therapist cut it short.

"He's tired," she said.

I hear those words now and I see pictures of him in those final days and I wonder how I could have been so deaf and blind.

"Listen to the dying," Elisabeth Kübler-Ross wrote. "They will tell you everything you need to know about when they are dying. And it is easy to miss."

I missed it.

Chapter 28

Natale

"You come for Natale? You come for Natale!"

Valerio's invitation to celebrate Christmas in Quarna was a delightful surprise—as was the sentence that followed:

"You stay as family. Not as guest."

The boundary between journalist and memoirist, between public and personal, between friendship and family, had disappeared. There was no more proscenium. I would have to balance my innate inquisitiveness against a private time for Valerio, his family, and my other families and friends in the village. Community celebrations and religious events were public, but in reality, they were private traditions for the Quarnesi. There were a few old-time Villeggianti, but no tourists. I was still a writer writing, but I would not carry a notepad, and there would be no sit-down interviews.

A light snow had fallen the eve before my arrival. The terracotta roof tiles were dusted as if with powdered sugar. Wisps of smoke swirled from chimneys. There were Christmas trees in the piazzas. No less so than in my Toledo childhood, some houses were trimmed tastefully, others had gaudy displays that surely inspired neighborly spats. There were nativity scenes throughout the village, from sax-playing wise men and shepherds on the approach to the village to a miniature crèche set in the hollow of an old tree. Every roadside *Madonnella* was jazzed up with garlands and *lumini*.

The view of the mountains was transformed. The verdant summer landscapes were now wintery pen-and-ink drawings. Even the sounds were new: Walking the trails through the woods, I could hear the crunch of snow on the frozen autumn leaves beneath my feet, a sound I had not heard since country hikes with Augie. Eyes wide open, I could see his paw prints before me and the divots where he poked his nose in the snow to suss out the scent of some hibernating creature.

Natale in Quarna was a flurry of events. At times it seemed the entire population moved as one. The morning after my arrival, the bells rang the call to worship for mass at Saliente. Unlike the mechanical bells at the main *chiesa*, the call for Saliente was a single bell pulled by a rope. It was still echoing as

I scurried downhill to a full house and gathered with the faithful spilling out of the doorway. To my delight, Guido was there with Mercedes—a rare winter visit, which meant at some point there would be a long walk, a Mexican meal, and meandering tales of Christmas yore.

There was no after-church-coffee-and-prosecco at Posta. All were heading up to Quarna Sopra for Mercato Natale, the annual Christmas market in the piazza. There was music, of course, and spirits were high. An elder I met on my first visit was dancing with his grandson held high, like Rafiki hoisting Simba. A young couple I knew from the Halloween whipped-cream hazing was now married with an infant in arms.

A jazz ensemble played Christmas tunes until the main event: a full-on white Italian gospel choir singing full-throated Black American gospel music. Organized and presented by Augusto, the imaginative mayor of Quarna Sopra, who also ran an arts academy in Omegna, the choir's performance was intoxicating. The crowd swayed to "Go Tell It on the Mountain" and "When the Saints Go Marching In" like the faithful at a Harlem Baptist church. Nearby, in a semicircle of booths, children sold handmade crafts and decorated cookies and plates of antipasti. I bought two of everything. Trash-can bonfires were all about for warming hands and butts.

In a flash, the entire population shifted from the piazza in Quarna Sopra to the Grassi Center in Quarna Sotto for a community concert. Everyone present was either a musician or related to a musician by no more than one or two degrees of separation. I got misty-eyed hearing a chorus of nursery school children I had known since before they were born, ensembles of pimply teenagers I knew when they were in grade school. The daughter of a friend played "Summertime" on the trumpet, the son of another played "My Grandfather's Clock" on the saxophone. Finally came the village band in full force with its traditional fare: a Sousa march, a medley of Italian pop songs, a rousing tribute to *Phantom of the Opera*, and the grand finale, a hands-in-the-air-everybody-clapping "We Will Rock You." In Quarna, the Three Tenors—Luciano Pavarotti, Jose Carreras, and Placido Domingo—were a bunch of nobodies compared to Queen and Freddie Mercury. Never once at any Quarna band concert can I recall hearing an instrumental performance of a Puccini or Verdi aria. "Bohemian Rhapsody" was in the Quarna canon.

Christmas Eve mass at the big *chiesa* in Quarna Sopra began with children reciting the story of the nativity. I had hoped for a traditional stage play with little actors costumed as animals and wise men, but, alas, the children were in street clothes reciting their lines against a PowerPoint backdrop. When the priest, in full vestments, appeared on the altar, a blast from the organ sent a bolt of musical lightning through my body: the wordless prelude, played with majesty on the church's eighteenth-century organ, was "White Christmas." I hadn't the heart to tell anyone that this ode they cherished as a religious hymn was a ballad written by Irving Berlin, a Russian-American Jewish immigrant, for a 1940s Hollywood movie musical starring Bing Crosby. Never had I heard music so out of time and out of place and yet so right for a village where music transcended all geographic, cultural, temporal, and spiritual boundaries.

After midnight mass, the grown-ups gathered in the piazza for mulled wine as the children anxiously awaited Babbo Natale. Finally, in a burst of fireworks, the sleigh (a decorated panel van) arrived to screams of delight. Out popped a well-padded Babbo Natale. I was chatting with Maria Rosa, Edo's mother, as Babbo Natale started handing out gifts to the children. She confessed a lingering bitterness toward the gift event. The tradition began two weeks after her birthday the year she turned fourteen, which the elders had established as the cutoff age. Her friends all received gifts. She was denied. Elegant and educated—the first Quarnese woman to attend law school—Maria Rosa still carried a grudge against Babbo Natale regardless of who was in the costume. Even this year, when the plump Babbo Natale with a long white beard was Edo.

Christmas lunch at Valerio's was a grand departure from the provincial Quarnese cuisine to which I had grown accustomed. There were no family-style bowls of soup or pasta or stew or rice or potatoes passed around the table. It was a tasting menu worthy of a Michelin-starred restaurant. Every element, spun from Valerio's feverish imagination, was cooked, crafted, layered, piped, and garnished to perfection. Watching him balance a pickled fig on a foie gras parfait was performance art.

On the buffet was a calligraphed menu:

Tartine of Eggplant with Caramelized Onion
Crostini with Stracchino cheese, Walnuts, and Radicchio
Savory & Sweet Canapés
Spicy Deviled Eggs a la Romana
Parfait of Salmon, Shrimp, and Avocado
Parfait of Foie gras with Apple Compote and Fig
Beignets filled with Nutella Mousse
Baked Sausage with Polenta
Veal with Tuna sauce
Pineapple and Lime sorbets
A Selection of Fruits and Cheeses

My calligraphed place card was at the head of the table. Rarely had I felt so honored. Two hours later, never had I felt so embarrassed. So full was I with rich food and wine that I nodded off at the table. Just as I was on the verge of tumbling out of my chair, Tati revived me with a double espresso, the Italian equivalent of smelling salts.

As eager as Valerio was to assimilate me into the family fold, there was a limit to what he could do. I could not expect Valerio to translate every moment of family dialogue, coded with shared history and inside jokes and *dialetto*. So, like the days of old, before opera houses offered subtitles, the best I could do was pay attention to the dramaturgy, the music, and the occasional word or gesture and hope to get the gist of their stories. There were all the elements of any family holiday supper in any country in any language: laughter, bickering, a tantrum, a spilled glass of wine on the good tablecloth. Nonna fussed over Nonno, whose appetite, normally robust, was diminished. He had lost considerable weight since my last visit and was gaunt. Valerio told me his father had been dealing with a stomach ailment, but he was on the mend. Perhaps the family could not hear the knell amid the merriment, but to an outsider it tolled clearly.

That evening there was aperitivo at the home of neighbors from my little piazza, Marie-Terese and Piero, and their family. Aperitivo quickly segued into dinner with a traditional *brodo*, broth with dumplings, followed by a game of *tombola*, an Italian cousin of bingo. So linked is *tombola* to Italian Christmas that they were truly shocked I had never heard of it. On Boxing Day, there was dinner with Arianna and Fabrizio and their two sons, who loved to speak English. The older brother, a shy high school student when I first met him, had finished an advanced degree and now had a good job in digital marketing. The younger brother, a pipsqueak when I first met him, was now in *liceo* and towered over his brother and father. His passions were physics, math, and helping at every community event. Their shy mother looked on with wonder at her children chatting in English. Their garrulous father, whom I knew well from the pub scene, looked at me with mock scorn and had the older son translate.

"If my sons are smart enough to learn English from you, how come you are not smart enough to learn Italian from them?" he asked.

My answer was that his boys were smarter than me and their education was more rigorous than mine. I was not being polite. Both observations were true.

The next night was dinner with my friends Gianni and Cristina at their home on the far side of Lake Orta. A retired engineer, Gianni and his wife shared a passion for the outdoors. They were intrepid skiers, hikers, sailors, and travelers. They were regular visitors to Quarna, where they maintained a beautifully renovated family home passed down through generations.

They were tremendously proud of their three adult children—two doctors and an engineer—and rightfully so. I had met them all, equally articulate and engaging. One of the sons, recently returned from a stint in Ukraine with Doctors Without Borders, joined us for dinner. The conversation was fascinating and the food terrific. There was roast beef, perfectly pink and thinly sliced—something I'd never seen served in a home in Italy—and a homemade green tomato and celery remoulade that was a revelation—but I kept getting distracted by their hypnotic Christmas tree. The glass ornaments, collected over a lifetime of travels, were as iridescent as a string of matched South Sea pearls. All I could think was, "How the hell did they carry them home when I cannot even pack a pencil that doesn't break?"

The following day I was invited for Christmas lunch with Nonna Dina and her family. The weather was so mild we could eat on the terrace table. The meal was prepared by her brother, a retired hotel chef, so when steak tartare was served, I was reasonably confident I would not die of salmonella. When I explained that steak tartare was a luxury back home, served only in small portions at fine restaurants, they howled. To them, it was as common as my grandmother's chopped liver.

The last dance on my card was the band's annual Christmas banquet at Circolo, a full-on affair with every member in attendance, along with an assortment of parents, siblings, spouses, and children. It was a replica of the band banquets of my childhood. There were rowdy songs, call-and-repeat chants, and peals of laughter.

Edo, sitting at my table, turned to me and said, "No outsider has ever been at the band dinner. You are as close to being a Quarnesi as any Fuorestiero can be."

New Year's Eve arrived, and with it a blessed reprieve from my social schedule. Valerio and Tati were having a quiet evening at home. The elders were gathering for a private dinner in Quarna Sopra. The young adults were celebrating at bars down the mountain. The teenagers were celebrating at a remote *baita* to revel out of sight of their parents. Circolo and Posta were offering holiday menus, but they were pricey and I was becoming more of a frugal Quarnesi with each visit.

I made the most of my quiet New Year's Eve in Quarna. I caught the indigo sunset from Matlucco, with donkeys braying "Buon Anno!" from a nearby meadow. I stopped at Circolo for a glass of prosecco. Back at the inn, I had plenty of salami and cheese and fruit, an ample supply of *tarallini*, a full bag of Nutella wafers, and a half-finished bottle of Nebbiolo. On Italian Netflix, I found *Puoi Baciare lo Sposo* (You May Kiss the Groom), a farce about a gay man coming out to his family in a tiny Italian village. How deprived we New Yorkers are with our curated art house Italian films! I thought. All those smoke-filled black-and-white dramas! We never get the silly popcorn movies. Here at the source, unfiltered, was colorful mediocrity at its very best. It was like discovering a good chianti in a box.

I was still in bed on New Year's Day, shaking off my Nutella hangover, when I received the inevitable text from Valerio.

"Cappuccino e brioche?"

He was going up to the *baita* for the day. Would I like to join him?

I jumped out of bed like a slumbering dog who leaps into a frenzy when his owner reaches for the leash.

"Sì-sì!" I typed.

Within minutes, I was ready for the brief drive in the Panda, followed by the twenty-minute hike to the *baita*. Valerio put a five-pound bag of foodstuffs in my backpack and a fifty-pound bag of cement in his own. Ryk was no less frenzied than I was for a day in nature.

Valerio had much work to do on the indoor shower he was creating in the shed and needed as much daylight as possible, so *cappuccino e brioche* would be an early pranzo. I expected the sack in my backpack contained salami and cheese and bread. But when we arrived, he chopped wood to feed the heat stove and put on a pot of water to boil for pasta. From my backpack, he pulled out garlic, leeks, radicchio, anchovies, and speck, which, in an ancient skillet over a propane stove, he sautéed in careful sequence to build flavor. He allowed me, after a bit of protest, to set the table, slice the bread, and open the wine.

"Buon Anno!" he said when we toasted.

Tears welled up in my eyes.

"The kindness is overwhelming," I said.

He looked bewildered.

"Is normal baita lunch," he said with a shrug.

After we finished eating, he made coffee and immediately went to work on his dream shower. He had tuned into an Italian rock station on his boom box and was singing along while mixing and troweling cement. Would that I could have helped, but I have no more skill with a trowel than with a saxophone. As close as we were in friendship, in the practical world, we were a galaxy apart. The best I could do was watch his artistry and write about it. Or better yet, leave him alone.

The *baita* was toasty from the heat stove. I could read in the loft, where the light was good; even in the digital age I never left home without a book or magazine. Or I could write. I never left home without a notebook. I could do the yoga or practice the mindfulness I learned at Mandali. Or I could catch up on the backlog of emergency American television sitcoms on my phone.

Or I could loll on the hillside and stare at the silver sky and the gray birches and the midnight green pines. I could find animal faces in the clouds. I could retreat into my imagination. In this space, in this time, with the comfort of good food and friendship, I could embrace a comforting forgetfulness. I could imagine Augie by my side and not feel sad.

Sometimes, despite one's best efforts, happiness is unavoidable.

Chapter 29

Becoming Quarnese

With the raucous festivities of Christmas and the quiet New Year's Day with Valerio, I began to feel a sense of closure to the double-helix of stories I wished to tell: the ethnographic history of a village struggling to survive and the emotional story of one man's journey out of grief. With each step of assimilation into Quarnese life, I felt a renewed sense of community. Along the way, I had evolved from Fuorestiero to Villeggianti. My stature in the caste system could go no further.

Or so I thought. The leap, a virtual if not bona fide conversion, occurred of all places at Marisa's beauty shop. As I waited for a haircut, Valerio—who had heard through the grapevine that I was next in line for Marisa's chair—texted to tell me that Marisa was shutting down her shop. The explanation was a bit muddled, but as I understood it, her landlord, who lived adjacent, had decided to expand his house. Instead of reopening at another location, Marisa chose to retire. This would be my last haircut in Quarna.

I was sad when Luigi the Butcher closed his shop. He and his wife, Anna Lucia, were warm and welcoming characters in my daily life. I was concerned when Maria Grazia closed her grocery in Quarna Sotto. I wasn't as fond of her, but where, I wondered, would the old nonnas get their daily bread and cleaning supplies? I was worried when I heard rumors that Giuseppe might soon retire and shut down his bar. Where would the women of Quarna Sopra have their morning coffee and the men have their morning wine? Where would the dwindling faithful buy cigarettes?

Marisa's closing did not just make me sad or worried. It made me angry. Marisa was exceptionally skilled. For ten euros, she could trim twenty years off my age. She did not speak a lick of English, but she communicated impeccably with kindness. Beyond my selfish needs, her artistry was essential to so many people in the community, from primping teenage girls to busy workmen to elderly women, for whom a wash and set was a social occasion.

After the final haircut and a tearful goodbye to Marisa, I marched to Giuseppe's, ordered a beer, ranted out loud to no one in particular, ordered a second beer, and texted Edo, demanding an emergency city council meeting so I could denounce this travesty.

"*Now* you are Quarnesi!" he replied.

My anger, I knew, had nothing to do with Marisa. Her years of hard work certainly merited a comfortable retirement. Nor had it anything to do with inconvenience. There were barbers in Omegna where I could go on market day or on a *cappuccino e brioche* adventure with Valerio. As for my concerns about the elderly women, I was told Marisa would be making house calls.

But Edo was right. My anger had nothing to do with hair. My anger was about change, the loss of tradition, and the fear of extinction for a village I loved. I was demanding that civic leaders solve an unsolvable problem. I wanted them to turn back time. By heart and soul, if not by blood and bones, I had become a Quarnesi.

There were nine visits to Quarna over seven years, some as short as three days, some as long as three months, some with Quarna as the prime destination, some with Quarna as an extension to other trips to Europe. Some visits to Quarna were journeys of discovery, some were journeys of celebration, some were journeys of escape. Some were treacherous, some were healing. Old Quarnesi I knew died. Young adult friends married and had children. (Or had children and got married. Or just had children. Or just got married. In modern Italian life, the sequence wasn't particularly important.) *Bambini* advanced from the yellow Quarna grade school shuttle bus to the public bus down to Omegna for middle school. *Ragazzi* matriculated from *liceo* to university.

A tax incentive encouraged renovation of private houses and public buildings. Construction cranes sprouted. A multimillion-euro campaign for federal and regional funds was proposed to construct a bypass road that would ease access to Quarna Sopra for visitors to Mandali. Meanwhile, the villagers of Quarna Sotto struggled to find the few thousand euros necessary to repair a crumbling stone staircase, an important shortcut for the elderly.

A wildfire scarred the mountains, but with moderate temperatures and a few heavy rains, dense shrubs and trees sprouted to conceal the wounds. Changing climate patterns had scattered the wolf population. Absent predators, the wild boar population grew. They in turn feasted on the eggs of the frogs that controlled mosquitos. Even lathered in repellant, I could no longer walk the path through the woods from Quarna Sotto to Quarna Sopra without being devoured.

The last old-time slate roofs began to disappear, replaced by modern terracotta tiles. Somewhere, I was told, there was a surviving thatched hut, but I never found it.

Valentina, the waitress at Circolo, was now the mother of a toddler. She shed the Goth look and, even under siege at pranzo rush hour, welcomed me with a smile and without any contempt for my Italian. Alessio finally relented and reduced the portions of pasta, but not the exceptional quality and beauty. Now and then, he created something off the menu for me.

Rampone & Cazzani continues to flourish. Claudio has grown the business through modern marketing strategies and old-school relationships; his brother, Simone, has maintained the standard of quality in the workshop; their father, Roberto, still meddles in the business as loving "retired" fathers do. The grocery store in Quarna Sopra does its best to fill the gaps left by the closing of the store in Quarna Sotto. A delivery system was created so that the elderly can get fresh bread every day. Giuseppe retired and his bar closed, but plans were underway to find a successor. A well-heeled Dutch woman in a relationship with a Quarnese man revived an old osteria with a vibrant new menu and live entertainment. An entrepreneurial Milanese man launched a pop-up microbrew pub at the Belvedere. Luigi the Butcher's daughter, Luisa, gave up an administrative job down in the valley to pursue her passion: baking. Each day, from her home, she sells breads, cakes, brioche, and pizzas to go. I go crazy for her olive focaccia.

Mandali leadership began acquiring additional properties for its programs, including Causello, the haunted mansion of my *Sunset Boulevard* imagination. Mandali staff, some with children, have made Quarna their permanent home. Mandali guests, enchanted with the village, have bought vacation homes.

Some Quarnesi still see the Mandali founders, staff, and guests as colonialist invaders. Others have come to value not just the jobs the retreat center has created, but also the global awareness of Quarna's existence it has created. Mandali has put Quarna on the map alongside Rampone & Cazzani.

The city councils and Pro Loco booster clubs of Quarna Sotto and Quarna Sopra still have a few old-timers reluctant to merge the two villages, but increasingly they are led by a new generation eager to end the centuries of conflict. Many new city council leaders are the mischievous young men and women who hazed me with whipped cream on my first Halloween visit. Should I ever need it, I have influence in high places.

"We will figure it out," the Quarnesi said to me when I first toured the messy old factory that became the Grassi Center. Indeed they did, spectacularly so. The acoustics are excellent and the performance space is flexible for all manner of events. There are rehearsal rooms, a library, a screening room, a barre for ballet, and, of course, a modest kitchen. A partnership was formed with the music conservatory of Novara, expanding the concert series with ever-higher standards. The Center features a burgeoning array of musical offerings with jazz, pop, classical, and masterclasses in various genres. Add in performances by the village band, visiting civic bands, impromptu jazz jam sessions, a week of rock bands during the Ferragosto celebrations, karaoke nights, '50s sock hops, and '70s disco nights, and rarely does a week go by where music is not as certain as mass on Sunday.

Over the years, I have invited and coaxed more than a dozen friends, family members, and colleagues to visit Quarna. Collin came for a visit even when our relationship was on the rocks to see what the fuss was all about. He saw immediately how Quarna was more than just a writing project or a retreat. It was a new community for me. It was a new relationship for me. If one can be slightly jealous of an entire village, he was.

All visitors received my basic guided tour, including the Belvedere, the churches, the cemeteries, Causello, the old mill, the museum, the Grassi Center, the waterfall, Monte Gioco, the fishpond, cappuccino at Posta, pranzo at Circolo, Dino's music box workshop, and the inevitable festival, concert, or procession. Gold-level guests were invited to coffee and cake at the home of Nonna Dina or Guido and Mercedes. Platinum-level guests were invited to a family dinner prepared by Valerio and Tati.

My interest in other Quarnesi waned as I became closer with my circle of families and friends. I remained "Buongiorno!" cordial to all and responded to "Where are you from?" and "Why are you here?" questions politely. But I became more selfish to preserve that portion of Quarna that was a peaceful escape from city life. Just as years ago I graduated from the "must-see, must-do" culture of New York City cognoscenti, in Quarna I no longer felt the urgency to chat with everybody, listen to every story, accept every dinner invitation, and attend every concert or religious event.

The landlord of my apartment in Pyk, eager to attract additional tenants, installed a high-speed internet connection. It eliminated my need to go to Valerio's for stable Wi-Fi to communicate with the outside world. Eventually, the landlord found a full-time tenant and I lost the apartment altogether, along with my treasured terrace and daily promenade of neighbors. I found other places to rent on my visits—some modern and charming, some ancient and creepy—and saw Quarna from new perspectives. In each new home, there were new neighbors with whom I bonded and who arrived with a metaphorical cow when I needed metaphorical milk.

I continued to learn scholarly history from Coppi Roberto, and oral history from various elders. A retired philosophy professor introduced me to the common birds of Quarna—the swallows, the tits, the eagles, the hawks, the cuckoos—and taught me their chirps and warbles in Italian vernacular. Tati taught me the names of the flowers in Italian: the common, the exotic, the wild, and the tame. Gabry, the train conductor, cut off his ponytail but continued to expose me to American bands I'd never heard of and teach me every vulgar expression in the Italian language. Nonna Dina demonstrated the traditional Quarnese yodel.

Even without a translator present, Gian Mario, the mayor of Quarna Sotto—who doesn't speak a word of English—waved me over to join him if we were both at Posta, having pranzo alone.

Sitting with a kindly man in silence is not so different from sharing a meal with my father many years ago. Sometimes, the quiet presence of another is enough—in any language.

If my perception of what constituted "family" in Quarna seemed distorted, the lens could be fuzzy in the other direction as well. One summer, during the annual Ferragosto holiday, I was invited for aperitivo at the home of my friends Gianni and Cristina and their extended clan of children, grandchildren, cousins, nieces, nephews, uncles, and aunts, many of whom, two or three generations removed from their Quarna roots, were urban professionals fluent in English. I moved about the room conversing effortlessly. While speaking with one of Gianni's cousins, his teenage son, earnest and polite, introduced himself in fine English.

"Now, how am I related to you?" he asked.

Chapter 30

After Augie

While I was tilting at windmills to preserve Quarna's heritage, my other village—the West Village—was hurtling toward extinction. After Augie the neighborhood became a casualty of gentrification. Gone are the old Italian men and women, gone are the bohemian artists and writers. Except for those heading to the venerable gay bars of yore, gone are the gay men of my generation. With the old guard gone, rent-controlled apartments landlords ignored for decades have been gutted and gussied up for young professionals paying multiples of the previous rent. Day and night, the sidewalks are overwhelmed with boisterous young people and bewildered tourists. The Hudson River esplanade is still lovely but so overrun with reckless bicyclists and zealous runners that a New York *passeggiata* has become a dance with death.

Every vacant warehouse and empty lot has been converted into luxury condos. Google transformed a massive railroad storage terminal into offices. Disney tore down an entire block to build a glassy, boxy East Coast headquarters. Village Cigars—the iconic triangular shop at the intersection of Christopher Street and Seventh Avenue—closed down, a victim of the war against tobacco. Cannabis shops have sprouted on every corner like weeds. Ridiculous lines form for the latest popular "it" thing. I have survived the manias of frozen yogurt, cupcakes, Cronuts, macarons, tacos, donuts, and now: artisanal pancakes. A pop-up shop popped up in our old laundromat. Some days it pops up with "experiences" I don't get. Some days the experiences come with a free designer coffee. That I get.

Basketball courts designed for urban youths have been reconfigured as pickleball courts for urban adults. Taxis are an endangered species. Ubers and Lyfts line my block in the morning, awaiting stunning young professionals en route to their jobs as attorneys, bankers, or self-proclaimed serial entrepreneurs. Lovable mutts attached to likable neighbors have been replaced by "-oodle" hybrids rushed through their routines by zombie dog-walkers clearly under the influence provided by the cannabis shops. Neighborhood businesses have shut down, their stores converted to restaurants for selfie-obsessed influencers and their followers. Affordable neighborhood gyms have been replaced by palatial fitness clubs that promise life extension. Svelte blonds stroll by in yoga outfits so revealing they make a Victorian middle-aged gay man quietly cluck his disapproval. Tall, handsome, shirtless men with perfect hair, their sculpted bodies slick with sweat, jog past my window on their way to and from the riverfront running path. Not all change is bad.

The *Friends* house remains a must-see tourist attraction, although it has been displaced as a must-selfie spot by the house on Cornelia Street where Taylor Swift briefly lived. Daniel Radcliffe, Hugh Jackman, and Nicole Kidman have moved away, replaced by Anderson Cooper and Bradley Cooper. Again, not all change is bad.

Collin and I reunited, not with some grand revelation but with a quiet realization that grief had led us on separate paths of healing and now our paths were converging again. We do not subtract the "break" from the totality of our life together. During our estrangement, we were both searching for some missing piece without realizing how much we had, including the memories of Augie that bonded us.

"He was our glue," Collin said.

Collin learned to forgive and forget my worst attributes. "You wouldn't be you without them" is his motto, sometimes uttered through gritted teeth. We both developed the skills essential for sustaining a long-term relationship: willful blindness and selective deafness. We have returned to the ordinary consonance and dissonance of domestic life. We cuddle, we laugh, we bicker. I attempt gourmet meals; he cleans up the mess. We watch comfort-food television in bed. We voice our mutual appreciation and say "I love you" at least once a day—by voice or text or touch. We take care of each other in times of physical or emotional distress. On Friday nights, when we eat our Sabbath salmon, we do so on a fish-patterned tablecloth purchased at the Thursday morning market in Omegna. We still set aside pieces of challah for Augie and cast them in the Hudson River from his favorite pier. We now speak of him with joy more than sorrow.

Yes, after Augie the West Village has changed. But early in the morning or late at night, when the bustle of the streets subsides; in the spring when the canopy of trees turns green or the fall when the leaves turn to blaze and brown; in the winter when the first snowflakes fall; when I sit on a stoop eating a tuna sandwich, I can conjure Augie: young, curious, alive, beside me.

The narrative of this story evolved too. A tale of discovery and music morphed into an ode to community and friendship that morphed into a travelogue of inner healing. The Quarnesi are a people with whom I have forged lifetime bonds. My gallant fantasies of saving the Quarnesi from extinction by telling their stories have been tempered by a humility born of ever-growing respect for their tenacity. The Quarnesi are more than capable of saving themselves. They have endured centuries of plagues, pestilence, and war. They have absorbed Walser nomads and Ukrainian refugees. They have evolved their economy from animal husbandry to lumber, woodcrafts, musical instruments, resort hotels, ecotourism, and now an upscale spirituality center.

My visits to Quarna are less frequent and of shorter duration; the reaffirmation of my life with Collin in New York and the renewal of my writing work keep me more grounded. Still, I stay in constant touch with Quarna by other means. Before I read the *New York Times* each morning, I check the overnight reports from the various Quarna social media sites to stay up-to-date on the news: civic projects, community events, a donkey in the road, a missing cat, found keys, tardy trash pickup, cell phone networks out of service.

My bond with Valerio remains tight. Each time I visit, our adventures are as fresh as they are inevitable. There are *cappuccino e brioche* days, elaborate aperitivos, and simple pasta-and-salad dinners with Tati and the Principessa. We share bottles of beer and Nebbiolo, we share stories of our lives. Our respective friends and families remain befuddled over our preposterous friendship. What could a rugged, straight Italian mountain man and a klutzy, gay American urbanite have in common? We dismiss their befuddlement with a shrug. If they don't understand the strange nature of our friendship, that's okay. Neither do we.

I am often asked by Quarnese and American friends alike if I would move to Quarna full time. In my imagination, the answer is yes. I even have a recurring dream in which I am struggling to find a passage over a mountain to Quarna. No need for a psychoanalyst to interpret that. The obstacles to making Quarna my forever home are very real. I have reaffirmed my life with Collin. I have reestablished order to my days. I do not have the unrelenting schedule of cultural events or the wide circle of friends and neighbors in New York that I have in Quarna, but I am making the effort to connect: I am dipping my toes into volunteering in the gay community, I have found a progressive Jewish congregation with a rabbi I admire, and I have joined a men's encounter group to share the weekly challenges of being human.

Of equal importance to sharing my life with Collin is proximity to my siblings and their families, for whom my love is unconditional, even if our visits are occasional. I don't need to live in the same city as them, but I prefer to be on the same continent. I want to be available if needed and to be present for every joyous occasion. I want to be a good brother and a great uncle (in both senses of the expression). I want to share stories of loony relatives, tales of Augie, and *cappuccino e brioche* adventures with Valerio. Eventually, I want to give everyone I love the platinum-level tour of Quarna.

Even if I wanted to become a permanent resident of Quarna, there are other obstacles. The process of getting a long-term Italian visa remains maddening. There would be the logistical and financial nightmares of buying and renovating a house. (I have neither the patience nor the fortitude of Frances Mayes or

Peter Mayle.) There is the matter of language. I have achieved a small measure of conversational Italian with a smattering of Quarnese *dialetto*. I can communicate slowly with a degree of comprehension, but I will never be able to participate in rapid-fire conversation with the requisite hand choreography.

There is the matter of faith. Even if I rarely attend a religious service, the city of New York, with its robust Jewish population, enables even a secular Jew a certain comfort in being among one's own. In Quarna, standing at the back of the church or watching a procession from a distance, I am always aware that I am at someone else's birthday party.

There is the matter of sexuality. I am now "out" to close Quarnese friends. I have received nothing but acceptance. As for those Quarnesi outside my immediate circle, I assume there are some who have figured it out and don't care, some who have not figured it out and don't care, and some who have figured it out and do care. As long as they say "Buongiorno!" when they pass me, I don't really care.

Finally, there is the matter of identity itself. I could be a Quarnesi heart and soul, but to the natives, I will always be an outsider, a Fuorestiero. I will always be a novelty. And the novelty of being a novelty wears off. One of the great gifts of life in a big city is anonymity. There is no such thing in a village. As the shtetl saying goes, "If you want to know what is going on in my house, ask my neighbor." I am as reluctant to know my neighbor's business as I am for them to know mine.

Loss, escape, discovery, friendship, adventure, and the embrace of the Quarnese stripped away the labels that had long defined and entrapped me. Call it insight or mindfulness (or vanity), but for the first time in my life, I saw the essence of myself: curious, adventurous, avowedly flawed, equally drawn to quiet contemplation and human connection. The journey out of grief led to a clarity that had long eluded me.

Postlude

Each January, Collin and I make a pilgrimage to East Hampton to honor Augie on the anniversary of his death, his *yahrzeit* as it is known in the Jewish tradition. Even in the years Collin and I were estranged, it was a journey we took together. (There is no custody for grief.) Our *yahrzeit* trips have become less a memorial and more a tribute. We stay at our favorite hotel and have dinner at our favorite restaurant. We visit the bay where Augie frolicked in the calm waters, and we visit the pond across from the old Springs General Store where he loved to watch the ducks. We drive to Two Mile Hollow Beach and, bright sun or silver clouds, calm seas or roiling breakers, gentle breeze or bracing gusts, we walk to the break in the dunes that was Augie's portal into adventure in life and portal into heaven in death. When we reach the site, we modify the traditional Jewish ritual of placing a pebble on the tombstone; instead, we place a few of his favorite treats on the scatter spot. We tuck yarmulkes under our stocking hats and recite Kaddish. We sit on the beach and split a tuna sandwich, Augie's favorite human food. If the wind is not too harsh, we nap on the beach with the sun on our faces. We imagine Augie digging a little trench and curling at our feet.

On one *yahrzeit* visit to East Hampton, Collin and I awoke from our nap on the beach and began our walk back to the car. In the distance we saw a dot on the horizon. The dot grew larger and larger, soon taking on the undeniable image of a dog racing toward us, eyes squinted, ears pinned back, tongue flapping in the wind. No one was chasing him or calling his name. There wasn't a human in sight. The closer the dog got, the more he resembled Augie—not a clone, but with a similar build and spirit of adventure. He raced right toward us, stopped for a moment to say hello, allowed us to scratch his head, and then sprinted toward Augie's portal and leapt into the dunes. That he did not even stop to gobble up Augie's memorial treats added to the surreality of the moment. (Signs and wonders don't eat, I suppose.) However agnostic I may be, I had to set skepticism aside. This was no illusion. As when the breath of God carried Augie's ashes into the dunes, a higher power was bringing a message of comfort, affirming that Augie was indeed at one with wind and water and earth and sky. And with us.

"By rights, my troubles should have cleared up," E. B. White writes of Fred, the dachshund he never ceased to mourn. "But I can't say they have. Here I am, seven years after his death, still sharing a fevered bed with him and, what is infinitely more burdensome, still feeling the compulsion to write about him."

The life and loss of Augie remains ever-present in my mind, in my dreams, in my writing, and in the stories I tell friends, family, and strangers. The sharp despair has faded, and I have fashioned a new structure for my days, but I still have not fully replaced the metronome, calendar, barometer, clock, and GPS that was Augie. There are still certain streets I avoid because they are too filled with meaning. His leash still hangs on a hook by the door.

The trauma of finding him dead on the floor is occasionally triggered, and there is a jag of tears, but time has edited the montage reel so that the rich memories are spliced in with the sorrowful: I can feel him relaxing into my arms when we met at the Humane Society; I can see him running through the woods and along the shore; I can see his dancing hysteria when I roasted a duck and hear the frenzy of barking when Collin came home; I can feel the softness of his ears and smell the scent of his ruff. Most of all I miss his unseen presence. Curled up on a settee in the corner of an anteroom at Versailles, Augie's aura could fill every room of the palace.

I no longer feel shame over the depth of my grief for Augie. All this because of a dog? Yes, all this because of a dog.

I feel less guilt and anger for not being with him at the end. Indeed, I have wondered whether my deafness and blindness to his imminent death was a gift, that in my decision to rush out and visit our friend Rick dying at Sloan Kettering, I had unwittingly done Augie a *mitzvah*, a blessed act of mercy. Had I been home and seen signs of distress, it is unlikely I would have calmly summoned a compassionate veterinarian with a potent syringe, as I had imagined. It is unlikely I would have calmly held Augie in my arms like a pietà, as I had imagined. It is more likely I would have rushed him to the hospital for extraordinary measures. I might well have had to make the excruciating choice to put him down. He might well have died frightened in the harsh glare of fluorescent hospital light. Instead he died in a sunbeam, an old dog in his bed.

"Lucky," his veterinarian had said.

Lucky indeed. For both of us.

"Acceptance is often confused with the notion of being all right or okay with what has happened," Elisabeth Kübler-Ross writes in *On Grief and Grieving*. "This is not the case. Most people don't ever feel okay or all right about the loss of a loved one." She continues: "We can never replace what has been lost, but we can make new connections, new meaningful relationships…we change, we grow, we evolve."

There are times—plenty of them—when I am not all right and do not feel okay about Augie's death. When I miss him terribly. When I do not feel whole. But through connection with Quarna and meaningful relationships with the Quarnesi I have changed, I have grown, I have evolved.

I am often asked, "Are you getting another dog?" The question is well-intentioned. And while not obscene—like asking one who has lost a child if they plan to have another—I do find it unsettling, as if a dog were a replaceable object. Many devoted animal people I know move on to another pet after a brief period of mourning. Whether to restore order to their lives, or the need for companionship, or an ethical sense of responsibility to provide a home for a stray, or simply their love for furry beasts—I honor their choice. But I do not plan to get another dog. I do not feel I have the emotional capacity for the inevitable loss.

I know I am not alone in my "grief aversion," as it is known in the literature. It is as common among pet owners as it is among humans who lose a spouse and choose not to remarry, whether from the fatigue of caretaking, the fear of emotional pain, or the sense that a chapter has closed.

For me, there are spiritual reasons as well. There is a story told in my family of my great-great-grandmother Alta Muschel, sitting on a park bench in New York City, attired in her widow's weeds. A gentleman approached, tipped his hat, and attempted to sit beside her. She smacked him with her parasol.

"Nur ein Mann!" she snapped.

"Just one man!" would be the literal translation from Yiddish. The greater meaning was that there had been just one man for her. Her husband was her *bashert*, her intended, and there could be no other.

That is precisely how I feel about Augie. *Nur ein Hund.* Just one dog. Augie was my canine *bashert*, my intended spirit animal, and there can be no other. With his life, he taught me how to love, trust, and connect. With his death, he transported me to an enchanted mountain village in a faraway land, where I learned to love, trust, and connect again. Augie guided me on an adventure of the heart and, as always, he guided me back home.

Acknowledgments

For nurturing this story with faith and tenacity and for guiding it through every step of this journey: my agent, Laurie Abkemeier of DeFiore and Company.

For shaping this story with heart: my editor, Anna Michels of Sourcebooks. For their dedicated expertise in production and marketing: the Sourcebooks team of Mary Wheelehan, Angela Corpus, Gianna Antolos, and Daisy Rankin.

For their enduring support of my writing career from the beginning: Robin Lee Perry and Mari Kuwabara-Wagg. For thoughtful reading of the manuscript in progress: Luca Battioni, Jeremy Benstein, Leif Bjaland, Susan Brooks, Dudley Cannada, Susan Feder, Catherine French, Caroline Livingston, Michael Mael, Regina Porter, Gordon Seabury, and Karen Seabury. For editorial assistance: Will Drickey.

For guiding me out of sorrow and continuing to guide me with gifted insight: Jeremy P. Ortman. For giving me and Augie a place at the beach to dream: Kim Richardson. For pointing the way to Stresa: Teresa Zak. For their enduring inspiration: in memory of Dr. Rick Martinez and Paul Berg.

For his extraordinary friendship and the embrace of his family: Valerio Coppi. For introducing me to the leaders of Quarna: Claudio Zolla. For his memories of Quarna's past: Guido Barone. For his vision of Quarna's future: Edoardo Casotti. For welcoming me into their village, their homes, and their hearts: the people of Quarna.

For bringing Augie into my life: William Berloni and the Humane Society of New York. For her generous support of the Humane Society in memory of Augie: Sandrea Goerlich Alexander. Representing the many dedicated veterinarians who cared for Augie over eighteen years: Jonathan S. Block, Django Martel, Lucy O'Byrne, Nancy Gustafson. For bringing him bliss in his final years: veterinary aqua-therapists Jean Marie Cooper and John Larson.

For loving Uncle Matt, *mishigas* and all: my siblings—Shari, Steven, and Claire—and their families. For loving, educating, and encouraging me to explore all that life has to offer: my parents, Arthur and Toby Sigman.

For his love, laughter, patience, and devotion—to me and to Augie: Collin Glidewell.

Reading Group Guide

1. Have you ever experienced the loss of a pet? What helped you cope? How did those close to you respond to your grief?

2. If you have lost a pet, was it during your childhood or in adulthood? How do you think these emotional experiences might differ?

3. If you currently have a pet, have you thought about rituals that might bring comfort when the time comes? If you hold religious or spiritual beliefs, do they include companion animals in the afterlife?

4. On his journey, the author discovered Quarna and asked to write about the village's heritage. How would you feel if a stranger asked to write about your town? Would you be willing to share your stories?

5. Have you ever traveled to a foreign country and felt "at home," as the author does in Quarna? What made you feel connected to an individual, a family, a village, or a city?

6. Have you ever felt an instant friendship with someone from a completely different culture, as the author does with Valerio? Have you shared unexpected adventures like their *cappuccino e brioche* outings?

7. What do you think of the author's decision to keep his gay and Jewish identity private? Have you ever felt the need to shield aspects of your identity in pursuit of a professional goal?

8. As the author lets go of his journalistic objectivity and assimilates into Quarna's community life, what changes do you notice in the story's tone? How do you think his growing connection to Quarna helped him process his grief?

9. Food plays an important role in the author's story of Quarna. What role does food play in your own community, culture, or family life? Are there specific meals or dishes tied to joyful occasions that resonate with you?

10. Have you traveled to Italy? How does the author's experience compare with yours? Are you more of a big-city tourist, or

would you be willing to explore a village off the beaten path on your own?

11. Throughout the story, the author weaves themes of loss, escape, discovery, and renewal. Which theme stood out to you most? Which theme would you emphasize when recommending this book?

12. Who would you recommend this book to? Someone who has lost a pet? Or someone who has never had a pet?

A Conversation with the Author

Did you learn anything new about yourself as a writer through the process of writing such a personal book?

I accepted that it is okay to personalize a nonfiction narrative without violating professional boundaries or the reader's trust: Fact and memoir can be ethically intertwined. I learned that the perspective through which you set out to observe a community changes as you make yourself a part of that community. And I learned that I would be a lousy sociologist or anthropologist. I'm just an old-school storyteller easily roped into the story I'm excited to tell.

How did it feel to become a "character" in the story of Quarna rather than simply the observing American writer?

Actors often speak of finding emotional freedom when inhabiting a role; when they walk on stage, they escape shyness, fear, and trauma. That's precisely what happened to me.

Becoming a Quarnese allowed me to escape the pain of losing Augie by inhabiting another world. Within reason, I could be whoever I wanted to be. But one can only live in an alternate reality for so long. Eventually I had to get off the stage and get back to life.

What do you hope readers take away from reading about Augie and your experiences in Quarna?

I want readers to know it is okay to grieve an animal deeply, that it can be equal to or more powerful than the grief they may feel for a human loss. I want to encourage readers to adopt—and adapt as necessary—secular or religious rituals as grab bars. I want to help validate for readers that, to the extent that time and resources allow, running away, seeking adventure, and embracing discovery can be valid forms of self-therapy. And if you are seeking escape and adventure, you can never go wrong with Italy.

For those going through the grieving process, what books would you most recommend?

Some of the mainstream literature on pet loss was inspirational, some a bit too sentimental. The academic literature on human/pet attachment theory was enormously informative but too dry for a personal narrative. Ultimately, the human grief books proved most comforting. Without question *On Grief and Grieving* by Elisabeth Kübler-Ross and David Kessler is a masterpiece. It speaks directly to the reader with remarkable empathy and clarity. Joan Didion's *The Year of Magical Thinking* validates the irrational side of grief and is well-balanced with Mary-Frances O'Connor's *The Grieving Brain*, which validates the rational side of grief. Of the elegiac dog books, Jon Katz's *Going Home* is best in show, a heartfelt classic.

What is a beloved memory of Augie that didn't make it into the book?

There are personal memories I want to keep to myself, painful memories I wish to forget, and delightful memories I've surely forgotten and will remember the moment this book comes off the press. I honestly did not anticipate writing this book or I would have taken notes on our life together, but I am glad I did not objectify Augie as a character in a story. Instead, we simply lived a life together for eighteen years. I think that is the most beloved memory of all.

About the Author

Matthew Sigman is a prize-winning music journalist who explores the creative process of composers, performers, artists, directors, and behind-the-scenes professionals in the performing arts. A three-time recipient of the ASCAP Deems Taylor Award, he has served as editor-in-chief of *Symphony* and *Opera America* magazines and has contributed features, interviews, criticism, and commentary to *Opera News*, *American Theatre*, *Chorus America*, *Classical Music*, and NPR's *Performance Today*. An avid traveler, a serious amateur chef, and a ferocious Scrabbler, he lives in New York City's West Village. You can visit him at matthewsigman.com.